*A Longman Cultural Edition*

William Shakespeare's

# HAMLET,
## Prince of Denmark

*Edited by*

**Constance Jordan**

**PEARSON**
Longman

New York   Boston   San Francisco
London   Toronto   Sydney   Tokyo   Singapore   Madrid
Mexico City   Munich   Paris   Cape Town   Hong Kong   Montreal

Vice President and Editor-in-Chief: Joseph P. Terry
Development Manager: Janet Lanphier
Development Editor: Anne Brunell Ehrenworth
Senior Marketing Manager: Melanie Craig
Production Coordinator: Shafiena Ghani
Project Coordination, Text Design, and Electronic Page Makeup: Dianne Hall
Cover Designer/Manager: John Callahan
Cover Illustration: *Hamlet and Horatio in the Cemetery* by Eugene Delacroix: The
    Bridgeman Art Library
Manufacturing Buyer: Roy L. Pickering, Jr.
Printer and Binder: R. R. Donnelly & Sons Company
Cover Printer: Coral Graphics Services, Inc.

Library of Congress Cataloging-in-Publication Data

Shakespeare, William, 1564–1616.
    [Hamlet]
    William Shakespeare's Hamlet, Prince of Denmark / edited by Constance Jordan.
        p. cm. — (A Longman cultural edition
    Includes bibliographical references.
    ISBN 0-321-14922-X (pbk.)
        1. Shakespeare, William, 1564–1616. Hamlet. 2. Hamlet (Legendary
character)—Drama. 3. Murder victims' families—Drama. 4. Fathers—Death—Drama.
5. Princes—Drama. 6. Revenge—Drama. 7. Denmark—Drama. I. Title: Hamlet,
Prince of Denmark. II. Jordan, Constance. III. Title. IV. Longman cultural edition.

PR2807.A2J67 2004
822.3'3—dc22                                                     2003060291

Please visit our website at http://www.ablongman.com

ISBN 0-321-14922-X

3 4 5 6 7 8 9 10—DOH—06 05 04

For Ethan, Simon, Devin, and Josie Marie

# Contents

# About the Cover Illustration

*Hamlet and Horatio in the Cemetery* (1859) by Eugene Delacroix (1798–1863)

The artist depicts Hamlet and Horatio at the newly dug grave of Ophelia, accompanied by the first of two gravediggers, who is referred to as "First Clown." In Shakespeare's theater, "clown" was the term traditionally reserved for the role of a country laborer who appears in comic scenes. Hamlet holds the skull of the late court jester Yorick, who has just been identified by the gravedigger, and declares: "Alas, poor Yorick . . . a fellow of infinite jest . . . where be your gibes now?" (ll. 183–189). These words preface the final scenes of the play, in which all the major characters are killed. Of them, Hamlet alone, having answered the gist of his own question, can express faith in the direction of providence (5.2.217–218).

# List of Illustrations

# *About Longman Cultural Editions*

Reading always seems to vibrate with the transformation of the day—now, yesterday, and centuries ago, when the presses first put printed language into wide circulation. Correspondingly, literary culture has always been a matter of change: of new practices confronting established traditions; of texts transforming under the pressure of new techniques of reading and new perspectives of understanding; of canons shifting and expanding; of informing traditions getting reviewed and renewed, recast and reformed by emerging cultural interests and concerns; of culture, too, as a variable "text"—a reading. Inspired by the innovative *Longman Anthology of British Literature*, Longman Cultural Editions respond creatively to the changes, past and recent, by presenting key texts in contexts that illuminate the lively intersections of literature, tradition, and culture. A principal work is made more interesting by materials that place it in relation to its past, present, and future, enabling us to see how it may be reworking traditional debates and practices, how it appears amid the conversations and controversies of its own historical moment, how it gains new significances in subsequent eras of reading and reaction. Readers new to the work will discover attractive paths for exploration, while those more experienced will encounter fresh perspectives and provocative juxtapositions.

Longman Cultural Editions serve not only several kinds of readers but also (appropriately) their several contexts, from various courses of study to independent adventure. Handsomely produced and affordably priced, our volumes offer appealing companions to *The Longman Anthology of British Literature,* in some cases enriching and expanding units originally developed for the *Anthol-*

*ogy,* and in other cases presenting this wealth for the first time. The logic and composition of the contexts vary across the series. The constants are the complete text of an important literary work, reliably edited, headed by an inviting introduction, and supplemented by helpful annotation; a table of dates to track its composition, publication, and public reception in relation to biographical, cultural, and historical events; and a guide for further inquiry and study. With these common measures and uncommon assets, Longman Cultural Editions encourage your literary pleasures with resources for lively reflection and adventurous inquiry.

Susan J. Wolfson
General Editor
Professor of English
Princeton University

# *About This Edition*

This edition of *Hamlet* reprints the authoritative text and notes to the play as edited by David Bevington for *The Complete Works of Shakespeare*, Fifth Ed. (Longman, 2004). Bevington's text is based mainly on the Second Quarto of 1604–1605 (Q2), with substitutions as needed from the Folio (F) and the First Quarto (Q1). The result, for the most part a conflation of Q2 and F, is the entire play that Shakespeare wrote. This text, however, is too long for any single production, and most stagings involve some careful cutting. For further discussion on the texts of *Hamlet*, see Paul Bertram and Bernice W. Kliman (eds.), *The Three-Text Hamlet: Parallel Texts of the First and Second Quartos and First Folio* (1991); Kathleen O. Irace (ed.), *The First Quarto of Hamlet* (1998); and Stanley Wells and Gary Taylor, "Hamlet," in *William Shakespeare: A Textual Companion* (1987), pp. 396–420. In this Longman Cultural Edition, a list of variants appears on pages 133–138.

Key issues in *Hamlet* and its history are illuminated by the Context materials, which show some of the cultural and ideological settings in which Shakespeare wrote and contemporary audiences saw the play: descriptions of the widely credited spirit world; accounts of the disease of melancholia; debates about purgatory, both Catholic and Protestant; prohibitions against the "wild justice" of revenge; and analyses of the causes of suicide, a mortal sin. To illustrate the varied responses to *Hamlet* on both the page and the stage, I have included some critical commentary and discussions of performances, drawn from the three centuries following the play's composition and first performances. The texts have been modernized to make them more accessible to twenty-first-century readers.

I am grateful to Clare Carroll, one of my coeditors on *The Longman Anthology of British Literature*, for supplying some of the account of Shakespeare's life and career that I use here. I especially thank Susan Wolfson, the general editor of the Cultural Editions series, for overseeing this volume from start to finish. I am also grateful to Anne Brunell Ehrenworth, Development Editor at Longman, who edited this manuscript with patience and great care. I wish further to thank my students and colleagues at Claremont Graduate University, particularly my research assistant Ambereen Dadabhoy, who went through Bevington's text and notes, supplying me with much useful information; my colleagues: Professors Marc Redfield and Molly Ierulli, who helped me find texts to illustrate past performances of the play; Carol Bliss, who guided me through databases for illustrations of the play; and Cynda Boland, who provided all-around support. This edition is dedicated to the next generation of Shakespeareans—they will see and know more than we do now.

Constance Jordan
Claremont Graduate University

# Introduction

Of all Shakespeare's tragedies, *Hamlet* is the best known. The figure of its hero, lonely, pensive, and shrouded in black, is recognized as a character quite independent of the play itself. He circulates within the limits of our cultures; he finds as many representations as readers and audiences. His face, whether Olivier's or Branagh's, Barrymore's or Gibson's, or that of one of the many other actors who have played the part, seems altogether familiar, a part of our world. And yet, what do we really know of Shakespeare's most enigmatic character?

Unlike Macbeth, the man of action to whom he is most often contrasted, Hamlet has appeared to epitomize the thoughtful hero. The great German playwright Goethe saw him as all-encompassing consciousness; the English poet Coleridge agreed. Their contemporary, the critic William Hazlitt, judged the play to be so dreamlike that he thought it should not be performed at all. And yet, *Hamlet* is action-packed, full of plots and quarrels, schemes and murders, plays and duels. The hero himself takes action, not once but a number of times—killing Polonius (although inadvertently); sending Rosencrantz and Guildenstern to their deaths (although they are guilty of no particular crime); tormenting Ophelia (although she appears to be ignorant of his motives). And he finally takes the revenge he has pledged himself to perform.

It's worth recognizing how many kinds of interpretations have yielded new visions of *Hamlet* and its hero over time. The hero of the Romantic poets now shares a place with others who speak to our present cultural concerns: Feminist criticism has shown us a Hamlet contending with Gertrude and Ophelia, contending, too, with questions about his own manliness; psychoanalytic criticism has exposed his unconscious drives, his unacknowledged desires; postmodern critical theory has shown how far he is a creature of language; and materialist criticism has revealed the social determinants of his career. Recent historicist criticism has helped us see the play and its hero in the complicated and, in a sense, conflicted cultural moment in which Shakespeare wrote and acted—a moment shaped by the troubles and triumphs of its fleeting present and its enduring memories. If some of these concerns may evoke little modern sympathy, they were fascinations for Shakespeare's contemporaries. Other issues, especially those having to do with questions of belief (or doubt), knowledge (or ignorance), loyalty (or treachery), and fortitude (or frailty) can still speak volumes to us.

From the beginning of the play, Shakespeare places his hero in a situation of almost unbearable constraints. Called to avenge his father's murder, Prince Hamlet must defy the social and political order if he is to accept the charge; he must rise above the law and be the judge and plaintiff in his own (and his father's) cause. The conventions of revenge tragedy, followed by Shakespeare himself in *Titus Andronicus*, represented revenge for honor's sake as a plausible if horrific act. Understood in terms of late Elizabethan England society, however, revenge was tantamount to treason. These are the terms that Shakespeare imports into his play; he makes Hamlet alone responsive to them. Neither Laertes nor Fortinbras, both vengeful characters, finds himself exactly in Hamlet's situation. Laertes desires a revenge that, although unlawful, is aided and abetted by the present king, a man who is supposedly the incarnation of the law. Fortinbras, the Norwegian prince whose father lost Denmark to the old king Hamlet, recovers this property not by taking action but by biding his time. The moment of his success is quite unforeseen—the vantage he acts upon at the end of the play is the "now" of an unanticipated present.

The social and political strictures that force Hamlet's careful questions of himself and his filial duty are compounded by other uncertainties. His father's ghost tells Hamlet that he comes from purgatory. Could a loyal Elizabethan subject believe in such a place? Protestant doctrine had dispensed with the idea of a nether world of purgation as a vital feature of Christian faith, calling it nothing more than a clerical fiction. Are we seeing a deluded Hamlet? And if purgatory does not seem strange to us, nor Hamlet's unquestioning acceptance of it unjustified by doctrine, what of the fact that it is his father's ghost that incites revenge? Catholic teaching maintained that souls in purgatory asked for graceful prayers, not earthly satisfactions. And finally, what was a ghost? Some who wrote about spiritual experiences said ghosts were merely figments of a supersensitive imagination. Others thought it possible that the real and material world was bound up with an invisible sphere of spirituality, but they usually remained unclear about how that spirituality manifested itself. Yet Shakespeare represents the ghost of the old king (an embodied character in the cast) as working his way through purgation, atoning for his sins. Shakespeare chose to dramatize such contested issues, conceiving a hero compelled to recognize and confront their complexities.

We should notice how quietly the play ends. Before the violence that brings the action to a conclusion, Hamlet's words to Horatio speak of a providence working in and through the natural world. He declares that he will defy "augury," the forecasting, planning, and anticipation of events: "If it be now, 'tis not to come; if it be not to come, it will be now; if it be not now, yet it will come, the readiness is all" (5.2.218–220). With these words, Hamlet gestures toward an essentially Calvinist eschatology. He implies that the terms of a particular death and the sense of ending it anticipates lie beyond human apprehension. All that matters is individual "readiness." True, there is something very bleak about the way Hamlet and his antagonists meet their death. Comforts for the dying which adhered to old Catholic rituals are represented as pernicious: the "unction" on Laertes' sword is a poison parody of the spiritual healing ointment of extreme unction; the wine in Claudius's "cup" is no eucharist but yet more poison—corrupted by the effects of a deadly "union" that separates the company forever.

These quotation-marked words draw vital historical meaning from current political and religious contexts. *Hamlet* is still embedded in these contexts, even as it speaks to subsequent ages. In addition to the rich and useful criticism that has informed its readings and performances, we can recognize a fundamental attitude of mind that embraces a creative skepticism, sustained at last by a comprehensive grasp of a providential design. Hamlet's testimony—arguably fatalistic were it not for its echo of Scripture (Matthew 10.29)—addresses the question that opens the play, "Who's there?" and reflects at length upon the noncommittal response it gets, "Nay, answer me." *Hamlet* tells us that we are ignorant of more than we know or can know, that what we do in the confidence of being right risks unintended, even ironic consequences. To question, to reflect, to think: these are the activities of a conscious mind. The Romantic poet John Keats saw them as Shakespeare's achievement of a "Negative Capability"—a capacity for being "in uncertainties, Mysteries, and doubts" (as he wrote in a letter of December 1817), and perhaps, too, a capacity for tempered inaction. The end of *Hamlet* is marked by a quietism made courageous by a belief in providence. Shakespeare's "romances" will show us a providence whose more generous dispensations justify desire and guarantee hope for a brave new world.

# Table of Dates

1588–97   England wages war with Spain.

1592      Shakespeare is mentioned as an actor and writer in a pamphlet by Robert Greene.

Thomas Kyd publishes his revenge play, *The Spanish Tragedy*, anonymously.

Christopher Marlowe's revenge play *The Jew of Malta* is performed.

1594      Shakespeare becomes a Charter Member of The Chamberlain's Men.

Shakespeare's revenge play *Titus Andronicus* is performed; Christopher Marlowe publishes *Dr. Faustus*, his last play.

1597      Francis Bacon publishes the first edition of *The Essays*.

1598      A play called *Hamlet*, now lost, is produced.

1599      The Chamberlain's Men occupy the Globe Theater.

1602      *Hamlet* is entered into the register of the Stationers' Company.

1603      Queen Elizabeth dies.

The "bad" quarto of *Hamlet* is published (Q1).

The "good" quarto of *Hamlet* is published (Q2).

1616      Shakespeare dies.

1623      Publication of the first collected edition of Shakespeare's plays in Folio.

# Introduction to
# William Shakespeare

## William Shakespeare (1564–1616)

England's greatest playwright began life modestly enough. He was the oldest son of John Shakespeare, glove manufacturer and seller, as well as alderman and bailiff, and Mary Arden, daughter of a Catholic farm owner who left property to her. As a member of one of the leading families of the market town of Stratford-on-Avon, Shakespeare most likely attended the local grammar school. The classical allusions and mastery of rhetoric in his plays show that he read the Latin poets Ovid and Virgil, and the playwrights Plautus and Seneca, all part of the standard humanist curriculum. He left school around the age of fifteen, at which point he may have had to help his father, who was having financial difficulties. (There are records of his continuing to suffer from debt in later years.)

A few years after leaving school, Shakespeare wed Anne Hathaway, whose family his parents had known for a long time. While Shakespeare and his wife grew up in what biographer Park Honan calls "the shadow of the old faith" (Roman Catholicism), he and his wife conformed to the Church of England. His marriage at age eighteen was early for a man of his time; Hathaway's age, twenty-six, was the average for a woman to be married. If they had promised marriage to one another at any point in their courtship, the Church of England would have viewed the promise as binding. Like many women of her time, Hathaway was pregnant when the marriage license was issued in November 1582; their first child, Susanna, was christened on May 26, 1583. Their twins, Judith and Hamnet, were born in 1585; the boy lived only to eleven. Shakespeare spent much of his married life away from home, in London and working in the theater, and retired to Stratford in 1610.

Mr. WILLIAM
SHAKESPEARES
COMEDIES,
HISTORIES, &
TRAGEDIES.

Published according to the True Originall Copies.

*Martin Droeshout sculpsit London.*

LONDON
Printed by Isaac Iaggard, and Ed. Blount. 1623.

Portrait of Shakespeare, title page of the Shakespeare First Folio
(London, 1623). Courtesy of The Library of Congress.

## Shakespeare's Career

There is a tradition that after leaving school, Shakespeare, under the name "Shakeshafte," served as a schoolmaster and acted in plays for the Hoghtons, a Catholic family in Lancashire. It may have been through the Hoghtons that Shakespeare encountered their friend Ferdinando Stanley, Lord Strange, who denounced his own father's papistry. The Hoghtons sponsored an acting troupe that performed at least two of Shakespeare's plays. Members of this troupe, under the patronage of Lord Strange, would become The Chamberlain's Men, one of the most successful London theatrical companies. Shakespeare became a shareholder in 1594, jointly owning and managing the company.

At this same time, through his connection with Richard Field, a Stratford man who had set up as a printer in London, Shakespeare published his first serious poetical works, *Venus and Adonis* (1593) and *The Rape of Lucrece* (1594), both dedicated to the Earl of Southampton. Shakespeare most likely wrote these works during 1592–1593 when the plague compelled city authorities to close the London theaters in an attempt to prohibit contagion in such crowded public gathering spots.

That Shakespeare did not go on to university, which at the time prepared young men for service in the government or church, may have been a blessing in disguise. He had to work to survive, and during the 1590s, he was quite busy in the London theater world writing plays and acting in them. He soon attracted the scorn of playwright Robert Greene, who referred to Shakespeare in 1592 as "an upstart crow, beautified with our feathers, that with his tiger's heart wrapped in a player's hide . . . is in his own conceit the only Shake-scene in a country."

Although we don't know for certain which roles Shakespeare played, legend has it that these included the ghost of Hamlet's father and a part in Ben Jonson's *Every Man in His Humor*. Already the object of envy and derision by Greene's account, Shakespeare became so popular that after 1598, even plays that were not written by him were printed with his name on them. The first complete edition of Shakespeare's *Comedies, Histories and Tragedies* did not appear until seven years after his death in the Folio of 1623.

Scholars have constructed a chronology of Shakespeare's plays based on recorded performances, the printing of individual Quarto editions, and the internal evidence of the plays themselves. By this reckoning, his output in the 1590s was staggering. Using Holin-shed's *Chronicles* as his chief source, Shakespeare wrote his first four history plays, culminating in one of his most often-performed works, *The Tragedy of Richard III,* celebrating the defeat of Richard's tyranny by Elizabeth I's grandfather Henry VII, who be-gan the reign of the Tudors. These history plays would be followed by four more, including one meditating on the dangers of absolute monarchy, *Richard II,* performed at the Globe at the prompting of Essex's faction to incite a revolt on the eve of their failed rebellion. Shakespeare also wrote two Roman plays, *The Tragedy of Julius Caesar,* which again concerns tyranny, this time in relation to the responsibilities of freedom demanded in the Roman republic; and *Titus Andronicus,* which portrays a world of horrendous vio-lence—mutilation, murder, and cannibalism.

In the genre of comedy, his work in this period includes: *The Comedy of Errors, The Taming of the Shrew, Two Gentlemen of Verona, Love's Labor's Lost, A Midsummer Night's Dream, The Merchant of Venice, The Merry Wives of Windsor, Much Ado About Nothing, As You Like It,* and *Twelfth Night.* These plays pursue themes that he would later take up in his romantic tragedy *Romeo and Juliet,* the dark comedies (or problem plays) *Measure for Measure* and *Troilus and Cressida,* and his first two great tragedies, *Hamlet* and *Othello*—treating, respectively, the disas-trous effects of revenge and the self-deceptions of love.

In the next century, these plays were followed by *King Lear* and *Macbeth,* tragedies of misrule and tyranny, and *Antony and Cleopatra,* on the conflict between passion and duty. Shakespeare's last tragedy, *Coriolanus,* representing the fate of an arrogant Ro-man general, was followed by *Timon of Athens,* the portrait of a misanthropist. Shakespeare concludes his playwriting with four comedies, more often known as "romances," depicting different kinds of conflict and reconciliation: *Pericles, Cymbeline, The Win-ter's Tale,* and *The Tempest.*

Clare Carroll
Constance Jordan

# HAMLET,
## Prince of Denmark

[by William Shakespeare]

# HAMLET,

## Prince of Denmark

[*Dramatis Personae*

GHOST *of Hamlet, the former King of Denmark*
CLAUDIUS, *King of Denmark, the former King's brother*
GERTRUDE, *Queen of Denmark, widow of the former King and now wife of Claudius*
HAMLET, *Prince of Denmark, son of the late King and of Gertrude*

POLONIUS, *councillor to the King*
LAERTES, *his son*
OPHELIA, *his daughter*
REYNALDO, *his servant*

HORATIO, *Hamlet's friend and fellow student*

VOLTIMAND,
CORNELIUS,
ROSENCRANTZ,
GUILDENSTERN, } *members of the Danish court*
OSRIC,
A GENTLEMAN,
A LORD,

BERNARDO,
FRANCISCO, } *officers and soldiers on watch*
MARCELLUS,

FORTINBRAS, *Prince of Norway*
CAPTAIN *in his army*

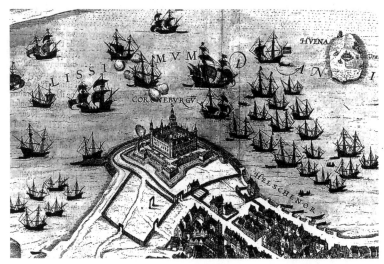

Freti Danici, *Elsinore Castle*. This eighteenth-century etching shows the superbly defensive situation of Kronenborg Castle (the site of the sixteenth-century Elsinore Castle) on a promontory at the very edge of the Baltic Sea. The castle's four corners are protected by v-shaped platforms, each fortified with several cannons, and the entire structure is surrounded by a moat. (By permission of the Folger Shakespeare Library.)

*Three or Four* PLAYERS, *taking the roles of* PROLOGUE, PLAYER KING,
    PLAYER QUEEN, *and* LUCIANUS
*Two* MESSENGERS
FIRST SAILOR
*Two* CLOWNS, *a gravedigger and his companion*
PRIEST
FIRST AMBASSADOR *from England*

*Lords, Soldiers, Attendants, Guards, other Players, Followers of Laertes,*
    *other Sailors, another Ambassador or Ambassadors from England*

SCENE: *Denmark*]

# [1.1]

*Enter Bernardo and Francisco, two sentinels, [meeting].*

BERNARDO  Who's there?
FRANCISCO
    Nay, answer me. Stand and unfold yourself.        2

---

**1.1 Location: Elsinore castle. A guard platform.**
**2 me** (Francisco emphasizes that *he* is the sentry currently on watch.)    **unfold yourself**
reveal your identity

BERNARDO    Long live the King!

FRANCISCO    Bernardo?

BERNARDO    He.

FRANCISCO
You come most carefully upon your hour.

BERNARDO
'Tis now struck twelve. Get thee to bed, Francisco.

FRANCISCO
For this relief much thanks. 'Tis bitter cold,
And I am sick at heart.

BERNARDO    Have you had quiet guard?

FRANCISCO    Not a mouse stirring.

BERNARDO    Well, good night.
If you do meet Horatio and Marcellus,
The rivals of my watch, bid them make haste.          14

*Enter Horatio and Marcellus.*

FRANCISCO
I think I hear them.—Stand, ho! Who is there?

HORATIO    Friends to this ground.                     16

MARCELLUS    And liegemen to the Dane.                 17

FRANCISCO    Give you good night.                       18

MARCELLUS
Oh, farewell, honest soldier. Who hath relieved you?

FRANCISCO
Bernardo hath my place. Give you good night.

*Exit Francisco.*

MARCELLUS    Holla! Bernardo!

BERNARDO    Say, what, is Horatio there?

HORATIO    A piece of him.

BERNARDO
Welcome, Horatio. Welcome, good Marcellus.

HORATIO
What, has this thing appeared again tonight?

BERNARDO    I have seen nothing.

MARCELLUS
Horatio says 'tis but our fantasy,                      27
And will not let belief take hold of him
Touching this dreaded sight twice seen of us.
Therefore I have entreated him along                    30
With us to watch the minutes of this night,            31
That if again this apparition come
He may approve our eyes and speak to it.               33

HORATIO
Tush, tush, 'twill not appear.

**14 rivals** partners   **16 ground** country, land   **17 liegemen to the Dane** men sworn to serve the Danish king   **18 Give** May God give   **27 fantasy** imagination   **30 along** to come along   **31 watch** keep watch during   **33 approve** corroborate

BERNARDO                     Sit down awhile
And let us once again assail your ears,
That are so fortified against our story,
What we have two nights seen.
HORATIO                          Well, sit we down,
And let us hear Bernardo speak of this.
BERNARDO   Last night of all,                                    39
When yond same star that's westward from the pole   40
Had made his course t'illume that part of heaven     41
Where now it burns, Marcellus and myself,
The bell then beating one—

            *Enter Ghost.*

MARCELLUS
Peace, break thee off! Look where it comes again!
BERNARDO
In the same figure like the King that's dead.
MARCELLUS
Thou art a scholar. Speak to it, Horatio.                46
BERNARDO
Looks 'a not like the King? Mark it, Horatio.            47
HORATIO
Most like. It harrows me with fear and wonder.
BERNARDO
It would be spoke to.
MARCELLUS            Speak to it, Horatio.                49
HORATIO
What art thou that usurp'st this time of night,          50
Together with that fair and warlike form
In which the majesty of buried Denmark                   52
Did sometimes march? By heaven, I charge thee, speak!    53
MARCELLUS
It is offended.
BERNARDO        See, it stalks away.
HORATIO
Stay! Speak, speak! I charge thee, speak!   *Exit Ghost.*
MARCELLUS   'Tis gone and will not answer.
BERNARDO
How now, Horatio? You tremble and look pale.
Is not this something more than fantasy?
What think you on't?                                     59
HORATIO
Before my God, I might not this believe

---

39 **Last . . . all** i.e., This *very* last night. (Emphatic.)   40 **pole** polestar, north star
41 **his** its   **t'illume** to illuminate   46 **scholar** one learned enough to know how to question a ghost properly   47 **'a** he   49 **It . . . to** (It was commonly believed that a ghost could not speak until spoken to)   50 **usurp'st** wrongfully takes over   52 **buried Denmark** the buried King of Denmark   53 **sometimes** formerly   59 **on't** of it

Without the sensible and true avouch                                    61
Of mine own eyes.
MARCELLUS            Is it not like the King?
HORATIO   As thou art to thyself.
Such was the very armor he had on
When he the ambitious Norway combated.                                  65
So frowned he once when, in an angry parle,                             66
He smote the sledded Polacks on the ice.                                67
'Tis strange.
MARCELLUS
Thus twice before, and jump at this dead hour,                          69
With martial stalk hath he gone by our watch.                           70
HORATIO
In what particular thought to work I know not,                          71
But in the gross and scope of mine opinion                              72
This bodes some strange eruption to our state.
MARCELLUS
Good now, sit down, and tell me, he that knows,                         74
Why this same strict and most observant watch
So nightly toils the subject of the land,                               76
And why such daily cast of brazen cannon                                77
And foreign mart for implements of war,                                 78
Why such impress of shipwrights, whose sore task                        79
Does not divide the Sunday from the week.
What might be toward, that this sweaty haste                            81
Doth make the night joint-laborer with the day?
Who is't that can inform me?
HORATIO                    That can I;
At least, the whisper goes so. Our last king,
Whose image even but now appeared to us,
Was, as you know, by Fortinbras of Norway,
Thereto pricked on by a most emulate pride,                             87
Dared to the combat; in which our valiant Hamlet—
For so this side of our known world esteemed him—                       89
Did slay this Fortinbras; who by a sealed compact                       90
Well ratified by law and heraldry                                       91
Did forfeit, with his life, all those his lands
Which he stood seized of, to the conqueror;                             93
Against the which a moiety competent                                    94

61 **sensible** confirmed by the senses   **avouch** warrant, evidence   65 **Norway** King of
Norway   66 **parle** parley   67 **sledded** traveling on sleds   **Polacks** Poles   69 **jump**
exactly   70 **stalk** stride   71 **to work** i.e., to collect my thoughts and try to understand
this   72 **gross and scope** general drift   74 **Good now** (an expression denoting entreaty
or expostulation.)   76 **toils** causes to toil   **subject** subjects   77 **cast** casting
78 **mart** shopping   79 **impress** impressment, conscription   81 **toward** in preparation
87 **Thereto . . . pride** (refers to old Fortinbras, not the Danish King)   **pricked on** incited
**emulate** emulous, ambitious   89 **this . . . world** i.e., all Europe, the Western world   90
**sealed** certified, confirmed   91 **heraldry** chivalry   93 **seized** possessed
94 **Against the** in return for   **moiety competent** corresponding portion

Was gagèd by our king, which had returned 95
To the inheritance of Fortinbras 96
Had he been vanquisher, as, by the same cov'nant 97
And carriage of the article designed, 98
His fell to Hamlet. Now, sir, young Fortinbras,
Of unimprovèd mettle hot and full, 100
Hath in the skirts of Norway here and there 101
Sharked up a list of lawless resolutes 102
For food and diet to some enterprise 103
That hath a stomach in't, which is no other— 104
As it doth well appear unto our state—
But to recover of us, by strong hand
And terms compulsatory, those foresaid lands
So by his father lost. And this, I take it,
Is the main motive of our preparations,
The source of this our watch, and the chief head 110
Of this posthaste and rummage in the land. 111
BERNARDO
I think it be no other but e'en so.
Well may it sort that this portentous figure 113
Comes armèd through our watch so like the King
That was and is the question of these wars. 115
HORATIO
A mote it is to trouble the mind's eye. 116
In the most high and palmy state of Rome, 117
A little ere the mightiest Julius fell, 118
The graves stood tenantless, and the sheeted dead 119
Did squeak and gibber in the Roman streets;
As stars with trains of fire and dews of blood, 121
Disasters in the sun; and the moist star 122
Upon whose influence Neptune's empire stands 123
Was sick almost to doomsday with eclipse. 124
And even the like precurse of feared events, 125
As harbingers preceding still the fates 126
And prologue to the omen coming on, 127
Have heaven and earth together demonstrated

95 **gagèd** engaged, pledged   **had returned** would have passed   96 **inheritance** possession   97 **cov'nant** i.e., the *sealed compact* of line 90   98 **carriage . . . designed** purport of the article referred to   100 **unimprovèd mettle** untried, undisciplined spirits   101 **skirts** outlying regions, outskirts   102–104 **Sharked . . . in't** rounded up (as a shark scoops up fish) a troop of lawless desperadoes to feed and supply an enterprise of considerable daring   110 **head** source   111 **posthaste and rummage** frenetic activity and bustle   113 **Well . . . sort** That would explain why   115 **question** focus of contention   116 **mote** speck of dust   117 **palmy** flourishing   118 **Julius** Julius Caesar   119 **sheeted** shrouded   121 **As** (This abrupt transition suggests that matter is possibly omitted between lines 120 and 121)   **trains** trails   122 **Disasters** unfavorable signs or aspects   **moist star** i.e., moon, governing tides   123 **Neptune's . . . stands** the sea depends   124 **Was . . . eclipse** was eclipsed nearly to the cosmic darkness predicted for the second coming of Christ and the ending of the world. (See Matthew 24.29 and Revelation 6.12.)   125 **precurse** heralding, foreshadowing   126 **harbingers** forerunners   **still** always   127 **omen** calamitous event

Unto our climatures and countrymen.                                129

    *Enter Ghost.*

But soft, behold! Lo, where it comes again!                        130
I'll cross it, though it blast me. (*It spreads his arms.*) Stay,
    illusion!                                                       131
If thou hast any sound or use of voice,
Speak to me!
If there be any good thing to be done
That may to thee do ease and grace to me,
Speak to me!
If thou art privy to thy country's fate,                           137
Which, happily, foreknowing may avoid,                             138
Oh, speak!
Or if thou hast uphoarded in thy life
Extorted treasure in the womb of earth,
For which, they say, you spirits oft walk in death,
Speak of it! (*The cock crows.*) Stay and speak!—Stop it,
    Marcellus.

MARCELLUS
Shall I strike at it with my partisan?                              144
HORATIO   Do, if it will not stand.     [*They strike at it.*]
BERNARDO   'Tis here!                                               146
HORATIO   'Tis here!           [*Exit Ghost.*]    147
MARCELLUS   'Tis gone.
We do it wrong, being so majestical,
To offer it the show of violence,
For it is as the air invulnerable,
And our vain blows malicious mockery.

BERNARDO
It was about to speak when the cock crew.

HORATIO
And then it started like a guilty thing
Upon a fearful summons. I have heard
The cock, that is the trumpet to the morn,                         156
Doth with his lofty and shrill-sounding throat
Awake the god of day, and at his warning,
Whether in sea or fire, in earth or air,
Th'extravagant and erring spirit hies                              160
To his confine; and of the truth herein
This present object made probation.                                162

---

129 **climatures** climes, regions   130 **soft** i.e., enough, break off   131 **cross** stand in its path,
confront   **blast** wither, strike with a curse   131 s.d. *his* its   137 **privy to** in on the secret of
138 **happily** haply, perchance   144 **partisan** long-handled spear   146–147 **'Tis Here! / 'Tis**
**here!** (Perhaps they attempt to strike at the Ghost, but are baffled by its seeming ability to
be here and there and nowhere.)   156 **trumpet** trumpeter   160 **extravagant and erring**
wandering beyond bounds. (The words have similar meaning.)   **hies** hastens
162 **probation** proof

MARCELLUS
It faded on the crowing of the cock.
Some say that ever 'gainst that season comes                164
Wherein our Savior's birth is celebrated,
This bird of dawning singeth all night long,
And then, they say, no spirit dare stir abroad;
The nights are wholesome, then no planets strike,           168
No fairy takes, nor witch hath power to charm,              169
So hallowed and so gracious is that time.                   170
HORATIO
So have I heard and do in part believe it.
But, look, the morn in russet mantle clad                   172
Walks o'er the dew of yon high eastward hill.
Break we our watch up, and by my advice
Let us impart what we have seen tonight
Unto young Hamlet; for upon my life,
This spirit, dumb to us, will speak to him.
Do you consent we shall acquaint him with it,
As needful in our loves, fitting our duty?
MARCELLUS
Let's do't, I pray, and I this morning know
Where we shall find him most conveniently.

*Exeunt.*

❖

# [1.2]

*Flourish. Enter Claudius, King of Denmark,*
*Gertrude the Queen, [the] Council, as Polonius*
*and his son Laertes, Hamlet, cum aliis [including*
*Voltimand and Cornelius].*

KING
Though yet of Hamlet our dear brother's death                1
The memory be green, and that it us befitted
To bear our hearts in grief and our whole kingdom
To be contracted in one brow of woe,
Yet so far hath discretion fought with nature
That we with wisest sorrow think on him
Together with remembrance of ourselves.
Therefore our sometime sister, now our queen,                8
Th'imperial jointress to this warlike state,                 9
Have we, as 'twere with a defeated joy—

---

164 'gainst just before   168 strike destroy by evil influence   169 takes bewitches
charm cast a spell, control by enchantment   170 gracious full of grace   172 russet red-
dish brown
1.2 Location: The castle.
0.2 s.d. as such as, including   0.3 s.d. cum aliis with others   1 our my (the royal "we";
also in the following lines)   8 sometime former   9 jointress woman possessing property
with her husband

With an auspicious and a dropping eye,                              11
With mirth in funeral and with dirge in marriage,
In equal scale weighing delight and dole—                          13
Taken to wife. Nor have we herein barred
Your better wisdoms, which have freely gone
With this affair along. For all, our thanks.
Now follows that you know young Fortinbras,                         17
Holding a weak supposal of our worth,                              18
Or thinking by our late dear brother's death
Our state to be disjoint and out of frame,                         20
Co-leaguèd with this dream of his advantage,                       21
He hath not failed to pester us with message
Importing the surrender of those lands                             23
Lost by his father, with all bonds of law,                         24
To our most valiant brother. So much for him.
Now for ourself and for this time of meeting.
Thus much the business is: we have here writ
To Norway, uncle of young Fortinbras—
Who, impotent and bed-rid, scarcely hears                          29
Of this his nephew's purpose—to suppress
His further gait herein, in that the levies,                       31
The lists, and full proportions are all made                       32
Out of his subject; and we here dispatch                           33
You, good Cornelius, and you, Voltimand,
For bearers of this greeting to old Norway,
Giving to you no further personal power
To business with the King more than the scope
Of these dilated articles allow.      [*He gives a paper.*]        38
Farewell, and let your haste commend your duty.                    39

CORNELIUS, VOLTIMAND
In that, and all things, will we show our duty.

KING
We doubt it nothing. Heartily farewell.                            41
                          [*Exeunt Voltimand and Cornelius.*]
And now, Laertes, what's the news with you?
You told us of some suit; what is't, Laertes?
You cannot speak of reason to the Dane                             44
And lose your voice. What wouldst thou beg, Laertes,               45
That shall not be my offer, not thy asking?

---

11 With . . . eye with one eye smiling and the other weeping   13 dole grief
17 Now . . . know Next, you need to be informed that   18 weak supposal low esti-
mate   20 disjoint . . . frame in a state of total disorder   21 Co-leaguèd . . . advantage
joined to his illusory sense of having the advantage over us and to his vision of future
success   23 Importing having for its substance   24 with . . . law (See 1.1.91, "Well ratified by law and heraldry.")   29 impotent helpless   31 His i.e., Fortinbras's   gait proceeding   31–33 in that . . . subject since the levying of troops and supplies is drawn entirely from the King of Norway's own subjects   38 dilated set out at length   39 let . . .
duty let your swift obeying of orders, rather than mere words, express your dutifulness.
41 nothing not at all   44 the Dane the Danish king   45 lose your voice waste your
speech

The head is not more native to the heart, 47
The hand more instrumental to the mouth, 48
Than is the throne of Denmark to thy father.
What wouldst thou have, Laertes?
LAERTES                             My dread lord,
    Your leave and favor to return to France, 51
    From whence though willingly I came to Denmark
    To show my duty in your coronation,
    Yet now I must confess, that duty done,
    My thoughts and wishes bend again toward France
    And bow them to your gracious leave and pardon. 56
KING
    Have you your father's leave? What says Polonius?
POLONIUS
    H'ath, my lord, wrung from me my slow leave 58
    By laborsome petition, and at last
    Upon his will I sealed my hard consent. 60
    I do beseech you, give him leave to go.
KING
    Take thy fair hour, Laertes. Time be thine, 62
    And thy best graces spend it at thy will. 63
    But now, my cousin Hamlet, and my son— 64
HAMLET
    A little more than kin, and less than kind. 65
KING
    How is it that the clouds still hang on you?
HAMLET
    Not so, my lord. I am too much in the sun. 67
QUEEN
    Good Hamlet, cast thy nighted color off, 68
    And let thine eye look like a friend on Denmark. 69
    Do not forever with thy vailèd lids 70
    Seek for thy noble father in the dust.
    Thou know'st 'tis common, all that lives must die, 72
    Passing through nature to eternity.
HAMLET
    Ay, madam, it is common.

47 native closely connected, related   48 instrumental serviceable   51 leave and favor
kind permission   56 bow . . . pardon entreatingly make a deep bow, asking your permission to depart   58 H'ath He has   60 sealed (as if sealing a legal document).   hard re-
luctant   62 Take thy fair hour Enjoy your time of youth   63 And . . . will and may
your time be spent in exercising your best qualities.   64 cousin any kin not of the immediate family   65 A little . . . kind Too close a blood relation, and yet we are less than
kinsmen in that our relationship lacks affection and is indeed unnatural. (Hamlet plays
on *kind* as [1] kindly and [2] belonging to nature, suggesting that Claudius is not the
same kind of being as the rest of humanity. The line is often delivered as an aside, though
it need not be.)   67 the sun i.e., the sunshine of the King's royal favor (with pun on *son*)
68 nighted color (1) mourning garments of black (2) dark melancholy   69 Denmark the
King of Denmark   70 vailèd lids lowered eyes   72 common of universal occurrence.
(But Hamlet plays on the sense of "vulgar" in line 74.)

QUEEN           If it be,
Why seems it so particular with thee?       75
HAMLET
  Seems, madam? Nay, it is. I know not "seems."
  'Tis not alone my inky cloak, good mother,
  Nor customary suits of solemn black,       78
  Nor windy suspiration of forced breath,       79
  No, nor the fruitful river in the eye,       80
  Nor the dejected havior of the visage,       81
  Together with all forms, moods, shapes of grief,       82
  That can denote me truly. These indeed seem,
  For they are actions that a man might play.
  But I have that within which passes show;
  These but the trappings and the suits of woe.
KING
  'Tis sweet and commendable in your nature, Hamlet,
  To give these mourning duties to your father.
  But you must know your father lost a father,
  That father lost, lost his, and the survivor bound
  In filial obligation for some term
  To do obsequious sorrow. But to persever       92
  In obstinate condolement is a course       93
  Of impious stubbornness. 'Tis unmanly grief.
  It shows a will most incorrect to heaven,
  A heart unfortified, a mind impatient,       96
  An understanding simple and unschooled.       97
  For what we know must be and is as common
  As any the most vulgar thing to sense,       99
  Why should we in our peevish opposition
  Take it to heart? Fie, 'tis a fault to heaven,
  A fault against the dead, a fault to nature,
  To reason most absurd, whose common theme
  Is death of fathers, and who still hath cried,       104
  From the first corpse till he that died today,       105
  "This must be so." We pray you, throw to earth
  This unprevailing woe and think of us       107
  As of a father; for let the world take note,
  You are the most immediate to our throne,       109
  And with no less nobility of love
  Than that which dearest father bears his son
  Do I impart toward you. For your intent       112

---

75 **particular** personal    78 **customary** customary to mourning    79 **suspiration** sighing
80 **fruitful** abundant    81 **havior** expression    82 **moods** outward expression of feeling
92 **obsequious** suited to obsequies or funerals    93 **condolement** sorrowing    96 **unfortified** i.e., against adversity    97 **simple** ignorant    99 **As . . . sense** as the most ordinary
experience    104 **still** always    105 **the first corpse** (Abel's)    107 **unprevailing** unavailing,
useless    109 **most immediate** next in succession    112 **impart toward** liberally bestow on
**For** As for

In going back to school in Wittenberg,                    113
It is most retrograde to our desire,                       114
And we beseech you bend you to remain                     115
Here in the cheer and comfort of our eye,
Our chiefest courtier, cousin, and our son.

QUEEN
Let not thy mother lose her prayers, Hamlet.
I pray thee, stay with us, go not to Wittenberg.

HAMLET
I shall in all my best obey you, madam.                  120

KING
Why, 'tis a loving and a fair reply.
Be as ourself in Denmark. Madam, come.
This gentle and unforced accord of Hamlet
Sits smiling to my heart, in grace whereof               124
No jocund health that Denmark drinks today               125
But the great cannon to the clouds shall tell,
And the King's rouse the heaven shall bruit again,       127
Respeaking earthly thunder. Come away.                   128

*Flourish. Exeunt all but Hamlet.*

HAMLET
Oh, that this too too sullied flesh would melt,          129
Thaw, and resolve itself into a dew!
Or that the Everlasting had not fixed
His canon 'gainst self-slaughter! Oh, God, God,          132
How weary, stale, flat, and unprofitable
Seem to me all the uses of this world!
Fie on't, ah fie! 'Tis an unweeded garden
That grows to seed. Things rank and gross in nature
Possess it merely. That it should come to this!         137
But two months dead—nay, not so much, not two.
So excellent a king, that was to this                    139
Hyperion to a satyr, so loving to my mother             140
That he might not beteem the winds of heaven            141
Visit her face too roughly. Heaven and earth,
Must I remember? Why, she would hang on him
As if increase of appetite had grown
By what it fed on, and yet within a month—
Let me not think on't; frailty, thy name is woman!—
A little month, or ere those shoes were old             147

---

113 **to school** i.e., to your studies   **Wittenberg** famous German university founded in 1502   114 **retrograde** contrary   115 **bend you** incline yourself   120 **in all my best** to the best of my ability   124 **to** i.e., at   **grace** thanksgiving   125 **jocund** merry   127 **rouse** drinking of a draft of liquor   **bruit again** loudly echo   128 **thunder** i.e., of trumpet and kettledrum, sounded when the King drinks; see 1.4.8–12.   129 **sullied** defiled. (The early quartos read "sallied"; the Folio, "solid.")   132 **canon** law   137 **merely** completely   139 **to** in comparison to   140 **Hyperion** Titan sun-god, father of Helios   **satyr** a lecherous creature of classical mythology, half-human but with a goat's legs, tail, ears, and horns   141 **beteem** allow   147 **or ere** even before

**8**

## The Doome, warning

Also there are certain men which haue no heads, but their eyes, nose, and mouth, are fixed in their breastes, so that their belly is close vnder the chin, supposed of those people that haūte ẏ seas to be *Polantines*, who in times past calling Mariners by their names, did in the nighte season deuoure them that came a shore.

*Scipodes and Cathani.* *Scipodes* and *Monomeri*, are people hauing but one foote, without bending their knæ at any time, and yet very swift. Plinie reporteth that in the great heate of the yeare, they lye vpon their backes and with the bignesse of their foote they shadow their bodies from the Sun.

*Cathaini* are a kinde of people of *Scithia*, betwéene *Gedrosa* and the riuer *Indus*: they say that no man liuing but themselues, haue the vse or sighte in both their eyes, but that all other mortall men are cleane voyde of sight, or else that they sée but with one eye, and the other to be blinde: they are of colour very white, their eyes are small and little, they are by nature without haire on their faces, their religion is nothing but mære superstition : they worship the Sun and Moone, and other fonde creatures, and some of them worship an Ore.

*Satiri.*

*Satyri* are foure footed beastes, very dāgerous, abyding vnder the Mountaines, from the Easterly windes with the *Indeas*, formed like vnto men, sauing that theyr nether parts arc like Goates, rough and hearie ouer-theyr bodye, voyde of all humanitie : their chiefe delight is to be in the solitarye woods, far from the companye of men, whome they flye from. Men in the olde time honored such like Monsters as gods of ẏ woods, as were *Fauni, Siltani.*, and *Pane*: these.

Stephen Batman, *The doome warning all men to the judgment* (1581). When Hamlet likens Claudius to a satyr (1.2.140), he refers to legendary monsters. As described by Stephen Batman, they are "foore footed beastes, very dangerous, abyding under the Mountaines . . . formed like to men, saving that theyr nether parts are like Goates." Here one converses with St. Jerome. (By permission of the Folger Shakespeare Library.)

With which she followed my poor father's body,
Like Niobe, all tears, why she, even she—                    149
Oh, God, a beast, that wants discourse of reason,            150
Would have mourned longer—married with my
    uncle,
My father's brother, but no more like my father
Than I to Hercules. Within a month,
Ere yet the salt of most unrighteous tears
Had left the flushing in her gallèd eyes,                    155
She married. Oh, most wicked speed, to post               156
With such dexterity to incestuous sheets!                   157
It is not, nor it cannot come to good.
But break, my heart, for I must hold my tongue.

        *Enter Horatio, Marcellus, and Bernardo.*

HORATIO
Hail to Your Lordship!
HAMLET                     I am glad to see you well.
Horatio!—or I do forget myself.
HORATIO
The same, my lord, and your poor servant ever.
HAMLET
Sir, my good friend; I'll change that name with you.        163
And what make you from Wittenberg, Horatio?—               164
Marcellus.
MARCELLUS   My good lord.
HAMLET
I am very glad to see you. [*To Bernardo*] Good even,
    sir.—
But what in faith make you from Wittenberg?
HORATIO
A truant disposition, good my lord.
HAMLET
I would not hear your enemy say so,
Nor shall you do my ear that violence
To make it truster of your own report                       171
Against yourself. I know you are no truant.
But what is your affair in Elsinore?
We'll teach you to drink deep ere you depart.
HORATIO
My lord, I came to see your father's funeral.

149 **Niobes** Tantalus's daughter, Queen of Thebes, who boasted that she had more sons
and daughters than Leto; for this, Apollo and Artemis, children of Leto, slew her fourteen children. She was turned by Zeus into a stone that continually dropped tears.
150 **wants . . . reason** lacks the faculty of reason   155 **gallèd** irritated, inflamed
156 **post** hasten   157 **incestuous** (In Shakespeare's day, the marriage of a man like
Claudius to his deceased brother's wife was considered incestuous.)   163 **change that
name** i.e., give and receive reciprocally the name of "friend" rather than talk of "servant." Or Hamlet may be saying, "No, I am *your* servant."   164 **what make you from**
what are you doing away from   171 **To . . . of** to make it trust

HAMLET
I prithee, do not mock me, fellow student;
I think it was to see my mother's wedding.
HORATIO
Indeed, my lord, it followed hard upon.                      179
HAMLET
Thrift, thrift, Horatio! The funeral baked meats             180
Did coldly furnish forth the marriage tables.                181
Would I had met my dearest foe in heaven                     182
Or ever I had seen that day, Horatio!                        183
My father!—Methinks I see my father.
HORATIO
Where, my lord?
HAMLET                In my mind's eye, Horatio.
HORATIO
I saw him once. 'A was a goodly king.                        186
HAMLET
'A was a man. Take him for all in all,
I shall not look upon his like again.
HORATIO
My lord, I think I saw him yesternight.
HAMLET    Saw? Who?
HORATIO    My lord, the King your father.
HAMLET    The King my father?
HORATIO
Season your admiration for a while                           193
With an attent ear till I may deliver,                       194
Upon the witness of these gentlemen,
This marvel to you.
HAMLET                For God's love, let me hear!
HORATIO
Two nights together had these gentlemen,
Marcellus and Bernardo, on their watch,
In the dead waste and middle of the night,                   199
Been thus encountered. A figure like your father,
Armèd at point exactly, cap-à-pie,                           201
Appears before them, and with solemn march
Goes slow and stately by them. Thrice he walked
By their oppressed and fear-surprisèd eyes
Within his truncheon's length, whilst they, distilled        205
Almost to jelly with the act of fear,                        206
Stand dumb and speak not to him. This to me
In dreadful secrecy impart they did,                         208

179 **hard** close    180 **baked meats** meat pies    181 **coldly** i.e., as cold leftovers
182 **dearest** closest (and therefore deadliest)    183 **Or ever** ere, before    186 **'A** He
193 **Season your admiration** Moderate your astonishment    194 **attent** attentive
199 **dead waste** desolate stillness    201 **at point** correctly in every detail    **cap-à-pie** from
head to foot    205 **truncheon** officer's staff    **distilled** dissolved    206 **act** action,
operation    208 **dreadful** full of dread

And I with them the third night kept the watch,
Where, as they had delivered, both in time,
Form of the thing, each word made true and good,
The apparition comes. I knew your father;
These hands are not more like.

HAMLET                                  But where was this?
MARCELLUS
My lord, upon the platform where we watch.
HAMLET
Did you not speak to it?
HORATIO                     My lord, I did,
But answer made it none. Yet once methought
It lifted up it head and did address                          217
Itself to motion, like as it would speak;                     218
But even then the morning cock crew loud,                     219
And at the sound it shrunk in haste away
And vanished from our sight.
HAMLET                         'Tis very strange.
HORATIO
As I do live, my honored lord, 'tis true,
And we did think it writ down in our duty
To let you know of it.
HAMLET
Indeed, indeed, sirs. But this troubles me.
Hold you the watch tonight?
ALL                            We do, my lord.
HAMLET   Armed, say you?
ALL   Armed, my lord.
HAMLET   From top to toe?
ALL   My lord, from head to foot.
HAMLET   Then saw you not his face?
HORATIO
Oh, yes, my lord, he wore his beaver up.                      232
HAMLET   What looked he, frowningly?                           233
HORATIO
A countenance more in sorrow than in anger.
HAMLET   Pale or red?
HORATIO   Nay, very pale.
HAMLET   And fixed his eyes upon you?
HORATIO   Most constantly.
HAMLET   I would I had been there.
HORATIO   It would have much amazed you.
HAMLET   Very like, very like. Stayed it long?
HORATIO
While one with moderate haste might tell a hundred.           242

---

**217 it** its   **217–218 did . . . speak** prepared to move as though it was about to speak
**219 even then** at that very instant   **232 beaver** visor on the helmet   **233 What** How
**242 tell** count

MARCELLUS, BERNARDO   Longer, longer.

HORATIO   Not when I saw't.

HAMLET   His beard was grizzled—no?

HORATIO
It was, as I have seen it in his life,
A sable silvered.

HAMLET                    I will watch tonight.
Perchance 'twill walk again.

HORATIO                              I warr'nt it will.

HAMLET
If it assume my noble father's person,
I'll speak to it though hell itself should gape
And bid me hold my peace. I pray you all,
If you have hitherto concealed this sight,
Let it be tenable in your silence still,                                    253
And whatsomever else shall hap tonight,
Give it an understanding but no tongue.
I will requite your loves. So, fare you well.
Upon the platform twixt eleven and twelve
I'll visit you.

ALL                    Our duty to Your Honor.

HAMLET
Your loves, as mine to you. Farewell.                           259
                                        *Exeunt [all but Hamlet].*
My father's spirit in arms! All is not well.
I doubt some foul play. Would the night were come!          261
Till then sit still, my soul. Foul deeds will rise,
Though all the earth o'erwhelm them, to men's eyes.
                                                              *Exit.*

❖

# [1.3]

*Enter Laertes and Ophelia, his sister.*

LAERTES
My necessaries are embarked. Farewell.
And, sister, as the winds give benefit
And convoy is assistant, do not sleep                              3
But let me hear from you.

OPHELIA                         Do you doubt that?

LAERTES
For Hamlet, and the trifling of his favor,                         5

---

253 **tenable** held   259 **Your loves** i.e., Say "Your loves" to me, not just your "duty."
261 **doubt** suspect
1.3 Location: Polonius's chambers.
3 **convoy is assistant** means of conveyance are available   5 **For** As for

Hold it a fashion and a toy in blood, 6
A violet in the youth of primy nature, 7
Forward, not permanent, sweet, not lasting, 8
The perfume and suppliance of a minute— 9
No more.

OPHELIA     No more but so?

LAERTES                    Think it no more.
For nature crescent does not grow alone 11
In thews and bulk, but as this temple waxes 12
The inward service of the mind and soul
Grows wide withal. Perhaps he loves you now, 14
And now no soil nor cautel doth besmirch 15
The virtue of his will; but you must fear, 16
His greatness weighed, his will is not his own. 17
For he himself is subject to his birth.
He may not, as unvalued persons do,
Carve for himself, for on his choice depends 20
The safety and health of this whole state,
And therefore must his choice be circumscribed
Unto the voice and yielding of that body 23
Whereof he is the head. Then if he says he loves you,
It fits your wisdom so far to believe it
As he in his particular act and place 26
May give his saying deed, which is no further
Than the main voice of Denmark goes withal. 28
Then weigh what loss your honor may sustain
If with too credent ear you list his songs, 30
Or lose your heart, or your chaste treasure open
To his unmastered importunity. 32
Fear it, Ophelia, fear it, my dear sister,
And keep you in the rear of your affection, 34
Out of the shot and danger of desire.
The chariest maid is prodigal enough 36
If she unmask her beauty to the moon. 37
Virtue itself scapes not calumnious strokes.
The canker galls the infants of the spring 39
Too oft before their buttons be disclosed, 40

---

**6 toy in blood** passing amorous fancy  **7 primy** in its prime, springtime  **8 Forward** precocious  **9 suppliance** pastime, something to fill the time  **11–14 For nature . . . withal** For nature, as it ripens, does not grow only in physical strength, but as the body matures the inner qualities of mind and soul grow along with it. (Laertes warns Ophelia that the mature Hamlet may not cling to his youthful interests.)  **15 soil nor cautel** blemish nor deceit  **16 The . . . will** the purity of his desire  **17 His greatness weighed** taking into account his high fortune  **20 Carve** i.e., choose  **23 voice and yielding** assent, approval  **26 in . . . place** in his particular restricted circumstances  **28 main voice** general assent  **withal** along with  **30 credent** credulous  **list** listen to  **32 unmastered** uncontrolled  **34 keep . . . affection** don't advance as far as your affection might lead you (a military metaphor)  **36 chariest** most scrupulously modest  **37 If she unmask** if she does no more than show  **moon** (symbol of chastity)  **39 canker galls** cankerworm destroys  **40 buttons be disclosed** buds be opened

And in the morn and liquid dew of youth                    41
Contagious blastments are most imminent.                    42
Be wary then; best safety lies in fear.
Youth to itself rebels, though none else near.              44

OPHELIA
I shall the effect of this good lesson keep
As watchman to my heart. But, good my brother,
Do not, as some ungracious pastors do,                      47
Show me the steep and thorny way to heaven,
Whiles like a puffed and reckless libertine                 49
Himself the primrose path of dalliance treads,
And recks not his own rede.

*Enter Polonius.*

LAERTES                    Oh, fear me not.                 51
I stay too long. But here my father comes.
A double blessing is a double grace;                        53
Occasion smiles upon a second leave.                        54

POLONIUS
Yet here, Laertes? Aboard, aboard, for shame!
The wind sits in the shoulder of your sail,
And you are stayed for. There—my blessing with thee!
And these few precepts in thy memory
Look thou character. Give thy thoughts no tongue,           59
Nor any unproportioned thought his act.                     60
Be thou familiar, but by no means vulgar.                   61
Those friends thou hast, and their adoption tried,          62
Grapple them unto thy soul with hoops of steel,
But do not dull thy palm with entertainment                 64
Of each new-hatched, unfledged courage. Beware             65
Of entrance to a quarrel, but being in,
Bear't that th'opposèd may beware of thee.                  67
Give every man thy ear, but few thy voice;
Take each man's censure, but reserve thy judgment.          69
Costly thy habit as thy purse can buy,                      70
But not expressed in fancy; rich, not gaudy,               71
For the apparel oft proclaims the man,
And they in France of the best rank and station

---

41 **liquid dew** i.e., time when dew is fresh and bright   42 **blastments** blights   44 **Youth . . . rebels** Youth yields to the rebellion of the flesh   47 **ungracious** ungodly   49 **puffed** bloated or swollen with pride   51 **recks** heeds   **rede** counsel   **fear me not** don't worry on my account   53–54 **A double . . . leave** The goddess Occasion or Opportunity smiles on the happy circumstance of being able to say good-bye twice and thus receive a second blessing.   59 **Look thou character** see to it that you inscribe   60 **unproportioned** badly calculated, intemperate   **his** its   61 **familiar** sociable   **vulgar** common   62 **and . . . tried** and their suitability to be your friends having been put to the test   64 **dull thy palm** i.e., shake hands so often as to make the gesture meaningless   65 **courage** swashbuckler   67 **Bear't that** manage it so that   69 **censure** opinion, judgment   70 **habit** clothing   71 **fancy** excessive ornament, decadent fashion

Are of a most select and generous chief in that.                           74
Neither a borrower nor a lender be,
For loan oft loses both itself and friend,
And borrowing dulleth edge of husbandry.                                   77
This above all: to thine own self be true,
And it must follow, as the night the day,
Thou canst not then be false to any man.
Farewell. My blessing season this in thee!                                 81
LAERTES
Most humbly do I take my leave, my lord.
POLONIUS
The time invests you. Go, your servants tend.                              83
LAERTES
Farewell, Ophelia, and remember well
What I have said to you.
OPHELIA    'Tis in my memory locked,
And you yourself shall keep the key of it.
LAERTES    Farewell.                              *Exit Laertes.*
POLONIUS
What is't, Ophelia, he hath said to you?
OPHELIA
So please you, something touching the Lord Hamlet.
POLONIUS    Marry, well bethought.                                         91
'Tis told me he hath very oft of late
Given private time to you, and you yourself
Have of your audience been most free and bounteous.
If it be so—as so 'tis put on me,                                         95
And that in way of caution—I must tell you
You do not understand yourself so clearly
As it behooves my daughter and your honor.                                98
What is between you? Give me up the truth.
OPHELIA
He hath, my lord, of late made many tenders                              100
Of his affection to me.
POLONIUS
Affection? Pooh! You speak like a green girl,
Unsifted in such perilous circumstance.                                  103
Do you believe his tenders, as you call them?
OPHELIA
I do not know, my lord, what I should think.
POLONIUS
Marry, I will teach you. Think yourself a baby
That you have ta'en these tenders for true pay

---

**74 Are . . . that** are of a most refined and well-bred preeminence in choosing what to wear   **77 husbandry** thrift   **81 season** mature   **83 invests** besieges, presses upon   **tend** attend, wait   **91 Marry** i.e., By the Virgin Mary (a mild oath)   **95 put on** impressed on, told to   **98 behooves** befits   **100 tenders** offers   **103 Unsifted** i.e., untried

Which are not sterling. Tender yourself more dearly,   108
Or—not to crack the wind of the poor phrase,   109
Running it thus—you'll tender me a fool.   110

OPHELIA
My lord, he hath importuned me with love
In honorable fashion.

POLONIUS
Ay, fashion you may call it. Go to, go to.   113

OPHELIA
And hath given countenance to his speech, my lord,   114
With almost all the holy vows of heaven.

POLONIUS
Ay, springes to catch woodcocks. I do know,   116
When the blood burns, how prodigal the soul   117
Lends the tongue vows. These blazes, daughter,
Giving more light than heat, extinct in both
Even in their promise as it is a-making,   120
You must not take for fire. From this time
Be something scanter of your maiden presence.   122
Set your entreatments at a higher rate   123
Than a command to parle. For Lord Hamlet,   124
Believe so much in him that he is young,   125
And with a larger tether may he walk
Than may be given you. In few, Ophelia,   127
Do not believe his vows, for they are brokers,   128
Not of that dye which their investments show,   129
But mere implorators of unholy suits,   130
Breathing like sanctified and pious bawds,   131
The better to beguile. This is for all:   132
I would not, in plain terms, from this time forth
Have you so slander any moment leisure   134
As to give words or talk with the Lord Hamlet.
Look to't, I charge you. Come your ways.   136

OPHELIA   I shall obey, my lord.      *Exeunt.*

108 **sterling** legal currency   **Tender . . . dearly** (1) Bargain for your favors at a higher rate—i.e., hold out for marriage (2) Show greater care of yourself   109 **crack the wind** i.e., run it until it is broken-winded   110 **tender . . . fool** (1) make a fool of me (2) present me with a *fool* or baby   113 **fashion** mere form, pretense   **Go to** (an expression of impatience.)   114 **countenance** credit, confirmation   116 **springes** snares **woodcocks** birds easily caught; here used to connote gullibility.   117 **prodigal** prodigally   120 **it** i.e., the promise   122 **something** somewhat   123–124 **Set . . . parle** i.e., As defender of your chastity, negotiate for something better than a surrender simply because the besieger requests an interview.   124 **For** As for   125 **so . . . him** this much concerning him   127 **In few** Briefly   128 **brokers** go-betweens, procurers   129 **dye** color or sort   **investments** clothes. (The vows are not what they seem.)   130 **mere implorators** out-and-out solicitors   131 **Breathing** speaking   132 **for all** once for all, in sum   134 **slander** abuse, misuse   **moment** moment's   136 **Come your ways** Come along

# [1.4]

*Enter Hamlet, Horatio, and Marcellus.*

HAMLET
The air bites shrewdly; it is very cold.                                    1
HORATIO
It is a nipping and an eager air.                                          2
HAMLET
What hour now?
HORATIO                           I think it lacks of twelve.              3
MARCELLUS
No, it is struck.
HORATIO                   Indeed? I heard it not.
It then draws near the season                                             5
Wherein the spirit held his wont to walk.                                 6
      *A flourish of trumpets, and two pieces go off*
                          *[within].*
What does this mean, my lord?
HAMLET
The King doth wake tonight and takes his rouse,                           8
Keeps wassail, and the swagg'ring upspring reels;                        9
And as he drains his drafts of Rhenish down,                             10
The kettledrum and trumpet thus bray out
The triumph of his pledge.
HORATIO                           Is it a custom?                          12
HAMLET Ay, marry, is't,
But to my mind, though I am native here
And to the manner born, it is a custom                                   15
More honored in the breach than the observance.                          16
This heavy-headed revel east and west                                    17
Makes us traduced and taxed of other nations.                            18
They clepe us drunkards, and with swinish phrase                         19
Soil our addition; and indeed it takes                                   20
From our achievements, though performed at height,                       21
The pith and marrow of our attribute.                                    22
So, oft it chances in particular men,
That for some vicious mole of nature in them,                            24
As in their birth—wherein they are not guilty,

---

1.4 **Location:** The guard platform.
1 **shrewdly** keenly, sharply   2 **eager** biting   3 **lacks of** is just short of   5 **season** time
6 **held his wont** was accustomed   6.1 s.d. *pieces* i.e., of ordnance, cannon   8 **wake** stay
awake and hold revel   **takes his rouse** carouses   9 **Keeps . . . reels** carouses, and ri-
otously dances a German dance called the upspring   10 **Rhenish** Rhine wine   12 **The
triumph . . . pledge** the celebration of his offering a toast   15 **manner** custom (of drinking)   16 **More . . . observance** better neglected than followed   17 **east and west** i.e.,
everywhere   18 **taxed of** censured by   19 **clepe** call   **with swinish phrase** i.e., by calling us swine   20 **addition** reputation   21 **at height** outstandingly   22 **The pith . . . attribute** the most essential part of the esteem that should be attributed to us   24 **for . . .
mole** on account of some natural defect in their constitutions

Since nature cannot choose his origin— 26
By their o'ergrowth of some complexion, 27
Oft breaking down the pales and forts of reason, 28
Or by some habit that too much o'erleavens 29
The form of plausive manners, that these men, 30
Carrying, I say, the stamp of one defect,
Being nature's livery or fortune's star, 32
His virtues else, be they as pure as grace, 33
As infinite as man may undergo, 34
Shall in the general censure take corruption 35
From that particular fault. The dram of evil 36
Doth all the noble substance often dout 37
To his own scandal.

    *Enter Ghost.*

HORATIO          Look, my lord, it comes! 38
HAMLET
Angels and ministers of grace defend us! 39
Be thou a spirit of health or goblin damned, 40
Bring with thee airs from heaven or blasts from hell, 41
Be thy intents wicked or charitable, 42
Thou com'st in such a questionable shape 43
That I will speak to thee. I'll call thee Hamlet,
King, father, royal Dane. Oh, answer me!
Let me not burst in ignorance, but tell
Why thy canonized bones, hearsèd in death, 47
Have burst their cerements; why the sepulcher 48
Wherein we saw thee quietly inurned 49
Hath oped his ponderous and marble jaws
To cast thee up again. What may this mean,
That thou, dead corpse, again in complete steel, 52
Revisits thus the glimpses of the moon, 53
Making night hideous, and we fools of nature 54
So horridly to shake our disposition 55

---

26 **his** its  27 **their o'ergrowth** . . . **complexion** the excessive growth in individuals of some natural trait  28 **pales** palings, fences (as of a fortification)  29–30 **o'erleavens** . . . **manners** i.e., infects the way we should behave (much as bad yeast spoils the dough). *Plausive* means "pleasing."  32 **Being** . . . **star** (that stamp of defect) being a sign identifying one as wearing the livery of, and hence being the servant to, nature (unfortunate inherited qualities) or fortune (mischance)  33 **His virtues else** i.e., the other qualities of *these men* (line 30)  34 **may undergo** can sustain  35 **in** . . . **censure** in overall appraisal, in people's opinion generally  36–38 **The dram** . . . **scandal** i.e., The small drop of evil blots out or works against the noble substance of the whole and brings it into disrepute. (To *dout* is to blot out. A famous crux.)  39 **ministers of grace** messengers of God  40 **Be** . . . **health** Whether you are a good angel  41 **Bring** whether you bring  42 **Be thy intents** whether your intentions are  43 **questionable** inviting question  47 **canonized** buried according to the canons of the church  **hearsèd** coffined  48 **cerements** grave clothes  49 **inurned** entombed  52 **complete steel** full armor  53 **the glimpses** . . . **moon** i.e., the sublunary world, all that is beneath the moon  54 **fools of nature** mere mortals, limited to natural knowledge and subject to nature  55 **So** . . . **disposition** to distress our mental composure so violently

With thoughts beyond the reaches of our souls?
Say, why is this? Wherefore? What should we do?
                                    [*The Ghost*] *beckons* [*Hamlet*].
HORATIO
It beckons you to go away with it,
As if it some impartment did desire                              59
To you alone.
MARCELLUS          Look with what courteous action
It wafts you to a more removèd ground.
But do not go with it.
HORATIO                    No, by no means.
HAMLET
It will not speak. Then I will follow it.
HORATIO
Do not, my lord!
HAMLET                Why, what should be the fear?
I do not set my life at a pin's fee,                             65
And for my soul, what can it do to that,                        66
Being a thing immortal as itself?
It waves me forth again. I'll follow it.
HORATIO
What if it tempt you toward the flood, my lord,                 69
Or to the dreadful summit of the cliff
That beetles o'er his base into the sea,                        71
And there assume some other horrible form
Which might deprive your sovereignty of reason                  73
And draw you into madness? Think of it.
The very place puts toys of desperation,                        75
Without more motive, into every brain
That looks so many fathoms to the sea
And hears it roar beneath.
HAMLET
It wafts me still.—Go on, I'll follow thee.
MARCELLUS
You shall not go, my lord.      [*They try to stop him.*]
HAMLET                    Hold off your hands!
HORATIO
Be ruled. You shall not go.
HAMLET                          My fate cries out,                81
And makes each petty artery in this body                        82
As hardy as the Nemean lion's nerve.                            83
Still am I called. Unhand me, gentlemen.

**59 impartment** communication   **65 fee** value   **66 for** as for   **69 flood** sea   **71 beetles**
**o'er** overhangs threateningly (like bushy eyebrows)   **his** its   **73 deprive . . . reason** take
away the rule of reason over your mind   **75 toys of desperation** fancies of desperate
acts, i.e., suicide   **81 My fate cries out** My destiny summons me   **82 petty** weak
**artery** blood vessel system through which the vital spirits were thought to have been
conveyed   **83 as the Nemean lion's nerve** as a sinew of the huge lion slain by Hercules
as the first of his twelve labors

By heaven, I'll make a ghost of him that lets me!                    85
I say, away!—Go on, I'll follow thee.
                                          *Exeunt Ghost and Hamlet.*
HORATIO
He waxes desperate with imagination.
MARCELLUS
Let's follow. 'Tis not fit thus to obey him.
HORATIO
Have after. To what issue will this come?                           89
MARCELLUS
Something is rotten in the state of Denmark.
HORATIO
Heaven will direct it.
MARCELLUS          Nay, let's follow him.      *Exeunt.*             91

❖

# [1.5]

*Enter Ghost and Hamlet.*

HAMLET
Whither wilt thou lead me? Speak. I'll go no further.
GHOST
Mark me.
HAMLET      I will.
GHOST                My hour is almost come,
When I to sulf'rous and tormenting flames
Must render up myself.
HAMLET                      Alas, poor ghost!
GHOST
Pity me not, but lend thy serious hearing
To what I shall unfold.
HAMLET      Speak. I am bound to hear.                               7
GHOST
So art thou to revenge, when thou shalt hear.
HAMLET      What?
GHOST      I am thy father's spirit,
Doomed for a certain term to walk the night,
And for the day confined to fast in fires,                          12
Till the foul crimes done in my days of nature                      13
Are burnt and purged away. But that I am forbid                     14
To tell the secrets of my prison house,

---

85 **lets** hinders   89 **Have after** Let's go after him.   **issue** outcome   91 **it** i.e., the outcome.
**1.5 Location:** The battlements of the castle.
7 **bound** (1) ready (2) obligated by duty and fate. (The Ghost, in line 8, answers in the second sense.)   12 **fast** do penance by fasting   13 **crimes** sins   **of nature** as a mortal   14 **But that** Were it not that

I could a tale unfold whose lightest word
Would harrow up thy soul, freeze thy young blood,                          17
Make thy two eyes like stars start from their spheres,                      18
Thy knotted and combinèd locks to part,                                      19
And each particular hair to stand on end
Like quills upon the fretful porcupine.
But this eternal blazon must not be                                          22
To ears of flesh and blood. List, list, oh, list!
If thou didst ever thy dear father love—
HAMLET   Oh, God!
GHOST
Revenge his foul and most unnatural murder.
HAMLET   Murder?
GHOST
Murder most foul, as in the best it is,                                      28
But this most foul, strange, and unnatural.
HAMLET
Haste me to know't, that I, with wings as swift
As meditation or the thoughts of love,
May sweep to my revenge.
GHOST                          I find thee apt;
And duller shouldst thou be than the fat weed                                33
That roots itself in ease on Lethe wharf,                                    34
Wouldst thou not stir in this. Now, Hamlet, hear.
'Tis given out that, sleeping in my orchard,                                 36
A serpent stung me. So the whole ear of Denmark
Is by a forgèd process of my death                                           38
Rankly abused. But know, thou noble youth,                                   39
The serpent that did sting thy father's life
Now wears his crown.
HAMLET   Oh, my prophetic soul! My uncle!
GHOST
Ay, that incestuous, that adulterate beast,                                  43
With witchcraft of his wit, with traitorous gifts—                          44
Oh, wicked wit and gifts, that have the power
So to seduce!—won to his shameful lust
The will of my most seeming-virtuous queen.
Oh, Hamlet, what a falling off was there!
From me, whose love was of that dignity
That it went hand in hand even with the vow                                  50
I made to her in marriage, and to decline

17 **harrow up** lacerate, tear   18 **spheres** i.e., eye-sockets, here compared to the orbits
or transparent revolving spheres in which, according to Ptolemaic astronomy, the heavenly bodies were fixed   19 **knotted . . . locks** hair neatly arranged and confined
22 **eternal blazon** revelation of the secrets of eternity   28 **in the best** even at best
33 **shouldst thou be** you would have to be   **fat** torpid, lethargic   34 **Lethe** the river
of forgetfulness in Hades   36 **orchard** garden   38 **forgèd process** falsified account
39 **abused** deceived   43 **adulterate** adulterous   44 **gifts** (1) talents (2) presents
50 **even with the vow** with the very vow

Upon a wretch whose natural gifts were poor
To those of mine!                                                              53
But virtue, as it never will be moved,                                         54
Though lewdness court it in a shape of heaven,                                 55
So lust, though to a radiant angel linked,
Will sate itself in a celestial bed                                            57
And prey on garbage.
But soft, methinks I scent the morning air.
Brief let me be. Sleeping within my orchard,
My custom always of the afternoon,
Upon my secure hour thy uncle stole,                                          62
With juice of cursèd hebona in a vial,                                         63
And in the porches of my ears did pour                                         64
The leprous distillment, whose effect                                          65
Holds such an enmity with blood of man
That swift as quicksilver it courses through
The natural gates and alleys of the body,                                      68
And with a sudden vigor it doth posset                                         69
And curd, like eager droppings into milk,                                      70
The thin and wholesome blood. So did it mine,
And a most instant tetter barked about,                                        72
Most lazar-like, with vile and loathsome crust,                                73
All my smooth body.
Thus was I, sleeping, by a brother's hand
Of life, of crown, of queen at once dispatched,                                76
Cut off even in the blossoms of my sin,
Unhouseled, disappointed, unaneled,                                            78
No reck'ning made, but sent to my account                                      79
With all my imperfections on my head.
Oh, horrible! Oh, horrible, most horrible!
If thou hast nature in thee, bear it not.                                      82
Let not the royal bed of Denmark be
A couch for luxury and damnèd incest.                                          84
But, howsomever thou pursues this act,
Taint not thy mind nor let thy soul contrive
Against thy mother aught. Leave her to heaven
And to those thorns that in her bosom lodge,
To prick and sting her. Fare thee well at once.

---

**53 To** compared with   **54 virtue, as it** just as virtue   **55 shape of heaven** heavenly form   **57 sate . . . bed** gratify its lustful appetite to the point of revulsion or ennui, even in a virtuously lawful marriage   **62 secure hour** time of being free from worries **63 hebona** a poison. (The word seems to be a form of *ebony*, though it is thought perhaps to be related to *henbane*, a poison, or to *ebenus*, "yew.")   **64 porches** gateways **65 leprous distillment** distillation causing leprosylike disfigurement   **68 gates** entryways **69–70 posset . . . curd** coagulate and curdle   **70 eager** sour, acid   **72 tetter** eruption of scabs   **barked** covered with a rough covering, like bark on a tree   **73 lazar-like** leperlike   **76 dispatched** suddenly deprived   **78 Unhouseled . . . unaneled** without having received the Sacrament or other last rites including confession, absolution, and the holy oil of extreme unction   **79 reck'ning** settling of accounts   **82 nature** i.e., the promptings of a son   **84 luxury** lechery

The glowworm shows the matin to be near, 90
And 'gins to pale his uneffectual fire. 91
Adieu, adieu, adieu! Remember me. *[Exit.]*

HAMLET
O all you host of heaven! O earth! What else?
And shall I couple hell? Oh, fie! Hold, hold, my heart, 94
And you, my sinews, grow not instant old, 95
But bear me stiffly up. Remember thee?
Ay, thou poor ghost, whiles memory holds a seat
In this distracted globe. Remember thee? 98
Yea, from the table of my memory 99
I'll wipe away all trivial fond records, 100
All saws of books, all forms, all pressures past 101
That youth and observation copied there,
And thy commandment all alone shall live
Within the book and volume of my brain,
Unmixed with baser matter. Yes, by heaven!
Oh, most pernicious woman!
Oh, villain, villain, smiling, damnèd villain!
My tables—meet it is I set it down 108
That one may smile, and smile, and be a villain.
At least I am sure it may be so in Denmark.
So, uncle, there you are. Now to my word: 111
It is "Adieu, adieu! Remember me."
I have sworn't.

*Enter Horatio and Marcellus.*

HORATIO  My lord, my lord!
MARCELLUS  Lord Hamlet!
HORATIO  Heavens secure him! 116
HAMLET  So be it.
MARCELLUS  Hillo, ho, ho, my lord!
HAMLET  Hillo, ho, ho, boy! Come, bird, come. 119
MARCELLUS  How is't, my noble lord?
HORATIO  What news, my lord?
HAMLET  Oh, wonderful!
HORATIO  Good my lord, tell it.
HAMLET  No, you will reveal it.
HORATIO  Not I, my lord, by heaven.
MARCELLUS  Nor I, my lord.

---

**90 matin** morning **91 his** its **94 couple** add **Hold** Hold together **95 instant** instantly **98 globe** (1) head (2) world (3) Globe Theater **99 table** tablet, slate **100 fond** foolish **101 All . . . past** all wise sayings, all shapes or images imprinted on the tablets of my memory, all past impressions **108 My tables . . . down** Editors often specify that Hamlet makes a note in his writing tablet, but he may simply mean that he is making a mental observation of lasting impression **111 there you are** i.e., there, I've noted that against you. **116 secure him** keep him safe **119 Hillo . . . come** (A falconer's call to a hawk in air. Hamlet mocks the hallooing as though it were a part of hawking.)

HAMLET
How say you, then, would heart of man once think it?                    127
But you'll be secret?
HORATIO, MARCELLUS   Ay, by heaven, my lord.
HAMLET
There's never a villain dwelling in all Denmark
But he's an arrant knave.                                               130
HORATIO
There needs no ghost, my lord, come from the grave
To tell us this.
HAMLET          Why, right, you are in the right.
And so, without more circumstance at all,                              133
I hold it fit that we shake hands and part,
You as your business and desire shall point you—
For every man hath business and desire,
Such as it is—and for my own poor part,
Look you, I'll go pray.
HORATIO
These are but wild and whirling words, my lord.
HAMLET
I am sorry they offend you, heartily;
Yes, faith, heartily.
HORATIO             There's no offense, my lord.
HAMLET
Yes, by Saint Patrick, but there is, Horatio,                          142
And much offense too. Touching this vision here,                       143
It is an honest ghost, that let me tell you.                           144
For your desire to know what is between us,
O'ermaster't as you may. And now, good friends,
As you are friends, scholars, and soldiers,
Give me one poor request.
HORATIO   What is't, my lord? We will.
HAMLET
Never make known what you have seen tonight.
HORATIO, MARCELLUS   My lord, we will not.
HAMLET   Nay, but swear't.
HORATIO   In faith, my lord, not I.                                     153
MARCELLUS   Nor I, my lord, in faith.
HAMLET   Upon my sword.   [*He holds out his sword.*]                   155
MARCELLUS   We have sworn, my lord, already.                           156
HAMLET   Indeed, upon my sword, indeed.
GHOST (*cries under the stage*)   Swear.

---

**127 once** ever   **130 But ... knave** (Hamlet jokingly gives a self-evident answer:
every villain is a thoroughgoing knave.)   **133 circumstance** ceremony, elaboration
**142 Saint Patrick** the keeper of Purgatory   **143 offense** (Hamlet deliberately changes
Horatio's "no offense taken" to "an offense against all decency.")   **144 honest** genuine
**153 In faith ... I** i.e., I swear not to tell what I have seen. (Horatio is not refusing to
swear.)   **155 sword** i.e., the hilt in the form of a cross   **156 We ... already** i.e., We
swore *in faith.*

HAMLET
Ha, ha, boy, say'st thou so? Art thou there, truepenny?    159
Come on, you hear this fellow in the cellarage.
Consent to swear.
HORATIO                    Propose the oath, my lord.
HAMLET
Never to speak of this that you have seen,
Swear by my sword.
GHOST [*beneath*]    Swear.              [*They swear.*]    164
HAMLET
*Hic et ubique?* Then we'll shift our ground.              165
                              [*He moves to another spot.*]
Come hither, gentlemen,
And lay your hands again upon my sword.
Swear by my sword
Never to speak of this that you have heard.
GHOST [*beneath*]    Swear by his sword.    [*They swear.*]
HAMLET
Well said, old mole. Canst work i'th'earth so fast?
A worthy pioneer!—Once more remove, good friends.         172
                              [*He moves again.*]
HORATIO
Oh, day and night, but this is wondrous strange!
HAMLET
And therefore as a stranger give it welcome.              174
There are more things in heaven and earth, Horatio,
Than are dreamt of in your philosophy.                    176
But come;
Here, as before, never, so help you mercy,                178
How strange or odd some'er I bear myself—
As I perchance hereafter shall think meet
To put an antic disposition on—                           181
That you, at such times seeing me, never shall,
With arms encumbered thus, or this headshake,             183
Or by pronouncing of some doubtful phrase
As "Well, we know," or "We could, an if we would,"        185
Or "If we list to speak," or "There be, an if they
     might,"                                               186
Or such ambiguous giving out, to note                     187

159 **truepenny** honest old fellow    164 **s.d.** *They swear* (Seemingly they swear here,
and at lines 170 and 190, as they lay their hands on Hamlet's sword. Triple oaths
would have particular force; these three oaths deal with what they have seen, what
they have heard, and what they promise about Hamlet's *antic disposition*.)    165 *Hic
et ubique?* Here and everywhere? (Latin)    172 **pioneer** foot soldier assigned to dig
tunnels and excavations    174 **as a stranger** i.e., needing your hospitality    176 **your
philosophy** this subject that is called "natural philosophy" or "science." (*Your* is not
personal.)    178 **so help you mercy** as you hope for God's mercy when you are judged
181 **antic** grotesque, strange    183 **encumbered** folded    185 **an if** if    186 **list** wished
**There . . . might** There are those who could talk if they were at liberty to do so.
187 **note** indicate

That you know aught of me—this do swear,                            188
So grace and mercy at your most need help you.
GHOST [*beneath*]   Swear.                            [*They swear.*]
HAMLET
Rest, rest, perturbèd spirit!—So, gentlemen,
With all my love I do commend me to you;                            192
And what so poor a man as Hamlet is
May do t'express his love and friending to you,                     194
God willing, shall not lack. Let us go in together,                 195
And still your fingers on your lips, I pray.                         196
The time is out of joint. Oh, cursèd spite                          197
That ever I was born to set it right!
                    [*They wait for him to leave first.*]
Nay, come, let's go together.                *Exeunt.*               199

❧

# [2.1]

*Enter old Polonius with his man* [*Reynaldo*].

POLONIUS
Give him this money and these notes, Reynaldo.
                    [*He gives money and papers.*]
REYNALDO   I will, my lord.
POLONIUS
You shall do marvelous wisely, good Reynaldo,                       3
Before you visit him, to make inquire                               4
Of his behavior.
REYNALDO          My lord, I did intend it.
POLONIUS
Marry, well said, very well said. Look you, sir,
Inquire me first what Danskers are in Paris,                        7
And how, and who, what means, and where they
    keep,                                                           8
What company, at what expense; and finding
By this encompassment and drift of question                        10
That they do know my son, come you more nearer                     11
Than your particular demands will touch it.                        12
Take you, as 'twere, some distant knowledge of him,                13

188 **aught** anything  192 **commend . . . you** give you my best wishes  194 **friending**
friendliness  195 **lack** be lacking  196 **still** always  197 **out of joint** in utter disorder
199 **let's go together** (Probably they wait for him to leave first, but he refuses this cere-
moniousness.)
**2.1 Location:** Polonius's chambers.
3 **marvelous** marvelously  4 **inquire** inquiry  7 **Danskers** Danes  8 **what means** what
wealth (they have)  **keep** dwell  10 **encompassment . . . question** roundabout way of
questioning  11–12 **come . . . it** you will find out more this way than by asking pointed
questions (*particular demands*).  13 **Take you** Assume, pretend

As thus, "I know his father and his friends,
And in part him." Do you mark this, Reynaldo?
REYNALDO   Ay, very well, my lord.
POLONIUS
"And in part him, but," you may say, "not well.
But if't be he I mean, he's very wild,
Addicted so and so," and there put on him                    19
What forgeries you please—marry, none so rank              20
As may dishonor him, take heed of that,
But, sir, such wanton, wild, and usual slips              22
As are companions noted and most known
To youth and liberty.
REYNALDO   As gaming, my lord.
POLONIUS   Ay, or drinking, fencing, swearing,
Quarreling, drabbing—you may go so far.                   27
REYNALDO   My lord, that would dishonor him.
POLONIUS
Faith, no, as you may season it in the charge.            29
You must not put another scandal on him
That he is open to incontinency;                          31
That's not my meaning. But breathe his faults so
   quaintly                                               32
That they may seem the taints of liberty,                 33
The flash and outbreak of a fiery mind,
A savageness in unreclaimèd blood,                        35
Of general assault.                                       36
REYNALDO   But, my good lord—
POLONIUS   Wherefore should you do this?
REYNALDO   Ay, my lord, I would know that.
POLONIUS   Marry, sir, here's my drift,
And I believe it is a fetch of warrant.                   41
You laying these slight sullies on my son,
As 'twere a thing a little soiled wi'th' working,         43
Mark you,
Your party in converse, him you would sound,              45
Having ever seen in the prenominate crimes                46
The youth you breathe of guilty, be assured               47
He closes with you in this consequence:                   48
"Good sir," or so, or "friend," or "gentleman,"
According to the phrase or the addition                   50
Of man and country.

---

**19 put on** impute to   **20 forgeries** invented tales   **rank** gross   **22 wanton** sportive, unrestrained   **27 drabbing** whoring   **29 season** temper, soften   **31 incontinency** habitual
sexual excess   **32 quaintly** artfully, subtly   **33 taints of liberty** faults resulting from free
living   **35–36 A savageness . . . assault** a wildness in untamed youth that assails all indiscriminately.   **41 fetch of warrant** legitimate trick   **43 wi'th' working** in the process of
being made, i.e., in everyday experience   **45 Your . . . converse** the person you are con-
versing with   **sound** sound out   **46 Having ever** if he has ever   **prenominate crimes**
aforenamed offenses   **47 breathe** speak   **48 closes . . . consequence** takes you into his
confidence as follows   **50 addition** title

REYNALDO    Very good, my lord.
POLONIUS    And then, sir, does 'a this—'a does—what
was I about to say? By the Mass, I was about to say
something. Where did I leave?
REYNALDO    At "closes in the consequence."
POLONIUS
At "closes in the consequence," ay, marry.
He closes thus: "I know the gentleman,
I saw him yesterday," or "th'other day,"
Or then, or then, with such or such, "and as you say,
There was 'a gaming," "there o'ertook in 's rouse,"                    60
"There falling out at tennis," or perchance                            61
"I saw him enter such a house of sale,"
Videlicet a brothel, or so forth. See you now,                         63
Your bait of falsehood takes this carp of truth;                       64
And thus do we of wisdom and of reach,                                 65
With windlasses and with assays of bias,                               66
By indirections find directions out.                                   67
So by my former lecture and advice                                     68
Shall you my son. You have me, have you not?                           69
REYNALDO
My lord, I have.
POLONIUS            God b'wi'ye; fare ye well.
REYNALDO    Good my lord.
POLONIUS
Observe his inclination in yourself.                                   72
REYNALDO    I shall, my lord.
POLONIUS    And let him ply his music.
REYNALDO    Well, my lord.
POLONIUS
Farewell.                          *Exit Reynaldo.*

*Enter Ophelia.*

How now, Ophelia, what's the matter?
OPHELIA
Oh, my lord, my lord, I have been so affrighted!
POLONIUS    With what, i'th' name of God?
OPHELIA
My lord, as I was sewing in my closet,                                 79
Lord Hamlet, with his doublet all unbraced,                            80
No hat upon his head, his stockings fouled,

60 o'ertook in 's rouse overcome by drink  61 falling out quarreling  63 Videlicet
namely  64 carp a fish  65 reach capacity, ability  66 windlasses i.e., circuitous paths
(literally, circuits made to head off the game in hunting)  assays of bias attempts
through indirection (like the curving path of the bowling ball, which is biased or
weighted to one side)  67 directions i.e., the way things really are  68 former lecture
just-ended set of instructions  69 have understand  72 in yourself in your own person
(as well as by asking questions of others)  79 closet private chamber
80 doublet close-fitting jacket  unbraced unfastened

Ungartered, and down-gyvèd to his ankle,     82
Pale as his shirt, his knees knocking each other,
And with a look so piteous in purport     84
As if he had been loosèd out of hell
To speak of horrors—he comes before me.

POLONIUS
   Mad for thy love?
OPHELIA           My lord, I do not know,
   But truly I do fear it.
POLONIUS           What said he?

OPHELIA
He took me by the wrist and held me hard.
Then goes he to the length of all his arm,
And, with his other hand thus o'er his brow
He falls to such perusal of my face
As 'a would draw it. Long stayed he so.     93
At last, a little shaking of mine arm
And thrice his head thus waving up and down,
He raised a sigh so piteous and profound
As it did seem to shatter all his bulk     97
And end his being. That done, he lets me go,
And with his head over his shoulder turned
He seemed to find his way without his eyes,
For out o' doors he went without their helps,
And to the last bended their light on me.

POLONIUS
Come, go with me. I will go seek the King.
This is the very ecstasy of love,     104
Whose violent property fordoes itself     105
And leads the will to desperate undertakings
As oft as any passion under heaven
That does afflict our natures. I am sorry.
What, have you given him any hard words of late?

OPHELIA
No, my good lord, but as you did command
I did repel his letters and denied
His access to me.
POLONIUS           That hath made him mad.
I am sorry that with better heed and judgment
I had not quoted him. I feared he did but trifle     114
And meant to wrack thee. But beshrew my jealousy!     115
By heaven, it is as proper to our age     116
To cast beyond ourselves in our opinions     117
As it is common for the younger sort

82 down-gyvèd fallen to the ankles (like gyves or fetters)   84 in purport in what it
expressed   93 As as if   97 As that   bulk body   104 ecstasy madness   105 property
fordoes nature destroys   114 quoted observed   115 wrack ruin, seduce   beshrew my
jealousy! a plague upon my suspicious nature!   116 proper . . . age characteristic of us
(old) men   117 cast beyond overshoot, miscalculate (a metaphor from hunting)

To lack discretion. Come, go we to the King.
This must be known, which, being kept close, might
   move                                               120
More grief to hide than hate to utter love.          121
Come.                           *Exeunt.*

❖

# [2.2]

*Flourish. Enter King and Queen, Rosencrantz,*
*and Guildenstern [with others].*

KING

Welcome, dear Rosencrantz and Guildenstern.
Moreover that we much did long to see you,        2
The need we have to use you did provoke
Our hasty sending. Something have you heard
Of Hamlet's transformation—so call it,
Sith nor th'exterior nor the inward man        6
Resembles that it was. What it should be,        7
More than his father's death, that thus hath put him
So much from th'understanding of himself,
I cannot dream of. I entreat you both
That, being of so young days brought up with him,  11
And sith so neighbored to his youth and havior,  12
That you vouchsafe your rest here in our court  13
Some little time, so by your companies
To draw him on to pleasures, and to gather
So much as from occasion you may glean,  16
Whether aught to us unknown afflicts him thus
That, opened, lies within our remedy.  18
QUEEN

Good gentlemen, he hath much talked of you,
And sure I am two men there is not living
To whom he more adheres. If it will please you
To show us so much gentry and good will  22
As to expend your time with us awhile
For the supply and profit of our hope,  24
Your visitation shall receive such thanks
As fits a kings's remembrance.

---

120 known made known (to the King)  close secret  120–121 might . . . love i.e., might cause more grief (because of what Hamlet might do) by hiding the knowledge of Hamlet's strange behavior to Ophelia than unpleasantness by telling it
2.2 Location: The castle.
2 Moreover that Besides the fact that  6 Sith nor since neither  7 that what  11–12 That . . . havior that, seeing as you were brought up with him from early youth (see 3.4.209, where Hamlet refers to Rosencrantz and Guildenstern as "my two schoolfellows"), and since you have been intimately acquainted with his youthful ways  13 vouchsafe your rest consent to stay  16 occasion opportunity  18 opened being revealed  22 gentry courtesy 24 supply . . . hope aid and furtherance of what we hope for  26 As fits . . . remembrance as would be a fitting gift of a king who rewards true service

ROSENCRANTZ          Both Your Majesties    26
  Might, by the sovereign power you have of us,    27
  Put your dread pleasures more into command    28
  Than to entreaty.
GUILDENSTERN    But we both obey,
  And here give up ourselves in the full bent    30
  To lay our service freely at your feet,
  To be commanded.
KING
  Thanks, Rosencrantz and gentle Guildenstern.
QUEEN
  Thanks, Guildenstern and gentle Rosencrantz.
  And I beseech you instantly to visit
  My too much changèd son.—Go, some of you,
  And bring these gentlemen where Hamlet is.
GUILDENSTERN
  Heavens make our presence and our practices    38
  Pleasant and helpful to him!
QUEEN              Ay, amen!

           *Exeunt Rosencrantz and Guildenstern*
                        *[with some attendants].*

   *Enter Polonius.*

POLONIUS
  Th'ambassadors from Norway, my good lord,
  Are joyfully returned.
KING
  Thou still hast been the father of good news.    42
POLONIUS
  Have I, my lord? I assure my good liege
  I hold my duty, as I hold my soul,
  Both to my God and to my gracious king;
  And I do think, or else this brain of mine
  Hunts not the trail of policy so sure    47
  As it hath used to do, that I have found
  The very cause of Hamlet's lunacy.
KING
  Oh, speak of that! That do I long to hear.
POLONIUS
  Give first admittance to th'ambassadors.
  My news shall be the fruit to that great feast.    52
KING
  Thyself do grace to them and bring them in.    53

                          *[Exit Polonius.]*

---

**27 of** over   **28 dread** inspiring awe   **30 in . . . bent** to the utmost degree of
our capacity (an archery metaphor)   **38 practices** doings   **42 still** always
**47 policy** statecraft   **52 fruit** dessert   **53 grace** honor (punning on *grace* said
before a *feast*, line 52)

He tells me, my dear Gertrude, he hath found
The head and source of all your son's distemper.

QUEEN

I doubt it is no other but the main,                                            56
His father's death and our o'erhasty marriage.

*Enter Ambassadors [Voltimand and Cornelius,*
*with Polonius].*

KING

Well, we shall sift him.—Welcome, my good friends!                 58
Say, Voltimand, what from our brother Norway?                       59

VOLTIMAND

Most fair return of greetings and desires.                               60
Upon our first, he sent out to suppress                                  61
His nephew's levies, which to him appeared
To be a preparation 'gainst the Polack,
But, better looked into, he truly found
It was against Your Highness. Whereat grieved
That so his sickness, age, and impotence                                66
Was falsely borne in hand, sends out arrests                          67
On Fortinbras, which he, in brief, obeys,
Receives rebuke from Norway, and in fine                               69
Makes vow before his uncle never more
To give th'assay of arms against Your Majesty.                        71
Whereon old Norway, overcome with joy,
Gives him three thousand crowns in annual fee
And his commission to employ those soldiers,
So levied as before, against the Polack,
With an entreaty, herein further shown,

                                                          *[giving a paper]*

That it might please you to give quiet pass
Through your dominions for this enterprise
On such regards of safety and allowance                               79
As therein are set down.

KING                                    It likes us well,                        80
And at our more considered time we'll read,                           81
Answer, and think upon this business.
Meantime we thank you for your well-took labor.
Go to your rest; at night we'll feast together.
Most welcome home!             *Exeunt Ambassadors.*

POLONIUS                              This business is well ended.
My liege, and madam, to expostulate                                    86

---

**56 doubt** fear, suspect   **58 sift him** question Polonius (or Hamlet) closely
**59 brother** fellow king   **60 desires** good wishes   **61 Upon our first** At our first words
on the business   **66 impotence** weakness   **67 borne in hand** deluded, taken advantage
of   **arrests** orders to desist   **69 in fine** in conclusion   **71 give th'assay** make trial of
strength, challenge   **79 On . . . allowance** i.e., with such considerations for the safety of
Denmark and permission for Fortinbras   **80 likes** pleases   **81 considered** suitable for
deliberation   **86 expostulate** expound, inquire into

What majesty should be, what duty is,
Why day is day, night night, and time is time,
Were nothing but to waste night, day, and time.
Therefore, since brevity is the soul of wit,                    90
And tediousness the limbs and outward flourishes,
I will be brief. Your noble son is mad.
Mad call I it, for, to define true madness,
What is't but to be nothing else but mad?
But let that go.
QUEEN                    More matter, with less art.
POLONIUS
Madam, I swear I use no art at all.
That he's mad, 'tis true; 'tis true 'tis pity,
And pity 'tis 'tis true—a foolish figure,                        98
But farewell it, for I will use no art.
Mad let us grant him, then, and now remains
That we find out the cause of this effect,
Or rather say, the cause of this defect,
For this effect defective comes by cause.                       103
Thus it remains, and the remainder thus.
Perpend.                                                         105
I have a daughter—have while she is mine—
Who, in her duty and obedience, mark,
Hath given me this. Now gather and surmise.                     108
[*He reads the letter.*] "To the celestial and my soul's
idol, the most beautified Ophelia"—
That's an ill phrase, a vile phrase; "beautified" is a
vile phrase. But you shall hear. Thus:            [*He reads.*]
"In her excellent white bosom, these, etc."                     113
QUEEN    Came this from Hamlet to her?
POLONIUS
Good madam, stay awhile, I will be faithful.                    115
                                                  [*He reads.*]
            "Doubt thou the stars are fire,
                Doubt that the sun doth move,
            Doubt truth to be a liar,                           118
                But never doubt I love.
O dear Ophelia, I am ill at these numbers. I have not           120
art to reckon my groans. But that I love thee best, O           121
most best, believe it. Adieu.
            Thine evermore, most dear lady, whilst this
                machine is to him, Hamlet."                     124

---

90 **wit** sense or judgment    98 **figure** figure of speech    103 **For . . . cause** i.e., for this
defective behavior, this madness, must have a cause    105 **Perpend** Consider.
108 **gather and surmise** draw your own conclusions    113 **"In . . . etc."** (The letter is
poetically addressed to her heart, where a letter would be kept by a young lady.)
115 **stay . . . faithful** i.e., hold on, I will do as you wish.    116 **Doubt** suspect
120 **ill . . . numbers** unskilled at writing verses    121 **reckon** (1) count (2) number
metrically, scan    124 **machine** i.e., body

This in obedience hath my daughter shown me,
And, more above, hath his solicitings,                                    126
As they fell out by time, by means, and place,                            127
All given to mine ear.
KING                      But how hath she                                128
Received his love?
POLONIUS              What do you think of me?
KING
As of a man faithful and honorable.
POLONIUS
I would fain prove so. But what might you think,                          131
When I had seen this hot love on the wing—
As I perceived it, I must tell you that,
Before my daughter told me—what might you,
Or my dear Majesty your queen here, think,
If I had played the desk or table book,                                   136
Or given my heart a winking, mute and dumb,                               137
Or looked upon this love with idle sight?                                 138
What might you think? No, I went round to work,                           139
And my young mistress thus I did bespeak:                                 140
"Lord Hamlet is a prince out of thy star;                                 141
This must not be." And then I prescripts gave her,                        142
That she should lock herself from his resort,
Admit no messengers, receive no tokens.
Which done, she took the fruits of my advice;
And he, repellèd—a short tale to make—
Fell into a sadness, then into a fast,
Thence to a watch, thence into a weakness,                                148
Thence to a lightness, and by this declension                             149
Into the madness wherein now he raves,
And all we mourn for.
KING [*to the Queen*]     Do you think 'tis this?
QUEEN    It may be, very like.
POLONIUS
Hath there been such a time—I would fain know
    that—
That I have positively said "'Tis so,"
When it proved otherwise?
KING                      Not that I know.
POLONIUS
Take this from this, if this be otherwise.                                156

126–128 **And . . . ear** and moreover she has told me when, how, and where his solicitings
of her occurred   **131 fain** gladly   **136–137 If . . . dumb** if I had acted as go-between,
passing love notes, or if I had refused to let my heart acknowledge what my eyes could see
**138 with idle sight** complacently or incomprehendingly   **139 round** roundly, plainly
**140 bespeak** address   **141 out of thy star** above your sphere, position   **142 prescripts**
orders   **148 watch** state of sleeplessness   **149 lightness** lightheadedness   **declension**
decline, deterioration (with a pun on the grammatical sense)   **156 Take this from this**
(The actor probably gestures, indicating that he means his head from his shoulders, or his
staff of office or chain from his hands or neck, or something similar.)

If circumstances lead me, I will find
Where truth is hid, though it were hid indeed
Within the center.

KING                          How may we try it further?                    159

POLONIUS
You know sometimes he walks four hours together
Here in the lobby.

QUEEN                          So he does indeed.

POLONIUS
At such a time I'll loose my daughter to him.              162
Be you and I behind an arras then.                           163
Mark the encounter. If he love her not
And be not from his reason fall'n thereon,                165
Let me be no assistant for a state,
But keep a farm and carters.

KING                                      We will try it.                      167

*Enter Hamlet [reading on a book].*

QUEEN
But look where sadly the poor wretch comes reading.

POLONIUS
Away, I do beseech you both, away.
I'll board him presently. Oh, give me leave.              170
                    *Exeunt King and Queen [with attendants].*
How does my good Lord Hamlet?

HAMLET    Well, God-a-mercy.                                     172

POLONIUS    Do you know me, my lord?

HAMLET    Excellent well. You are a fishmonger.         174

POLONIUS    Not I, my lord.

HAMLET    Then I would you were so honest a man.

POLONIUS    Honest, my lord?

HAMLET    Ay, sir. To be honest, as this world goes, is to
be one man picked out of ten thousand.

POLONIUS    That's very true, my lord.

HAMLET    For if the sun breed maggots in a dead dog,
being a good kissing carrion—Have you a daughter?        182

POLONIUS    I have, my lord.

HAMLET    Let her not walk i'th' sun. Conception is a       184
blessing, but as your daughter may conceive, friend, look to't.

POLONIUS [*aside*]    How say you by that? Still harping
on my daughter. Yet he knew me not at first; 'a said
I was a fishmonger. 'A is far gone. And truly in my

**159 center** center of the earth, traditionally an extraordinarily inaccessible place
**try** test    **162 loose** (as one might release an animal that is being mated)    **163 arras**
hanging, tapestry    **165 thereon** on that account    **167 carters** wagon drivers    **170 I'll ...**
**leave** I'll accost him at once. Please leave us alone; leave him to me.    **172 God-a-mercy**
God have mercy, i.e., thank you.    **174 fishmonger** fish merchant    **182 a good kissing**
**carrion** i.e., a good piece of flesh for kissing, or for the sun to kiss    **184 i'th' sun** in
public (with additional implication of the sunshine of princely favors)    **Conception**
(1) Understanding (2) Pregnancy

youth I suffered much extremity for love, very near
this. I'll speak to him again.—What do you read,
my lord?

HAMLET  Words, words, words.

POLONIUS  What is the matter, my lord?                          194

HAMLET  Between who?

POLONIUS  I mean, the matter that you read, my lord.

HAMLET  Slanders, sir; for the satirical rogue says here
that old men have gray beards, that their faces are
wrinkled, their eyes purging thick amber and plum-tree          199
gum, and that they have a plentiful lack of wit, together       200
with most weak hams. All which, sir, though I
most powerfully and potently believe, yet I hold it not
honesty to have it thus set down, for yourself, sir, shall      203
grow old as I am, if like a crab you could go backward.         204

POLONIUS [*aside*]  Though this be madness, yet there is
method in't.—Will you walk out of the air, my lord?            206

HAMLET  Into my grave.

POLONIUS  Indeed, that's out of the air. [*Aside*] How
pregnant sometimes his replies are! A happiness that            209
often madness hits on, which reason and sanity could
not so prosperously be delivered of. I will leave him           211
and suddenly contrive the means of meeting between              212
him and my daughter.—My honorable lord, I will
most humbly take my leave of you.

HAMLET  You cannot, sir, take from me anything that I
will more willingly part withal—except my life, except         216
my life, except my life.

*Enter Guildenstern and Rosencrantz.*

POLONIUS  Fare you well, my lord.

HAMLET  These tedious old fools!

POLONIUS  You go to seek the Lord Hamlet. There he is.

ROSENCRANTZ [*to Polonius*]  God save you, sir!

[*Exit Polonius.*]

GUILDENSTERN  My honored lord!

ROSENCRANTZ  My most dear lord!

HAMLET  My excellent good friends! How dost thou,
Guildenstern? Ah, Rosencrantz! Good lads, how do
you both?

ROSENCRANTZ
As the indifferent children of the earth.                       227

---

**194 matter** substance. (But Hamlet plays on the sense of "basis for a dispute.")
**199 purging** discharging   **amber** i.e., resin, like the resinous *plum-tree gum*   **200 wit**
understanding   **203 honesty** decency, decorum   **204 old** as old   **206 out of the air** (The
open air was considered dangerous for sick people.)   **209 pregnant** quick-witted, full of
meaning   **happiness** felicity of expression   **211 prosperously** successfully   **212 sud-**
**denly** immediately   **216 withal** with   **227 indifferent** ordinary, at neither extreme of
fortune or misfortune

GUILDENSTERN
Happy in that we are not overhappy.
On Fortune's cap we are not the very button.
HAMLET   Nor the soles of her shoe?
ROSENCRANTZ   Neither, my lord.
HAMLET   Then you live about her waist, or in the middle     232
of her favors?     233
GUILDENSTERN   Faith, her privates we.     234
HAMLET   In the secret parts of Fortune? Oh, most true,
she is a strumpet. What news?     236
ROSENCRANTZ   None, my lord, but the world's grown
honest.
HAMLET   Then is doomsday near. But your news is not
true. Let me question more in particular. What have
you, my good friends, deserved at the hands of
Fortune that she sends you to prison hither?
GUILDENSTERN   Prison, my lord?
HAMLET   Denmark's a prison.
ROSENCRANTZ   Then is the world one.
HAMLET   A goodly one, in which there are many
confines, wards, and dungeons, Denmark being one     247
o'th' worst.
ROSENCRANTZ   We think not so, my lord.
HAMLET   Why then 'tis none to you, for there is nothing
either good or bad but thinking makes it so. To me it
is a prison.
ROSENCRANTZ   Why then, your ambition makes it one.
'Tis too narrow for your mind.
HAMLET   Oh, God, I could be bounded in a nutshell and
count myself a king of infinite space, were it not that
I have bad dreams.
GUILDENSTERN   Which dreams indeed are ambition, for
the very substance of the ambitious is merely the     259
shadow of a dream.
HAMLET   A dream itself is but a shadow.
ROSENCRANTZ   Truly, and I hold ambition of so airy
and light a quality that it is but a shadow's shadow.
HAMLET   Then are our beggars bodies, and our monarchs     264
and outstretched heroes the beggars' shadows.     265
Shall we to th' court? For, by my fay, I cannot reason.     266

---

**232–233 the middle . . . favors** i.e., her genitals   **234 her privates we** (1) we dwell in her privates, her genitals, in the middle of her favors (2) we are her ordinary footsoldiers.
**236 strumpet** (Fortune was proverbially thought of as fickle.)   **247 confines** places of confinement   **259 the very . . . ambitious** that seemingly very substantial thing that the ambitious pursue   **264–265 Then . . . shadows** (Hamlet pursues their argument about ambition to its absurd extreme: If ambition is only a shadow of a shadow, then beggars (who are presumably without ambition) must be real, whereas monarchs and heroes are only their shadows—*outstretched* like elongated shadows, made to look bigger than they are.)   **266 fay** faith

ROSENCRANTZ, GUILDENSTERN  We'll wait upon you.                   267
HAMLET  No such matter. I will not sort you with the            268
rest of my servants, for, to speak to you like an honest
man, I am most dreadfully attended. But, in the               270
beaten way of friendship, what make you at Elsinore?          271
ROSENCRANTZ  To visit you, my lord, no other occasion.
HAMLET  Beggar that I am, I am even poor in thanks;
but I thank you, and sure, dear friends, my thanks are
too dear a halfpenny. Were you not sent for? Is it your       275
own inclining? Is it a free visitation? Come, come, deal      276
justly with me. Come, come. Nay, speak.
GUILDENSTERN  What should we say, my lord?
HAMLET  Anything but to th' purpose. You were sent            279
for, and there is a kind of confession in your looks
which your modesties have not craft enough to color.          281
I know the good King and Queen have sent for you.
ROSENCRANTZ  To what end, my lord?
HAMLET  That you must teach me. But let me conjure            284
you, by the rights of our fellowship, by the consonancy       285
of our youth, by the obligation of our ever-preserved         286
love, and by what more dear a better proposer                 287
could charge you withal, be even and direct with me           288
whether you were sent for or no.
ROSENCRANTZ  [*aside to Guildenstern*]  What say you?
HAMLET  [*aside*]  Nay, then, I have an eye of you.—If       291
you love me, hold not off.                                    292
GUILDENSTERN  My lord, we were sent for.
HAMLET  I will tell you why; so shall my anticipation        294
prevent your discovery, and your secrecy to the King          295
and Queen molt no feather. I have of late—but                296
wherefore I know not—lost all my mirth, forgone all
custom of exercises; and indeed it goes so heavily with
my disposition that this goodly frame, the earth,
seems to me a sterile promontory; this most excellent
canopy, the air, look you, this brave o'erhanging             301
firmament, this majestical roof fretted with golden           302
fire, why, it appeareth nothing to me but a foul and

---

**267 wait upon** accompany, attend. (But Hamlet uses the phrase in the sense of providing menial service.)  **268 sort** class, categorize  **270 dreadfully attended** waited upon in slovenly fashion  **271 beaten way** familiar path, tried-and-true course  **make** do  **275 too dear a halfpenny** (1) too expensive at even a halfpenny, i.e., of little worth (2) too expensive *by* a halfpenny in return for worthless kindness.  **276 free** voluntary  **279 Anything but to th' purpose** Anything except a straightforward answer. (Said ironically.)  **281 color** disguise  **284 conjure** adjure, entreat  **285–286 the consonancy of our youth** our closeness in our younger days  **287 better** more skillful  **288 charge** urge  **even** straight, honest  **291 of on**  **292 hold not off** don't hold back  **294–295 so . . . discovery** in that way my saying it first will spare you from having to reveal the truth  **296 molt no feather** i.e., not diminish in the least  **301 brave** splendid  **302 fretted** adorned (with fretwork, as in a vaulted ceiling)

pestilent congregation of vapors. What a piece of work    304
is a man! How noble in reason, how infinite in faculties,
in form and moving how express and admirable, in    306
action how like an angel, in apprehension how like a    307
god! The beauty of the world, the paragon of animals!
And yet, to me, what is this quintessence of dust?    309
Man delights not me—no, nor woman neither,
though by your smiling you seem to say so.
ROSENCRANTZ   My lord, there was no such stuff in my
thoughts.
HAMLET   Why did you laugh, then, when I said man
delights not me?
ROSENCRANTZ   To think, my lord, if you delight not in
man, what Lenten entertainment the players shall    317
receive from you. We coted them on the way, and    318
hither are they coming to offer you service.
HAMLET   He that plays the king shall be welcome; His
Majesty shall have tribute of me. The adventurous    321
knight shall use his foil and target, the lover shall not    322
sigh gratis, the humorous man shall end his part in    323
peace, the clown shall make those laugh whose lungs    324
are tickle o'th' sear, and the lady shall say her mind    325
freely, or the blank verse shall halt for't. What players    326
are they?
ROSENCRANTZ   Even those you were wont to take such
delight in, the tragedians of the city.    329
HAMLET   How chances it they travel? Their residence,    330
both in reputation and profit, was better both ways.
ROSENCRANTZ   I think their inhibition comes by the    332
means of the late innovation.    333
HAMLET   Do they hold the same estimation they did
when I was in the city? Are they so followed?
ROSENCRANTZ   No, indeed are they not.
HAMLET   How comes it? Do they grow rusty?    337

---

**304 congregation** mass   **piece of work** masterpiece   **306 express** well-framed, exact,
expressive   **307 apprehension** power of comprehending   **309 quintessence** very essence
(literally, the fifth essence beyond earth, water, air, and fire, supposed to be extractable
from them)   **317 Lenten entertainment** meager reception (appropriate to Lent)
**318 coted** overtook and passed by   **321 tribute** (1) applause (2) homage paid in money
of from   **322 foil and target** sword and shield   **323 gratis** for nothing   **humorous man**
eccentric character, dominated by one trait or "humor"   **323–324 in peace** i.e., with full
license   **325 tickle o'th' sear** hair trigger, ready to laugh easily. (A *sear* is part of a gun-
lock.)   **326 halt** limp   **329 tragedians** actors   **330 residence** remaining in their usual
place, i.e., in the city   **332 inhibition** formal prohibition (against acting plays in the city)
**333 late innovation** i.e., recent new fashion in satirical plays performed by boy actors
in the "private" theaters; or the Earl of Essex's abortive rebellion in 1601 against
Elizabeth's government (a much debated passage of seemingly topical reference)
**337 How . . . rusty?** Have they lost their polish, gone out of fashion? (This passage,
through line 362, alludes to the rivalry between the children's companies and the adult
actors, given strong impetus by the reopening of the Children of the Chapel at the
Blackfriars Theater in late 1600.)

ROSENCRANTZ  Nay, their endeavor keeps in the wonted                338
pace. But there is, sir, an aerie of children, little eyases,       339
that cry out on the top of question and are most                    340
tyrannically clapped for't. These are now the fashion, and          341
so berattle the common stages—so they call them—                    342
that many wearing rapiers are afraid of goose quills                343
and dare scarce come thither.
HAMLET  What, are they children? Who maintains 'em?
How are they escotted? Will they pursue the quality no              346
longer than they can sing? Will they not say afterwards,           347
if they should grow themselves to common                            348
players—as it is most like, if their means are no                   349
better—their writers do them wrong to make them                     350
exclaim against their own succession?                               351
ROSENCRANTZ  Faith, there has been much to-do on                    352
both sides, and the nation holds it no sin to tar them to           353
controversy. There was for a while no money bid for                 354
argument unless the poet and the player went to cuffs               355
in the question.                                                    356
HAMLET  Is't possible?
GUILDENSTERN  Oh, there has been much throwing
about of brains.
HAMLET  Do the boys carry it away?                                  360
ROSENCRANTZ  Ay, that they do, my lord—Hercules             361
and his load too.                                                   362
HAMLET  It is not very strange; for my uncle is King of
Denmark, and those that would make mouths at him                   364
while my father lived give twenty, forty, fifty, a
hundred ducats apiece for his picture in little. 'Sblood,          366
there is something in this more than natural, if philosophy
could find it out.
                                    *A flourish [of trumpets within].*
GUILDENSTERN  There are the players.
HAMLET  Gentlemen, you are welcome to Elsinore. Your
hands, come then. Th'appurtenance of welcome is                    371

**338 keeps . . . wonted** continues in the usual  **339 aerie** nest  **eyases** young hawks
**340 cry . . . question** speak shrilly, dominating the controversy (in decrying the public
theaters)  **341 tyrannically** vehemently  **342 berattle . . . stages** clamor against the public
theaters  **343 many wearing rapiers** i.e., many men of fashion, afraid to patronize the
common players for fear of being satirized by the poets writing for the boy actors
**goose quills** i.e., pens of satirists  **346 escotted** maintained  **quality** (acting) profession
**346–347 no longer . . . sing** i.e., only until their voices change  **348 common** regular, adult
**349 like** likely  **349–350 if . . . better** if they find no better way to support themselves
**351 succession** i.e., future careers  **352 to-do** ado  **353 tar** incite (as in inciting dogs to attack a chained bear)  **354–356 There . . . question** i.e., For a while, no money was offered
by the acting companies to playwrights for the plot to a play unless the satirical poets who
wrote for the boys and the adult actors came to blows in the play itself.  **360 carry it away**
i.e., win the day  **361–362 Hercules . . . load** (Thought to be an allusion to the sign of the
Globe Theatre, which allegedly was Hercules bearing the world on his shoulders.)
**364 mouths** faces  **366 ducats** gold coins  **in little** in miniature  **'Sblood** By God's
(Christ's) blood  **371 Th'appurtenance** The proper accompaniment

fashion and ceremony. Let me comply with you in this 372
garb, lest my extent to the players, which, I tell you, 373
must show fairly outwards, should more appear like 374
entertainment than yours. You are welcome. But my 375
uncle-father and aunt-mother are deceived.

GUILDENSTERN   In what, my dear lord?

HAMLET   I am but mad north-north-west. When the 378
wind is southerly I know a hawk from a handsaw. 379

*Enter Polonius.*

POLONIUS   Well be with you, gentlemen!

HAMLET   Hark you, Guildenstern, and you too; at each
ear a hearer. That great baby you see there is not yet
out of his swaddling clouts. 383

ROSENCRANTZ   Haply he is the second time come to 384
them, for they say an old man is twice a child.

HAMLET   I will prophesy he comes to tell me of the
players. Mark it.—You say right, sir, o' Monday 387
morning, 'twas then indeed. 388

POLONIUS   My lord, I have news to tell you.

HAMLET   My lord, I have news to tell you. When Roscius 390
was an actor in Rome—

POLONIUS   The actors are come hither, my lord.

HAMLET   Buzz, buzz! 393

POLONIUS   Upon my honor—

HAMLET   Then came each actor on his ass.

POLONIUS   The best actors in the world, either for
tragedy, comedy, history, pastoral, pastoral-comical,
historical-pastoral, tragical-historical, tragical-comical-
historical-pastoral, scene individable, or poem 399
unlimited. Seneca cannot be too heavy, nor Plautus too 400
light. For the law of writ and the liberty, these are the 401
only men.

HAMLET   O Jephthah, judge of Israel, what a treasure 403
hadst thou!

---

**372 comply** observe the formalities of courtesy   **373 garb** i.e., manner   **my extent** that
which I extend, i.e., my polite behavior   **374 show fairly outwards** show every evidence
of cordiality   **375 entertainment** a (warm) reception   **378 north-north-west** just off true
north, only partly   **379 I . . . handsaw** (Speaking in his mad guise, Hamlet perhaps suggests that he can tell true from false. A *handsaw* may be a *hernshaw* or heron. Still, a
supposedly mad disposition might compare hawks and handsaws.)   **383 swaddling clouts**
cloths in which to wrap a newborn baby   **384 Haply** Perhaps   **387–388 You say . . .**
**then indeed** (Said to impress upon Polonius the idea that Hamlet is in serious conversation with his friends.)   **390 Roscius** a famous Roman actor who died in 62 B.C.
**393 Buzz** (An interjection used to denote stale news.)   **399–400 scene . . . unlimited**
plays that are unclassifiable and all-inclusive (an absurdly catchall conclusion to Polonius's pompous list of categories)   **400 Seneca** writer of Latin tragedies   **Plautus** writer
of Latin comedies   **401 law . . . liberty** dramatic composition both according to the rules
and disregarding the rules   **these** i.e., the actors   **403 Jephthah . . . Israel** (Jephthah
had to sacrifice his daughter; see Judges 11. Hamlet goes on to quote from a ballad on
the theme.)

POLONIUS   What a treasure had he, my lord?
HAMLET   Why,
"One fair daughter, and no more,
The which he lovèd passing well."                                    408
POLONIUS [*aside*]   Still on my daughter.
HAMLET   Am I not i'th' right, old Jephthah?
POLONIUS   If you call me Jephthah, my lord, I have a
daughter that I love passing well.
HAMLET   Nay, that follows not.                                      413
POLONIUS   What follows then, my lord?                              414
HAMLET   Why,
"As by lot, God wot,"                                              416
and then, you know,
"It came to pass, as most like it was"—                            418
the first row of the pious chanson will show you more,             419
for look where my abridgement comes.                               420

*Enter the Players.*

You are welcome, masters; welcome, all. I am glad to               421
see thee well. Welcome, good friends. Oh, old friend!
Why, thy face is valanced since I saw thee last. Com'st            423
thou to beard me in Denmark? What, my young lady                   424
and mistress! By'r Lady, Your Ladyship is nearer to                425
heaven than when I saw you last, by the altitude of a              426
chopine. Pray God your voice, like a piece of uncurrent            427
gold, be not cracked within the ring. Masters, you                 428
are all welcome. We'll e'en to't like French falconers,           429
fly at anything we see. We'll have a speech straight.              430
Come, give us a taste of your quality. Come, a                     431
passionate speech.
FIRST PLAYER   What speech, my good lord?
HAMLET   I heard thee speak me a speech once, but it
was never acted, or if it was, not above once, for the
play, I remember, pleased not the million; 'twas caviar           436
to the general. But it was—as I received it, and                  437

---

**408 passing** surpassingly   **413 that follows not** i.e., just because you resemble Jephthah
in having a daughter does not logically prove that you love her   **414 What . . . lord?**
What does follow logically? (But Hamlet, pretending madness, answers with a fragment
of a ballad, as if Polonius had asked, "What comes next?" See 419n.)   **416 lot** chance
**wot** knows   **418 like** likely, probable   **419 the first . . . more** the first stanza of this bib-
lically based ballad will satisfy your stated desire to know *what follows* (line 414).
**420 my abridgment** something that cuts short my conversation; also, a diversion
**421 masters** good sirs   **423 valanced** fringed (with a beard)   **424 beard** confront, challenge (with obvious pun)   **young lady** i.e., boy playing women's parts   **425 By'r Lady**
By Our Lady   **425–426 nearer to heaven** i.e., taller   **427 chopine** thick-soled shoe of
Italian fashion   **427 uncurrent** not passable as lawful coinage   **428 cracked . . . ring** i.e.,
changed from adolescent to male voice, no longer suitable for women's roles. (Coins
featured rings enclosing the sovereign's head; if the coin was sufficiently clipped to
invade within this ring, it was unfit for currency.)   **429 e'en to't** go at it   **430 straight**
at once   **431 quality** professional skill   **436–437 caviar to the general** i.e., an expensive
delicacy not generally palatable to uneducated tastes

others, whose judgments in such matters cried in the 438
top of mine—an excellent play, well digested in the 439
scenes, set down with as much modesty as cunning. I 440
remember one said there were no sallets in the lines to 441
make the matter savory, nor no matter in the phrase
that might indict the author of affectation, but called it 443
an honest method, as wholesome as sweet, and by very
much more handsome than fine. One speech in't I 445
chiefly loved: 'twas Aeneas' tale to Dido, and there-
about of it especially when he speaks of Priam's 447
slaughter. If it live in your memory, begin at this line: 448
let me see, let me see—
  "The rugged Pyrrhus, like th' Hyrcanian beast"— 450
'Tis not so. It begins with Pyrrhus:
  "The rugged Pyrrhus, he whose sable arms, 452
Black as his purpose, did the night resemble
When he lay couchèd in th' ominous horse, 454
Hath now this dread and black complexion
    smeared
With heraldry more dismal. Head to foot 456
Now is he total gules, horridly tricked 457
With blood of fathers, mothers, daughters, sons,
Baked and impasted with the parching streets, 459
That lend a tyrannous and a damnèd light 460
To their lord's murder. Roasted in wrath and fire, 461
And thus o'ersizèd with coagulate gore, 462
With eyes like carbuncles, the hellish Pyrrhus 463
Old grandsire Priam seeks."
So proceed you.
POLONIUS  'Fore God, my lord, well spoken, with good
accent and good discretion.
FIRST PLAYER        "Anon he finds him
Striking too short at Greeks. His antique sword, 469
Rebellious to his arm, lies where it falls,

---

**438–439 cried in the top of** i.e., spoke with greater authority than  **439 digested**
arranged, ordered  **440 modesty** moderation, restraint  **cunning** skill  **441 sallets** i.e.,
something savory, spicy improprieties  **443 indict** convict  **445 handsome** well-propor-
tioned  **fine** elaborately ornamented, showy  **447–448 Priam's slaughter** the slaying
of the ruler of Troy, when the Greeks finally took the city  **450 Pyrrhus** a Greek hero in
the Trojan War, also known as Neoptolemus, son of Achilles—another avenging son
**th' Hyrcanian beast** i.e., the tiger. (On the death of Priam, see Virgil, *Aeneid*, 2.506 ff.;
compare the whole speech with Marlowe's *Dido Queen of Carthage*, 2.1.214 ff. On the
*Hyrcanian* tiger, see *Aeneid*, 4.366–367. Hyrcania is on the Caspian Sea.)  **452 rugged**
shaggy, savage  **sable** black (for reasons of camouflage during the episode of the Trojan
horse)  **454 couchèd** concealed  **ominous horse** fateful Trojan horse, by which the
Greeks gained access to Troy  **456 dismal** calamitous  **457 total gules** entirely red (a
heraldic term)  **tricked** spotted and smeared (heraldic)  **459 Baked . . . streets** roasted
and encrusted, like a thick paste, by the parching heat of the streets (because of the fires
everywhere)  **460 tyrannous** cruel  **461 their lord's** i.e., Priam's  **462 o'ersizèd** covered
as with size or glue  **463 carbuncles** large fiery-red precious stones thought to emit their
own light  **469 antique** ancient, long-used

Repugnant to command. Unequal matched,                                   471
Pyrrhus at Priam drives, in rage strikes wide,
But with the whiff and wind of his fell sword                            473
Th'unnervèd father falls. Then senseless Ilium,                          474
Seeming to feel this blow, with flaming top
Stoops to his base, and with a hideous crash                             476
Takes prisoner Pyrrhus' ear. For, lo! His sword,
Which was declining on the milky head                                    478
Of reverend Priam, seemed i'th'air to stick.
So as a painted tyrant Pyrrhus stood,                                    480
And, like a neutral to his will and matter,                              481
Did nothing.
But as we often see against some storm                                   483
A silence in the heavens, the rack stand still,                          484
The bold winds speechless, and the orb below                             485
As hush as death, anon the dreadful thunder
Doth rend the region, so, after Pyrrhus' pause,                          487
A rousèd vengeance sets him new a-work,
And never did the Cyclops' hammers fall                                  489
On Mars's armor forged for proof eterne                                  490
With less remorse than Pyrrhus' bleeding sword                           491
Now falls on Priam.
Out, out, thou strumpet Fortune! All you gods
In general synod take away her power!                                     494
Break all the spokes and fellies from her wheel,                         495
And bowl the round nave down the hill of heaven                          496
As low as to the fiends!"
POLONIUS   This is too long.
HAMLET   It shall to the barber's with your beard.—Prithee,
say on. He's for a jig or a tale of bawdry, or he                         500
sleeps. Say on; come to Hecuba.                                          501
FIRST PLAYER
"But who, ah woe! had seen the moblèd queen"—                            502
HAMLET   "The moblèd queen?"
POLONIUS   That's good. "Moblèd queen" is good.
FIRST PLAYER
"Run barefoot up and down, threat'ning the flames                        505
With bisson rheum, a clout upon that head                                506

---

471 **Repugnant** disobedient, resistant   473 **fell** cruel   474 **Th'** unnervèd the strength-
less   **senseless Ilium** inanimate citadel of Troy   476 **his** its   478 **declining** descending   **milky** white-haired   480 **painted** motionless, as in a painting   481 **like . . . matter** i.e., as though suspended between his intention and its fulfillment   483 **against** just
before   484 **rack** mass of clouds   485 **orb** globe, earth   487 **region** sky   489 **Cyclops** giant armor makers in the smithy of Vulcan   490 **proof** proven or tested resistance to assault   491 **remorse** pity   494 **synod** assembly   495 **fellies** pieces of wood
forming the rim of a wheel   496 **nave** hub   **hill of heaven** Mount Olympus   500 **jig**
comic song and dance often given at the end of a play   501 **Hecuba** wife of Priam
502 **who . . . had** anyone who had (also in line 510)   **moblèd** muffled   505 **threat'ning
the flames** i.e., weeping hard enough to dampen the flames   506 **bisson rheum** blind-
ing tears   **clout** cloth

Guillaume de La Perriere, *La Morosophie* (1553). Fortune was often described as a fatal figure whose ever-turning wheel signified the rise and fall of persons, families, and states (see 2.2.493–494). But she was also a charming figure whose music could both charm and tempt the listener: "blest are those / Whose blood and judgment are so well commeddled [i.e, commingled] / That they are not a pipe for Fortune's finger / To sound what stop she please" (3.2.67–70). (By permission of the Folger Shakespeare Library.)

Where late the diadem stood, and, for a robe,                        507
About her lank and all o'erteemèd loins                              508
A blanket, in the alarm of fear caught up—
Who this had seen, with tongue in venom steeped,
'Gainst Fortune's state would treason have
  pronounced.                                                        511
But if the gods themselves did see her then
When she saw Pyrrhus make malicious sport
In mincing with his sword her husband's limbs,
The instant burst of clamor that she made,
Unless things mortal move them not at all,
Would have made milch the burning eyes of heaven,                   517
And passion in the gods."                                           518
POLONIUS   Look whe'er he has not turned his color and               519
  has tears in 's eyes. Prithee, no more.
HAMLET   'Tis well; I'll have thee speak out the rest of
  this soon.—Good my lord, will you see the players well
  bestowed? Do you hear, let them be well used, for they            523
  are the abstract and brief chronicles of the time. After          524
  your death you were better have a bad epitaph than
  their ill report while you live.
POLONIUS   My lord, I will use them according to their
  desert.
HAMLET   God's bodikin, man, much better. Use every                  529
  man after his desert, and who shall scape whipping?
  Use them after your own honor and dignity. The less               531
  they deserve, the more merit is in your bounty. Take
  them in.
POLONIUS   Come, sirs.                                  [*Exit.*]
HAMLET   Follow him, friends. We'll hear a play tomorrow.
  [*As they start to leave, Hamlet detains the First
  Player.*] Dost thou hear me, old friend? Can you play
  *The Murder of Gonzago?*
FIRST PLAYER   Ay, my lord.
HAMLET   We'll ha 't tomorrow night. You could, for a               540
  need, study a speech of some dozen or sixteen lines              541
  which I would set down and insert in 't, could you not?
FIRST PLAYER   Ay, my lord.
HAMLET   Very well. Follow that lord, and look you mock
  him not.                                  *Exeunt players.*
  My good friends, I'll leave you till night. You are welcome
  to Elsinore.

---

507 late lately   508 all o'erteemèd utterly worn out with bearing children
511 state rule, managing   pronounced proclaimed   517 milch milky, moist with tears
burning eyes of heaven i.e., stars, heavenly bodies   518 passion overpowering emotion
519 whe'er whether   523 bestowed lodged   524 abstract summary account
529 God's bodikin By God's (Christ's) little body, *bodykin.* (Not to be confused with
*bodkin,* "dagger.")   531 after according to   540 ha 't have it   541 study memorize

ROSENCRANTZ  Good my lord!

*Exeunt [Rosencrantz and Guildenstern].*

HAMLET

Ay, so, goodbye to you.—Now I am alone.

Oh, what a rogue and peasant slave am I!

Is it not monstrous that this player here,

But in a fiction, in a dream of passion,                                        552

Could force his soul so to his own conceit                                      553

That from her working all his visage wanned,                                    554

Tears in his eyes, distraction in his aspect,                                   555

A broken voice, and his whole function suiting                                  556

With forms to his conceit? And all for nothing!                                 557

For Hecuba!

What's Hecuba to him, or he to Hecuba,

That he should weep for her? What would he do

Had he the motive and the cue for passion

That I have? He would drown the stage with tears

And cleave the general ear with horrid speech,                                  563

Make mad the guilty and appall the free,                                        564

Confound the ignorant, and amaze indeed                                         565

The very faculties of eyes and ears. Yet I,

A dull and muddy-mettled rascal, peak                                           567

Like John-a-dreams, unpregnant of my cause,                                     568

And can say nothing—no, not for a king

Upon whose property and most dear life                                          570

A damned defeat was made. Am I a coward?                                        571

Who calls me villain? Breaks my pate across?                                    572

Plucks off my beard and blows it in my face?

Tweaks me by the nose? Gives me the lie i'th' throat                            574

As deep as to the lungs? Who does me this?

Ha, 'swounds, I should take it; for it cannot be                                576

But I am pigeon-livered and lack gall                                           577

To make oppression bitter, or ere this                                          578

I should ha' fatted all the region kites                                        579

With this slave's offal. Bloody, bawdy villain!                                 580

Remorseless, treacherous, lecherous, kindless villain!                          581

Oh, vengeance!

552 **But** merely   553 **force . . . conceit** bring his innermost being so entirely into accord with his conception (of the role)   554 **from her working** as a result of, or in response to, his soul's activity   **wanned** grew pale   555 **aspect** look, glance   556–557 **his whole . . . conceit** all his bodily powers responding with actions to suit his thought   563 **the general ear** everyone's ear   **horrid** horrible   564 **appall** (Literally, make pale.)   **free** innocent   565 **Confound the ignorant** i.e., dumbfound those who know nothing of the crime that has been committed   **amaze** stun   567 **muddy-mettled** dull-spirited   567–568 **peak . . . cause** mope, like a dreaming idler, not quickened by my cause   570 **property** person and function   571 **damned defeat** damnable act of destruction   572 **pate** head   574 **Gives . . . throat** Calls me an out-and-out liar   576 **'swounds** by his (Christ's) wounds   577 **pigeon-livered** (The pigeon or dove was popularly supposed to be mild because it secreted no gall.)   578 **To . . . bitter** to make things bitter for oppressors   579 **region kites** kites (birds of prey) of the air   580 **offal** entrails   581 **Remorseless** Pitiless   **kindless** unnatural

Why, what an ass am I! This is most brave,                                          583
That I, the son of a dear father murdered,
Prompted to my revenge by heaven and hell,
Must like a whore unpack my heart with words
And fall a-cursing, like a very drab,                                               587
A scullion! Fie upon't, foh! About, my brains!                                      588
Hum, I have heard
That guilty creatures sitting at a play
Have by the very cunning of the scene                                               591
Been struck so to the soul that presently                                           592
They have proclaimed their malefactions;
For murder, though it have no tongue, will speak
With most miraculous organ. I'll have these players
Play something like the murder of my father
Before mine uncle. I'll observe his looks;
I'll tent him to the quick. If 'a do blench,                                         598
I know my course. The spirit that I have seen
May be the devil, and the devil hath power
T'assume a pleasing shape; yea, and perhaps,
Out of my weakness and my melancholy,
As he is very potent with such spirits,                                             603
Abuses me to damn me. I'll have grounds                                             604
More relative than this. The play's the thing                                       605
Wherein I'll catch the conscience of the King.       *Exit.*

❖

# [3.1]

*Enter King, Queen, Polonius, Ophelia,*
*Rosencrantz, Guildenstern, lords.*

KING
  And can you by no drift of conference                                              1
  Get from him why he puts on this confusion,
  Grating so harshly all his days of quiet
  With turbulent and dangerous lunacy?
ROSENCRANTZ
  He does confess he feels himself distracted,
  But from what cause 'a will by no means speak.
GUILDENSTERN
  Nor do we find him forward to be sounded,                                          7
  But with a crafty madness keeps aloof

583 **brave** fine, admirable (said ironically)   587 **drab** whore   588 **scullion** menial
kitchen servant (apt to be foul-mouthed)   **About** About it, to work   591 **cunning** art,
skill   **scene** dramatic presentation   592 **presently** at once   598 **tent** probe   **the quick**
the tender part of a wound, the core   **blench** quail, flinch   603 **spirits** humors (of
melancholy)   604 **Abuses** deludes   605 **relative** cogent, pertinent
**3.1 Location: The castle.**
1 **drift of conference** course of talk   7 **forward** willing   **sounded** questioned

When we would bring him on to some confession
Of his true state.
QUEEN          Did he receive you well?
ROSENCRANTZ   Most like a gentleman.
GUILDENSTERN
But with much forcing of his disposition.          12
ROSENCRANTZ
Niggard of question, but of our demands          13
Most free in his reply.
QUEEN          Did you assay him          14
To any pastime?
ROSENCRANTZ
Madam, it so fell out that certain players
We o'erraught on the way. Of these we told him,          17
And there did seem in him a kind of joy
To hear of it. They are here about the court,
And, as I think, they have already order
This night to play before him.
POLONIUS          'Tis most true,
And he beseeched me to entreat Your Majesties
To hear and see the matter.
KING
With all my heart, and it doth much content me
To hear him so inclined.
Good gentlemen, give him a further edge          26
And drive his purpose into these delights.
ROSENCRANTZ
We shall, my lord.
                *Exeunt Rosencrantz and Guildenstern.*
KING          Sweet Gertrude, leave us too,
For we have closely sent for Hamlet hither,          29
That he, as 'twere by accident, may here
Affront Ophelia.          31
Her father and myself, lawful espials,          32
Will so bestow ourselves that seeing, unseen,
We may of their encounter frankly judge,
And gather by him, as he is behaved,
If't be th'affliction of his love or no
That thus he suffers for.
QUEEN          I shall obey you.
And for your part, Ophelia, I do wish
That your good beauties be the happy cause
Of Hamlet's wildness. So shall I hope your virtues
Will bring him to his wonted way again,
To both your honors.

---

**12 disposition** inclination   **13 Niggard of question** Laconic   **demands** questions
**14 assay** try to win   **17 o'erraught** overtook   **26 edge** incitement   **29 closely** privately
**31 Affront** confront, meet   **32 espials** spies

OPHELIA          Madam, I wish it may.

                                                        [*Exit Queen.*]

POLONIUS

Ophelia, walk you here.—Gracious, so please you,                          43
We will bestow ourselves. [*To Ophelia*] Read on this
   book,            [*giving her a book*]                          44
That show of such an exercise may color                          45
Your loneliness. We are oft to blame in this—                          46
'Tis too much proved—that with devotion's visage                          47
And pious action we do sugar o'er
The devil himself.

KING [*aside*]   Oh, 'tis too true!
How smart a lash that speech doth give my
   conscience!
The harlot's cheek, beautied with plast'ring art,
Is not more ugly to the thing that helps it                          53
Than is my deed to my most painted word.                          54
Oh, heavy burden!

POLONIUS

I hear him coming. Let's withdraw, my lord.                          56
                  [*The King and Polonius withdraw.*]

    *Enter Hamlet.* [*Ophelia pretends to read a book.*]

HAMLET

To be, or not to be, that is the question:
Whether 'tis nobler in the mind to suffer
The slings and arrows of outrageous fortune,
Or to take arms against a sea of troubles
And by opposing end them. To die, to sleep—
No more—and by a sleep to say we end
The heartache and the thousand natural shocks
That flesh is heir to. 'Tis a consummation
Devoutly to be wished. To die, to sleep;
To sleep, perchance to dream. Ay, there's the rub,                          66
For in that sleep of death what dreams may come,
When we have shuffled off this mortal coil,                          68
Must give us pause. There's the respect                          69
That makes calamity of so long life.                          70
For who would bear the whips and scorns of time,

---

43 **Gracious** Your Grace (i.e., the King)   44 **bestow** conceal   45 **exercise** religious
exercise. (The book she reads is one of devotion.)   **color** give a plausible appearance to
46 **loneliness** being alone   47 **too much proved** too often shown to be true, too often
practiced   53 **to . . . helps it** in comparison with the cosmetic that fashions the cheek's
false beauty   54 **painted word** deceptive utterances   56.1 s.d. *withdraw* (The King and
Polonius may retire behind an arras. The stage directions specify that they "enter" again
near the end of the scene.)   66 **rub** (literally, an obstacle in the game of bowls)
68 **shuffled** sloughed, cast   **coil** turmoil   69 **respect** consideration   70 **of . . . life** so
long-lived, something we willingly endure for so long (also suggesting that long life is
itself a calamity)

Th'oppressor's wrong, the proud man's contumely,    72
The pangs of disprized love, the law's delay,    73
The insolence of office, and the spurns    74
That patient merit of th'unworthy takes,    75
When he himself might his quietus make    76
With a bare bodkin? Who would fardels bear,    77
To grunt and sweat under a weary life,
But that the dread of something after death,
The undiscovered country from whose bourn    80
No traveler returns, puzzles the will,
And makes us rather bear those ills we have
Than fly to others that we know not of?
Thus conscience does make cowards of us all;
And thus the native hue of resolution    85
Is sicklied o'er with the pale cast of thought,    86
And enterprises of great pitch and moment    87
With this regard their currents turn awry    88
And lose the name of action.—Soft you now,    89
The fair Ophelia.—Nymph, in thy orisons    90
Be all my sins remembered.
OPHELIA               Good my lord,    91
How does Your Honor for this many a day?
HAMLET
I humbly thank you; well, well, well.
OPHELIA
My lord, I have remembrances of yours,
That I have longèd long to redeliver.
I pray you, now receive them.    [*She offers tokens.*]
HAMLET
No, not I, I never gave you aught.
OPHELIA
My honored lord, you know right well you did,
And with them words of so sweet breath composed
As made the things more rich. Their perfume lost,
Take these again, for to the noble mind
Rich gifts wax poor when givers prove unkind.
There, my lord.            [*She gives tokens.*]
HAMLET    Ha, ha! Are you honest?    104
OPHELIA    My lord?
HAMLET    Are you fair?    106
OPHELIA    What means Your Lordship?

---

**72 contumely** insolent abuse    **73 disprized** unvalued    **74 office** officialdom    **spurns** insults    **75 of . . . takes** receives from unworthy persons    **76 quietus** acquittance; here, death    **77 a bare bodkin** a mere dagger, unsheathed    **fardels** burdens    **80 bourn** frontier, boundary    **85 native hue** natural color, complexion    **86 cast** tinge, shade of color    **87 pitch** height (as of a falcon's flight)    **moment** importance    **88 regard** respect, consideration    **currents** courses    **89 Soft you** i.e., Wait a minute, gently    **90–91 in . . . remembered** i.e., pray for me, sinner that I am    **104 honest** (1) truthful (2) chaste    **106 fair** (1) beautiful (2) just, honorable

HAMLET   That if you be honest and fair, your honesty   108
should admit no discourse to your beauty.   109
OPHELIA   Could beauty, my lord, have better commerce   110
than with honesty?
HAMLET   Ay, truly, for the power of beauty will sooner
transform honesty from what it is to a bawd than the
force of honesty can translate beauty into his likeness.   114
This was sometime a paradox, but now the time gives   115
it proof. I did love you once.   116
OPHELIA   Indeed, my lord, you made me believe so.
HAMLET   You should not have believed me, for virtue   118
cannot so inoculate our old stock but we shall relish of   119
it. I loved you not.   120
OPHELIA   I was the more deceived.
HAMLET   Get thee to a nunnery. Why wouldst thou be a   122
breeder of sinners? I am myself indifferent honest, but   123
yet I could accuse me of such things that it were better
my mother had not borne me: I am very proud,
revengeful, ambitious, with more offenses at my beck   126
than I have thoughts to put them in, imagination to
give them shape, or time to act them in. What should
such fellows as I do crawling between earth and
heaven? We are arrant knaves all; believe none of us.
Go thy ways to a nunnery. Where's your father?
OPHELIA   At home, my lord.
HAMLET   Let the doors be shut upon him, that he may
play the fool nowhere but in 's own house. Farewell.
OPHELIA   Oh, help him, you sweet heavens!
HAMLET   If thou dost marry, I'll give thee this plague for
thy dowry: be thou as chaste as ice, as pure as snow,
thou shalt not escape calumny. Get thee to a nunnery,
farewell. Or, if thou wilt needs marry, marry a fool, for
wise men know well enough what monsters you   140
make of them. To a nunnery, go, and quickly too.
Farewell.
OPHELIA   Heavenly powers, restore him!
HAMLET   I have heard of your paintings too, well   144
enough. God hath given you one face, and you make
yourselves another. You jig, you amble, and you   146

---

108 **your honesty** your chastity   109 **discourse to** familiar dealings with   110 **commerce**
dealings, intercourse   114 **his** its   115–116 **This . . . proof** This was formerly an unfash-
ionable view, but now the present age confirms how true it is.   118–120 **virtue . . . of it**
virtue cannot be grafted onto our sinful condition without our retaining some taste of the
old stock.   122 **nunnery** convent (with an awareness that the word was also used derisively to denote a brothel)   123 **indifferent honest** reasonably virtuous   126 **beck** command   140 **monsters** (an illusion to the horns of a cuckold)   **you** i.e., you women
144 **paintings** use of cosmetics   146–148 **You jig . . . ignorance** i.e., You prance about
frivolously and speak with affected coynesss, you put new labels on God's creatures
(by your use of cosmetics), and you excuse your affectations on the grounds of pretended
ignorance.

lisp, you nickname God's creatures, and make your          147
wantonness your ignorance. Go to, I'll no more on't;       148
it hath made me mad. I say we will have no more
marriage. Those that are married already—all but
one—shall live. The rest shall keep as they are. To a
nunnery, go.                                        *Exit.*

OPHELIA
Oh, what a noble mind is here o'erthrown!
The courtier's, soldier's, scholar's, eye, tongue, sword,
Th'expectancy and rose of the fair state,                  155
The glass of fashion and the mold of form,                 156
Th'observed of all observers, quite, quite down!           157
And I, of ladies most deject and wretched,
That sucked the honey of his music vows,                   159
Now see that noble and most sovereign reason
Like sweet bells jangled out of tune and harsh,
That unmatched form and feature of blown youth             162
Blasted with ecstasy. Oh, woe is me,                       163
T'have seen what I have seen, see what I see!

    *Enter King and Polonius.*

KING
Love? His affections do not that way tend;                 165
Nor what he spake, though it lacked form a little,
Was not like madness. There's something in his soul
O'er which his melancholy sits on brood,                   168
And I do doubt the hatch and the disclose                  169
Will be some danger; which for to prevent,
I have in quick determination
Thus set it down: he shall with speed to England           172
For the demand of our neglected tribute.
Haply the seas and countries different
With variable objects shall expel                          175
This something-settled matter in his heart,                176
Whereon his brains still beating puts him thus             177
From fashion of himself. What think you on't?              178
POLONIUS
It shall do well. But yet do I believe
The origin and commencement of his grief
Sprung from neglected love.—How now, Ophelia?

---

**148 on't** of it    **155 Th'expectancy and rose** the hope and ornament    **156 The glass** . . .
**form** the mirror of true self-fashioning and the pattern of courtly behavior    **157 Th'ob-**
**served . . . observers** i.e., the center of attention and honor in the court    **159 music** musical, sweetly uttered    **162 blown** blossoming    **163 Blasted with ecstasy** blighted with
madness    **165 affections** emotions, feelings    **168 sits on brood** sits like a bird on a nest,
about to *hatch* mischief (line 169)    **169 doubt** suspect, fear    **disclose** disclosure, hatch-
ing    **172 set it down** resolved    **175 variable objects** various sights and surroundings to
divert him    **176 This something . . . heart** the strange matter settled in his heart
**177 still** continually    **178 From . . . himself** out of his natural manner

You need not tell us what Lord Hamlet said;
We heard it all.—My lord, do as you please,
But, if you hold it fit, after the play
Let his queen-mother all alone entreat him
To show his grief. Let her be round with him;                                    186
And I'll be placed, so please you, in the ear
Of all their conference. If she find him not,                                    188
To England send him, or confine him where
Your wisdom best shall think.
KING                                    It shall be so.
Madness in great ones must not unwatched go.

                                                                    *Exeunt.*

## [3.2]

*Enter Hamlet and three of the Players.*

HAMLET   Speak the speech, I pray you, as I pronounced
it to you, trippingly on the tongue. But if you mouth
it, as many of our players do, I had as lief the town crier                       3
spoke my lines. Nor do not saw the air too much with
your hand, thus, but use all gently; for in the very
torrent, tempest, and, as I may say, whirlwind of your
passion, you must acquire and beget a temperance
that may give it smoothness. Oh, it offends me to the
soul to hear a robustious periwig-pated fellow tear a                             9
passion to tatters, to very rags, to split the ears of the
groundlings, who for the most part are capable of                                11
nothing but inexplicable dumb shows and noise. I                                 12
would have such a fellow whipped for o'erdoing Termagant.                         13
It out-Herods Herod. Pray you, avoid it.                                         14
FIRST PLAYER   I warrant Your Honor.
HAMLET   Be not too tame neither, but let your own
discretion be your tutor. Suit the action to the word,
the word to the action, with this special observance,
that you o'erstep not the modesty of nature. For                                 19
anything so o'erdone is from the purpose of playing,                             20
whose end, both at the first and now, was and is to
hold as 'twere the mirror up to nature, to show virtue

---

186 **round** blunt   188 **find him not** fails to discover what is troubling him
**3.2 Location: The castle.**
3 **our players** players nowadays   **I had as lief** I would just as soon   9 **robustious** violent, boisterous   **periwig-pated** wearing a wig   11 **groundlings** spectators who paid least and stood in the yard of the theater   **capable of** able to understand   12 **dumb shows and noise** noisy spectacle (rather than thoughtful drama)   13 **Termagant** a supposed deity of the Mohammedans, not found in any English medieval play but elsewhere portrayed as violent and blustering   14 **Herod** Herod of Jewry. (A character in *The Slaughter of the Innocents* and other cycle plays. The part was played with great noise and fury.)   19 **modesty** restraint, moderation   20 **from** contrary to

her feature, scorn her own image, and the very age 23
and body of the time his form and pressure. Now this 24
overdone or come tardy off, though it makes the 25
unskillful laugh, cannot but make the judicious grieve, 26
the censure of the which one must in your allowance 27
o'erweigh a whole theater of others. Oh, there be players
that I have seen play, and heard others praise, and
that highly, not to speak it profanely, that, neither 30
having th'accent of Christians nor the gait of Christian, 31
pagan, nor man, have so strutted and bellowed 32
that I have thought some of nature's journeymen had 33
made men and not made them well, they imitated
humanity so abominably. 35
FIRST PLAYER   I hope we have reformed that indifferently 36
with us, sir.
HAMLET   Oh, reform it altogether. And let those that play
your clowns speak no more than is set down for them;
for there be of them that will themselves laugh, to set 40
on some quantity of barren spectators to laugh too, 41
though in the meantime some necessary question of
the play be then to be considered. That's villainous,
and shows a most pitiful ambition in the fool that uses
it. Go make you ready.          [*Exeunt Players.*]

   *Enter Polonius, Guildenstern, and Rosencrantz.*

How now, my lord, will the King hear this piece of
work?
POLONIUS   And the Queen too, and that presently. 48
HAMLET   Bid the players make haste.     [*Exit Polonius.*]
Will you two help to hasten them?
ROSENCRANTZ
Ay, my lord.                    *Exeunt they two.*
HAMLET          What ho, Horatio!

   *Enter Horatio.*

HORATIO   Here, sweet lord, at your service.
HAMLET
Horatio, thou art e'en as just a man
As e'er my conversation coped withal. 54

---

23 **scorn** i.e., something foolish and deserving of scorn   23–24 **and the . . . pressure** and
the present state of affairs its likeness as seen in an impression, such as wax   25 **come
tardy off** falling short   25–26 **the unskillful** those lacking in judgment   27 **the censure . . .
one** the judgment of even one of whom   **your allowance** your scale of values
30 **not . . . profanely** (Hamlet anticipates his idea in lines 33–34 that some men were not
made by God at all.)   31 **Christians** i.e., ordinary decent folk   32 **nor man** i.e., nor any
human being at all   33 **journeymen** common workmen   35 **abominably** (Shakespeare's
usual spelling, "abhominably," suggests a literal though etymologically incorrect meaning, "removed from human nature.")   36 **indifferently** tolerably   40 **of them** some
among them   41 **barren** i.e., of wit   48 **presently** at once   54 **my . . . withal** my dealings encountered

HORATIO
Oh, my dear lord—
HAMLET                              Nay, do not think I flatter,
For what advancement may I hope from thee
That no revenue hast but thy good spirits
To feed and clothe thee? Why should the poor be
    flattered?
No, let the candied tongue lick absurd pomp,                    59
And crook the pregnant hinges of the knee                       60
Where thrift may follow fawning. Dost thou hear?                61
Since my dear soul was mistress of her choice
And could of men distinguish her election,                      63
Sh' hath sealed thee for herself, for thou hast been            64
As one, in suffering all, that suffers nothing,
A man that Fortune's buffets and rewards
Hast ta'en with equal thanks; and blest are those
Whose blood and judgment are so well commeddled                 68
That they are not a pipe for Fortune's finger
To sound what stop she please. Give me that man                 70
That is not passion's slave, and I will wear him
In my heart's core, ay, in my heart of heart,
As I do thee.—Something too much of this.—
There is a play tonight before the King.
One scene of it comes near the circumstance
Which I have told thee of my father's death.
I prithee, when thou see'st that act afoot,
Even with the very comment of thy soul                          78
Observe my uncle. If his occulted guilt                         79
Do not itself unkennel in one speech,                           80
It is a damnèd ghost that we have seen,
And my imaginations are as foul
As Vulcan's stithy. Give him heedful note,                      83
For I mine eyes will rivet to his face,
And after we will both our judgments join
In censure of his seeming.
HORATIO                         Well, my lord.                  86
If 'a steal aught the whilst this play is playing               87
And scape detecting, I will pay the theft.

    *[Flourish.] Enter trumpets and kettledrums,*
    *King, Queen, Polonius, Ophelia, [Rosencrantz,*

---

59 **candied** sugared, flattering   60 **pregnant** compliant   61 **thrift** profit   63 **could . . . election** could make distinguishing choices among persons   64 **sealed thee** (literally, as one would seal a legal document to mark possession)   68 **blood** passion   **commeddled** commingled   70 **stop** hole in a wind instrument for controlling the sound   78 **very . . . soul** your most penetrating observation and consideration   79 **occulted** hidden   80 **unkennel** (as one would say of a fox driven from its lair)   83 **Vulcan's stithy** the smithy, the place of stiths (anvils) of the Roman god of fire and metalworking   86 **censure of his seeming** judgment of his appearance or behavior   87 **If 'a steal aught** If he gets away with anything

*Guildenstern, and other lords, with guards*
*carrying torches].*

HAMLET   They are coming to the play. I must be idle.                    89
Get you a place. [*The King, Queen, and courtiers sit.*]
KING   How fares our cousin Hamlet?                                       91
HAMLET   Excellent, i'faith, of the chameleon's dish: I eat              92
the air, promise-crammed. You cannot feed capons so.                     93
KING   I have nothing with this answer, Hamlet. These                    94
words are not mine.                                                      95
HAMLET   No, nor mine now. [*To Polonius*] My lord, you                  96
played once i'th'university, you say?
POLONIUS   That did I, my lord, and was accounted a
good actor.
HAMLET   What did you enact?
POLONIUS   I did enact Julius Caesar. I was killed i'th'                101
Capitol; Brutus killed me.                                              102
HAMLET   It was a brute part of him to kill so capital a                103
calf there.—Be the players ready?                                      104
ROSENCRANTZ   Ay, my lord. They stay upon your                         105
patience.
QUEEN   Come hither, my dear Hamlet, sit by me.
HAMLET   No, good mother, here's metal more attractive.                 108
POLONIUS [*to the King*]   Oho, do you mark that?
HAMLET   Lady, shall I lie in your lap?                                 110
                              [*Lying down at Ophelia's feet.*]
OPHELIA   No, my lord.
HAMLET   I mean, my head upon your lap?
OPHELIA   Ay, my lord.
HAMLET   Do you think I meant country matters?                          114
OPHELIA   I think nothing, my lord.
HAMLET   That's a fair thought to lie between maids'
legs.
OPHELIA   What is, my lord?
HAMLET   Nothing.                                                      119

---

**89 idle** (1) unoccupied (2) mad   **91 cousin** i.e., close relative   **92 chameleon's dish**
(Chameleons were supposed to feed on air. Hamlet deliberately misinterprets the King's
*fares* as "feeds." By his phrase *eat the air* he also plays on the idea of feeding himself
with the promise of succession, of being the *heir*.)   **93 capons** roosters castrated and
*crammed* with feed to make them succulent   **94 have . . . with** make nothing of, or gain
nothing from   **95 are not mine** do not respond to what I asked   **96 nor mine now**
(Once spoken, words are proverbially no longer the speaker's own—and hence should be
uttered warily.)   **101–102 i'th' Capitol** (where Caesar was assassinated, according to
*Julius Caesar*, 3.1)   **103 brute** (The Latin meaning of *brutus,* "stupid," was often used
punningly with the name Brutus.)   **part** (1) deed (2) role   **104 calf** fool   **105 stay**
**upon** await   **108 metal** substance that is *attractive,* i.e., magnetic, but with suggestion
also of *mettle,* "disposition"   **110 Lady . . . lap?** (Onstage, Hamlet often lies at Ophelia's feet, but he could instead offer to do this and continue to stand.)   **114 country**
**matters** sexual intercourse (with a bawdy pun on the first syllable of *country*)
**119 Nothing** The figure zero or naught, suggesting the female sexual anatomy. (*Thing*
not infrequently has a bawdy connotation of male or female anatomy, and the reference
here could be male.)

OPHELIA  You are merry, my lord.
HAMLET  Who, I?
OPHELIA  Ay, my lord.
HAMLET  Oh, God, your only jig maker. What should a       123
man do but be merry? For look you how cheerfully my
mother looks, and my father died within 's two hours.       125
OPHELIA  Nay, 'tis twice two months, my lord.
HAMLET  So long? Nay then, let the devil wear black, for
I'll have a suit of sables. O heavens! Die two months       128
ago, and not forgotten yet? Then there's hope a great
man's memory may outlive his life half a year. But, by'r
Lady, 'a must build churches, then, or else shall 'a
suffer not thinking on, with the hobbyhorse, whose       132
epitaph is "For oh, for oh, the hobbyhorse is forgot."       133

*The trumpets sound. Dumb show follows.*

*Enter a King and a Queen [very lovingly]; the*
*Queen embracing him, and he her. [She kneels,*
*and makes show of protestation unto him.] He*
*takes her up, and declines his head upon her neck.*
*He lies him down upon a bank of flowers. She,*
*seeing him asleep, leaves him. Anon comes in*
*another man, takes off his crown, kisses it, pours*
*poison in the sleeper's ears, and leaves him. The*
*Queen returns, finds the King dead, makes*
*passionate action. The Poisoner with some three or*
*four come in again, seem to condole with her. The*
*dead body is carried away. The Poisoner woos the*
*Queen with gifts; she seems harsh awhile, but in*
*the end accepts love.*

*[Exeunt players.]*
OPHELIA  What means this, my lord?
HAMLET  Marry, this' miching mallico; it means       135
mischief.
OPHELIA  Belike this show imports the argument of the       137
play.

*Enter Prologue.*

---

123 **only jig maker** very best composer of jigs, i.e., pointless merriment. (Hamlet
replies sardonically to Ophelia's observation that he is merry by saying, "If you're
looking for someone who is really merry, you've come to the right person.")
125 **within 's** within this (i.e., these)   128 **suit of sables** garments trimmed with the
dark fur of the sable and hence suited for a person in mourning   132 **suffer . . . on**
undergo oblivion   133 **"For . . . forgot"** (Verse of a song occurring also in *Love's La-*
*bor's Lost*, 3.1.27–28. The hobbyhorse was a character made up to resemble a horse
and rider, appearing in the morris dance and such May-game sports. This song laments
the disappearance of such customs under pressure from the Puritans.)   **133.12 s.d.**
*condole with* offer sympathy to   135 **this' miching mallico** this is sneaking mischief
137 **Belike** Probably   **argument** plot

HAMLET   We shall know by this fellow. The players can-
not keep counsel; they'll tell all.                                              140
OPHELIA   Will 'a tell us what this show meant?
HAMLET   Ay, or any show that you will show him. Be                              142
not you ashamed to show, he'll not shame to tell you                            143
what it means.
OPHELIA   You are naught, you are naught. I'll mark the                         145
play.
PROLOGUE
     For us, and for our tragedy,
     Here stooping to your clemency,                                            148
     We beg your hearing patiently.            [*Exit.*]
HAMLET   Is this a prologue, or the posy of a ring?                             150
OPHELIA   'Tis brief, my lord.
HAMLET   As woman's love.

     *Enter [two Players as] King and Queen.*

PLAYER KING   Full thirty times hath Phoebus' cart gone round                   153
     Neptune's salt wash and Tellus' orbèd ground,                              154
     And thirty dozen moons with borrowed sheen                                155
     About the world have times twelve thirties been,
     Since love our hearts and Hymen did our hands                              157
     Unite commutual in most sacred bands.                                      158
PLAYER QUEEN   So many journeys may the sun and moon
     Make us again count o'er ere love be done!
     But, woe is me, you are so sick of late,
     So far from cheer and from your former state,
     That I distrust you. Yet, though I distrust,                              163
     Discomfort you, my lord, it nothing must.                                 164
     For women's fear and love hold quantity;                                  165
     In neither aught, or in extremity.                                        166
     Now, what my love is, proof hath made you know,                           167
     And as my love is sized, my fear is so.
     Where love is great, the littlest doubts are fear;                        169
     Where little fears grow great, great love grows there.
PLAYER KING
     Faith, I must leave thee, love, and shortly too;
     My operant powers their functions leave to do.                            172
     And thou shalt live in this fair world behind,                            173

---

**140 counsel** secret   **142–143 Be not you** Provided you are not   **145 naught** indecent.
(Ophelia is reacting to Hamlet's pointed remarks about not being ashamed to show all.)
**148 stooping** bowing   **150 posy . . . ring** brief motto in verse inscribed in a ring
**153 Phoebus' cart** the sun-god's chariot, making its yearly cycle   **154 salt wash** the sea
**Tellus** goddess of the earth, of the *orbèd* ground   **155 borrowed** i.e., reflected
**157 Hymen** god of matrimony   **158 commutual** mutually   **bands** bonds
**163 distrust** am anxious about   **164 Discomfort . . . must** it must not distress you at all.
**165 hold quantity** keep proportion with one another   **166 In . . . extremity** (women feel)
either no anxiety if they do not love or extreme anxiety if they do love.   **167 proof** experience   **169 the littlest** even the littlest   **172 My . . . to do** my vital functions are shut-
ting down   **173 behind** after I have gone

Honored, beloved; and haply one as kind
For husband shalt thou—
PLAYER QUEEN                    Oh, confound the rest!
Such love must needs be treason in my breast.
In second husband let me be accurst!
None wed the second but who killed the first.                    178
HAMLET   Wormwood, wormwood.                                     179
PLAYER QUEEN   The instances that second marriage move           180
Are base respects of thrift, but none of love.                  181
A second time I kill my husband dead
When second husband kisses me in bed.
PLAYER KING   I do believe you think what now you speak,
But what we do determine oft we break.
Purpose is but the slave to memory,                              186
Of violent birth, but poor validity,                            187
Which now, like fruit unripe, sticks on the tree,               188
But fall unshaken when they mellow be.
Most necessary 'tis that we forget                               190
To pay ourselves what to ourselves is debt.                     191
What to ourselves in passion we propose,
The passion ending, doth the purpose lose.
The violence of either grief or joy
Their own enactures with themselves destroy.                    195
Where joy most revels, grief doth most lament;                  196
Grief joys, joy grieves, on slender accident.                   197
This world is not for aye, nor 'tis not strange                 198
That 'even our loves should with our fortunes change;
For 'tis a question left us yet to prove,
Whether love lead fortune, or else fortune love.
The great man down, you mark his favorite flies;                202
The poor advanced makes friends of enemies.                     203
And hitherto doth love on fortune tend;                         204
For who not needs shall never lack a friend,                    205
And who in want a hollow friend doth try                        206
Directly seasons him his enemy.                                  207
But, orderly to end where I begun,

178 None (1) Let no woman; or (2) No woman does   but who except the one who
179 Wormwood i.e., How bitter. (Literally, a bitter-tasting plant.)   180 instances
motives   move motivate   181 base . . . thrift ignoble considerations of material
prosperity   186 Purpose . . . memory Our good intentions are subject to forgetfulness
187 validity strength, durability   188 Which i.e., purpose   190–191 Most . . . debt
It's inevitable that in time we forget the obligations we have imposed on ourselves.
195 enactures fulfillments   196–197 Where . . . accident The capacity for extreme joy
and grief go together, and often one extreme is instantly changed into its opposite on
the slightest provocation.   198 aye ever   202 down fallen in fortune   203 The poor
. . . enemies when one of humble station is promoted, you see his enemies suddenly
becoming his friends.   204 hitherto up to this point in the argument, or, to this
extent   tend attend   205 who not needs he who is not in need (of wealth)
206 who in want he who, being in need   try test (his generosity)   207 seasons
him ripens him into

Our wills and fates do so contrary run                                          209
That our devices still are overthrown;                                          210
Our thoughts are ours, their ends none of our own.                              211
So think thou wilt no second husband wed,
But die thy thoughts when thy first lord is dead.

PLAYER QUEEN
    Nor earth to me give food, nor heaven light,                   214
Sport and repose lock from me day and night,                                    215
To desperation turn my trust and hope,
An anchor's cheer in prison be my scope!                                        217
Each opposite that blanks the face of joy                                       218
Meet what I would have well and it destroy!                                     219
Both here and hence pursue me lasting strife                                    220
If, once a widow, ever I be wife!

HAMLET    If she should break it now!

PLAYER KING    'Tis deeply sworn. Sweet, leave me here awhile;
My spirits grow dull, and fain I would beguile                                  224
The tedious day with sleep.

PLAYER QUEEN            Sleep rock thy brain,
And never come mischance between us twain!

                        *[He sleeps.] Exit [Player Queen].*

HAMLET    Madam, how like you this play?

QUEEN    The lady doth protest too much, methinks.                       228

HAMLET    Oh, but she'll keep her word.

KING    Have you heard the argument? Is there no                          230
offense in't?

HAMLET    No, no, they do but jest, poison in jest. No offense            232
i'th' world.                                                                    233

KING    What do you call the play?

HAMLET    *The Mousetrap.* Marry, how? Tropically.                        235
This play is the image of a murder done in Vienna.
Gonzago is the Duke's name, his wife, Baptista. You                             237
shall see anon. 'Tis a knavish piece of work, but what
of that? Your Majesty, and we that have free souls, it                          239
touches us not. Let the galled jade wince, our withers                          240
are unwrung.                                                                    241

---

209 **Our . . . run** what we want and what we get go so contrarily   210 **devices** intentions   **still** continually   211 **ends** results   214 **Nor** Let neither   215 **Sport . . . night** may day deny me its pastimes and night its repose   217 **anchor's cheer** anchorite's or hermit's fare   **my scope** the extent of my happiness   218–219 **Each . . . destroy!** May every adverse thing that causes the face of joy to turn pale meet and destroy everything that I desire to see prosper!   220 **hence** in the life hereafter   224 **spirits** vital spirits 228 **doth . . . much** makes too many promises and protestations   230 **argument** plot 232 **jest** make believe   232–233 **offense** crime, injury. (Hamlet playfully alters the King's use of the word in line 231 to mean "cause for objection.")   235 **Tropically** Figuratively. (The First Quarto reading, "trapically," suggests a pun on *trap* in *Mousetrap*.) 237 **Duke's** i.e., King's (an inconsistency that may be due to Shakespeare's possible acquaintance with a historical incident, the alleged murder of the Duke of Urbino by Luigi Gonzaga in 1538)   239 **free** guiltless   240 **galled jade** horse whose hide is rubbed by saddle or harness   **withers** the part between the horse's shoulder blades   241 **unwrung** not rubbed sore

*Enter Lucianus.*

This is one Lucianus, nephew to the King.

OPHELIA   You are as good as a chorus, my lord.                    243

HAMLET   I could interpret between you and your love,          244
if I could see the puppets dallying                                       245

OPHELIA   You are keen, my lord, you are keen.                   246

HAMLET   It would cost you a groaning to take off mine
edge.                                                                                        249

OPHELIA   Still better, and worse.                                         249

HAMLET   So you mis-take your husbands.—Begin,             250
murderer; leave thy damnable faces and begin. Come, the
croaking raven doth bellow for revenge.

LUCIANUS
Thoughts black, hands apt, drugs fit, and time
agreeing,
Confederate season, else no creature seeing,                      254
Thou mixture rank, of midnight weeds collected,
With Hecate's ban thrice blasted, thrice infected,             256
Thy natural magic and dire property                                    257
On wholesome life usurp immediately.

                    [*He pours the poison into the sleeper's ear.*]

HAMLET   'A poisons him i'th' garden for his estate. His       259
name's Gonzago. The story is extant, and written in
very choice Italian. You shall see anon how the
murderer gets the love of Gonzago's wife.

                                                              [*Claudius rises.*]

OPHELIA   The King rises.

HAMLET   What, frighted with false fire?                              264

QUEEN   How fares my lord?

POLONIUS   Give o'er the play.

KING   Give me some light. Away!

POLONIUS   Lights, lights, lights!
                                    *Exeunt all but Hamlet and Horatio.*

HAMLET
        "Why, let the strucken deer go weep,                          269

---

**243 chorus** (In many Elizabethan plays, the forthcoming action was explained by an actor known as the "chorus"; at a puppet show, the actor who spoke the dialogue was known as an "interpreter," as indicated by the lines following.)   **244 interpret** (1) ventriloquize the dialogue, as in puppet show (2) act as pander   **245 puppets dallying** (with suggestion of sexual play, continued in *keen*, "sexually aroused," *groaning*, "moaning in pregnancy," and *edge*, "sexual desire" or "impetuosity")   **246 keen** sharp, bitter   **249 Still . . . worse** More keen, always *bettering* what other people say with witty wordplay, but at the same time more offensive.   **250 So** Even thus (in marriage)   **mis-take** take falseheartedly and cheat on. (The marriage vows say "for better, for worse.")   **254 Confederate . . . seeing** the time and occasion conspiring (to assist me), and also no one seeing me   **256 Hecate's ban** the curse of Hecate, the goddess of witchcraft   **257 dire property** baleful quality   **259 estate** i.e., the kingship   **His** i.e., the King's   **264 false fire** the blank discharge of a gun loaded with powder but no shot   **269–272 Why . . . away** (Perhaps this comes from an old ballad, with allusion to the popular belief that a wounded deer retires to weep and die; compare with *As You Like It*, 2.1.33–66.)

The hart ungallèd play. 270
For some must watch, while some must sleep; 271
Thus runs the world away." 272
Would not this, sir, and a forest of feathers—if the 273
rest of my fortunes turn Turk with me—with two 274
Provincial roses on my razed shoes, get me a fellowship 275
in a cry of players? 276
HORATIO  Half a share.
HAMLET  A whole one, I.
"For thou dost know, O Damon dear, 279
This realm dismantled was 280
Of Jove himself, and now reigns here 281
A very, very—pajock." 282
HORATIO  You might have rhymed.
HAMLET  Oh, good Horatio, I'll take the ghost's word for
a thousand pound. Didst perceive?
HORATIO  Very well, my lord.
HAMLET  Upon the talk of the poisoning?
HORATIO  I did very well note him.

*Enter Rosencrantz and Guildenstern.*

HAMLET  Aha! Come, some music! Come, the
recorders.
"For if the King like not the comedy,
Why then, belike, he likes it not, perdy." 292
Come, some music.
GUILDENSTERN  Good my lord, vouchsafe me a word
with you.
HAMLET  Sir, a whole history.
GUILDENSTERN  The King, sir—
HAMLET  Ay, sir, what of him?
GUILDENSTERN  Is in his retirement marvelous 299
distempered. 300
HAMLET  With drink, sir?
GUILDENSTERN  No, my lord, with choler. 302

---

270 **ungallèd** unafflicted  271 **watch** remain awake  272 **Thus . . . away** Thus the world goes.  273 **this** i.e., this success with the play I have just presented  **feathers** (allusion to the plumes that Elizabethan actors were fond of wearing)  274 **turn Turk with** turn renegade against, go back on  275 **Provincial roses** rosettes of ribbon, named for roses grown in a part of France  **razed** with ornamental slashing  275–276 **fellowship . . . players** partnership in a theatrical company  276 **cry** pack (of hounds, etc.)  279 **Damon** the friend of Pythias, as Horatio is friend of Hamlet; or, a traditional pastoral name  280–282 **This realm . . . pajock** i.e., Jove, representing divine authority and justice, has abandoned this realm to its own devices, leaving in his stead only a peacock or vain pretender to virtue (though the rhyme-word expected in place of *pajock* or "peacock" suggests that the realm is now ruled over by an "ass").  280 **dismantled** stripped, divested  292 **perdy** (a corruption of the French *par dieu*, "by God")  299 **retirement** withdrawal to his chambers  300 **distempered** out of humor. (But Hamlet deliberately plays on the wider application to any illness of mind or body, as in lines 335–336, especially to drunkenness.)  302 **choler** anger. (But Hamlet takes the word in its more basic humoral sense of "bilious disorder.")

HAMLET  Your wisdom should show itself more richer
to signify this to the doctor, for for me to put him to his
purgation would perhaps plunge him into more                            305
choler.
GUILDENSTERN  Good my lord, put your discourse into
some frame and start not so wildly from my affair.                      308
HAMLET  I am tame, sir. Pronounce.
GUILDENSTERN  The Queen, your mother, in most great
affliction of spirit, hath sent me to you.
HAMLET  You are welcome.
GUILDENSTERN  Nay, good my lord, this courtesy is not
of the right breed. If it shall please you to make me a                 314
wholesome answer, I will do your mother's commandment;
if not, your pardon and my return shall be the                          316
end of my business.
HAMLET  Sir, I cannot.
ROSENCRANTZ  What, my lord?
HAMLET  Make you a wholesome answer; my wit's
diseased. But, sir, such answer as I can make, you shall
command, or rather, as you say, my mother. Therefore
no more, but to the matter. My mother, you say—
ROSENCRANTZ  Then thus she says: your behavior hath
struck her into amazement and admiration.                               325
HAMLET  Oh, wonderful son, that can so 'stonish a mother!
But is there no sequel at the heels of this mother's
admiration? Impart.
ROSENCRANTZ  She desires to speak with you in her
closet ere you go to bed.                                               330
HAMLET  We shall obey, were she ten times our mother.
Have you any further trade with us?
ROSENCRANTZ  My lord, you once did love me.
HAMLET  And do still, by these pickers and stealers.                    334
ROSENCRANTZ  Good my lord, what is your cause of
distemper? You do surely bar the door upon your own
liberty if you deny your griefs to your friend.                         337
HAMLET  Sir, I lack advancement.
ROSENCRANTZ  How can that be, when you have the
voice of the King himself for your succession in
Denmark?
HAMLET  Ay, sir, but "While the grass grows"—the            342
proverb is something musty.                                             343

305 **purgation** (Hamlet hints at something going beyond medical treatment to bloodlet-
ting and the extraction of confession.)  308 **frame** order  **start** shy or jump away (like
a horse; the opposite of *tame* in line 309)  314 **breed** (1) kind (2) breeding, manners
316 **pardon** permission to depart  325 **admiration** bewilderment  330 **closet** private
chamber  334 **pickers and stealers** i.e., hands (so called from the catechism, "to keep
my hands from picking and stealing")  337 **liberty** i.e., being freed from *distemper*, line
336; but perhaps with a veiled threat as well  **deny** refuse to share  342 "**While** . . .
**grows**" (The rest of the proverb is "the silly horse starves"; Hamlet implies that his
hopes of succession are distant in time at best.)  343 **something** somewhat

*Enter the Players with recorders.*

Oh, the recorders. Let me see one. [*He takes a recorder.*]
To withdraw with you: why do you go about to recover                345
the wind of me, as if you would drive me into a toil?               346
GUILDENSTERN   Oh, my lord, if my duty be too bold, my              347
love is too unmannerly.                                             348
HAMLET   I do not well understand that. Will you play              349
upon this pipe?
GUILDENSTERN   My lord, I cannot.
HAMLET   I pray you.
GUILDENSTERN   Believe me, I cannot.
HAMLET   I do beseech you.
GUILDENSTERN   I know no touch of it, my lord.
HAMLET   It is as easy as lying. Govern these ventages             356
with your fingers and thumb, give it breath with your
mouth, and it will discourse most eloquent music.
Look you, these are the stops.
GUILDENSTERN   But these cannot I command to any
utterance of harmony. I have not the skill.
HAMLET   Why, look you now, how unworthy a thing
you make of me! You would play upon me, you would
seem to know my stops, you would pluck out the heart
of my mystery, you would sound me from my lowest            365
note to the top of my compass, and there is much           366
music, excellent voice, in this little organ, yet cannot   367
you make it speak. 'Sblood, do you think I am easier
to be played on than a pipe? Call me what instrument
you will, though you can fret me, you cannot play           370
upon me.

*Enter Polonius.*

God bless you, sir!
POLONIUS   My lord, the Queen would speak with you,
and presently.                                             374
HAMLET   Do you see yonder cloud that's almost in
shape of a camel?
POLONIUS   By th' Mass and 'tis, like a camel indeed.
HAMLET   Methinks it is like a weasel.
POLONIUS   It is backed like a weasel.
HAMLET   Or like a whale.

---

**343.1 s.d. *Players*** actors   **345 withdraw** speak privately   **345–346 recover the wind** get
to the windward side (thus allowing the game to scent the hunter and thereby be driven
in the opposite direction into the *toil* or net)   **346 toil** snare   **347–348 if . . . unmannerly** if I am using an unmannerly boldness, it is my love that occasions it.   **349 I . . .
that** i.e., I don't understand how genuine love can be unmannerly.   **356 ventages** finger-
holes or *stops* (line 359) of the recorder   **365 sound** (1) fathom (2) produce sound in
**366 compass** range (of voice)   **367 organ** musical instrument   **370 fret** irritate (with a
quibble on the *frets* or ridges on the fingerboard of some stringed instruments to regulate
the fingering)   **374 presently** at once

POLONIUS   Very like a whale.

HAMLET   Then I will come to my mother by and by.
[*Aside*] They fool me to the top of my bent.—I will        383
come by and by.

POLONIUS   I will say so.                                    [*Exit.*]

HAMLET   "By and by" is easily said. Leave me, friends.
                                    [*Exeunt all but Hamlet.*]
'Tis now the very witching time of night,                    387
When churchyards yawn and hell itself breathes out
Contagion to this world. Now could I drink hot
    blood
And do such bitter business as the day
Would quake to look on. Soft, now to my mother.
O heart, lose not thy nature! Let not ever                   392
The soul of Nero enter this firm bosom.                      393
Let me be cruel, not unnatural;
I will speak daggers to her, but use none.
My tongue and soul in this be hypocrites:
How in my words somever she be shent,                        397
To give them seals never my soul consent!        *Exit.*     398

❖

# [3.3]

*Enter King, Rosencrantz, and Guildenstern.*

KING
I like him not, nor stands it safe with us                   1
To let his madness range. Therefore prepare you.
I your commission will forthwith dispatch,                   3
And he to England shall along with you.
The terms of our estate may not endure                       5
Hazard so near 's as doth hourly grow
Out of his brows.

GUILDENSTERN        We will ourselves provide.               7
Most holy and religious fear it is                           8
To keep those many many bodies safe
That live and feed upon Your Majesty.

---

383 **They fool . . . bent** They humor my odd behavior to the limit of my ability or endurance (literally, the extent to which a bow may be bent)   387 **witching time** time when spells are cast and evil is abroad   392 **nature** natural feeling   393 **Nero** (This infamous Roman emperor put to death his mother, Agrippina, who had murdered her husband, Claudius.)   397–398 **How . . . consent!** However much she is to be rebuked by my words, may my soul never consent to ratify those words with deeds of violence!
3.3 **Location: The castle.**
1 **him** i.e., his behavior   3 **dispatch** prepare, cause to be drawn up   5 **terms of our estate** circumstances of my royal position   7 **Out . . . brows** i.e., from his brain, in the form of plots and threats   **We . . . provide** We'll put ourselves in readiness.
8 **religious fear** sacred concern

ROSENCRANTZ

The single and peculiar life is bound                               11
With all the strength and armor of the mind
To keep itself from noyance, but much more                          13
That spirit upon whose weal depends and rests                       14
The lives of many. The cess of majesty                              15
Dies not alone, but like a gulf doth draw                           16
What's near it with it; or it is a massy wheel                      17
Fixed on the summit of the highest mount,
To whose huge spokes ten thousand lesser things
Are mortised and adjoined, which, when it falls,                    20
Each small annexment, petty consequence,                            21
Attends the boist'rous ruin. Never alone                            22
Did the King sigh, but with a general groan.

KING

Arm you, I pray you, to this speedy voyage,                         24
For we will fetters put about this fear,
Which now goes too free-footed.

ROSENCRANTZ                          We will haste us.
    *Exeunt gentlemen [Rosencrantz and Guildenstern].*

    *Enter Polonius.*

POLONIUS

My lord, he's going to his mother's closet.
Behind the arras I'll convey myself                                 28
To hear the process. I'll warrant she'll tax him home,             29
And, as you said—and wisely was it said—
'Tis meet that some more audience than a mother,                    31
Since nature makes them partial, should o'erhear
The speech of vantage. Fare you well, my liege.                     33
I'll call upon you ere you go to bed
And tell you what I know.

KING                          Thanks, dear my lord.
    *Exit [Polonius].*
Oh, my offense is rank! It smells to heaven.
It hath the primal eldest curse upon't,                             37
A brother's murder. Pray can I not,
Though inclination be as sharp as will;                             39
My stronger guilt defeats my strong intent,

---

**11 single and peculiar** individual and private **13 noyance** harm **14 weal** well-being
**15 cess** decease, cessation **16 gulf** whirlpool **17 massy** massive **20 mortised** fastened
(as with a fitted joint) **when it falls** i.e., when it descends, like the wheel of Fortune,
bringing a king down with it **21 Each . . . consequence** i.e., every hanger-on and
unimportant person or thing connected with the King **22 Attends** participates in
**24 Arm** Provide, prepare **28 arras** screen of tapestry placed around the walls of household apartments. (On the Elizabethan stage, the arras was presumably over a door or
aperture in the tiring-house facade.) **29 process** proceedings **tax him home** reprove
him severely **31 meet** fitting **33 of vantage** from an advantageous place, or, in addition
**37 the primal eldest curse** the curse of Cain, the first murderer, who killed his brother
Abel **39 Though . . . will** though my desire is as strong as my determination

And like a man to double business bound 41
I stand in pause where I shall first begin,
And both neglect. What if this cursèd hand
Were thicker than itself with brother's blood,
Is there not rain enough in the sweet heavens
To wash it white as snow? Whereto serves mercy 46
But to confront the visage of offense? 47
And what's in prayer but this twofold force,
To be forestallèd ere we come to fall, 49
Or pardoned being down? Then I'll look up.
My fault is past. But oh, what form of prayer
Can serve my turn? "Forgive me my foul murder"?
That cannot be, since I am still possessed
Of those effects for which I did the murder:
My crown, mine own ambition, and my queen.
May one be pardoned and retain th'offense? 56
In the corrupted currents of this world 57
Offense's gilded hand may shove by justice, 58
And oft 'tis seen the wicked prize itself 59
Buys out the law. But 'tis not so above.
There is no shuffling, there the action lies 61
In his true nature, and we ourselves compelled, 62
Even to the teeth and forehead of our faults, 63
To give in evidence. What then? What rests? 64
Try what repentance can. What can it not?
Yet what can it, when one cannot repent?
O wretched state, O bosom black as death,
O limèd soul that, struggling to be free, 68
Art more engaged! Help, angels! Make assay. 69
Bow, stubborn knees, and heart with strings of steel,
Be soft as sinews of the newborn babe!
All may be well.          [*He kneels.*]

    *Enter Hamlet.*

HAMLET
Now might I do it pat, now 'a is a-praying; 73
And now I'll do't. [*He draws his sword.*] And so 'a goes
   to heaven,
And so am I revenged. That would be scanned: 75

---

**41 bound** (1) destined (2) obliged. (The King wants to repent and still enjoy what he has
gained.)   **46–47 Whereto . . . offense?** What function does mercy serve other than to
meet sin face to face?   **49 forestallèd** prevented (from sinning)   **56 th'offense** the thing
for which one offended   **57 currents** courses of events   **58 gilded hand** hand offering
gold as a bribe   **shove by** thrust aside   **59 wicked prize** prize won by wickedness
**61 There . . . lies** There in heaven can be no evasion, there the deed lies exposed to view
**62 his** its   **63 to the teeth and forehead** face to face, concealing nothing   **64 give in** provide   **rests** remains   **68 limèd** caught as with birdlime, a sticky substance used to
ensnare birds   **69 engaged** entangled   **assay** trial (said to himself, or to the angels to try
him)   **73 pat** opportunely   **75 would be scanned** needs to be looked into, or, would be
interpreted as follows

A villain kills my father, and for that,
I, his sole son, do this same villain send
To heaven.
Why, this is hire and salary, not revenge.
'A took my father grossly, full of bread,                               80
With all his crimes broad blown, as flush as May;                      81
And how his audit stands who knows save heaven?                        82
But in our circumstance and course of thought                          83
'Tis heavy with him. And am I then revenged,
To take him in the purging of his soul,
When he is fit and seasoned for his passage?                           86
No!
Up, sword, and know thou a more horrid hent.                           88
                                    [*He puts up his sword.*]
When he is drunk asleep, or in his rage,                               89
Or in th'incestuous pleasure of his bed,
At game, a-swearing, or about some act                                 91
That has no relish of salvation in't—                                  92
Then trip him, that his heels may kick at heaven,
And that his soul may be as damned and black
As hell, whereto it goes. My mother stays.                             95
This physic but prolongs thy sickly days.          *Exit.*             96
KING
My words fly up, my thoughts remain below.
Words without thoughts never to heaven go.        *Exit.*

❖

# [3.4]

*Enter [Queen] Gertrude and Polonius.*

POLONIUS
'A will come straight. Look you lay home to him.                       1
Tell him his pranks have been too broad to bear with,                 2
And that Your Grace hath screened and stood
    between
Much heat and him. I'll silence me even here.                          4
Pray you, be round with him.                                           5

---

**80 grossly, full of bread** i.e., enjoying his worldly pleasures rather than fasting. (See Ezekiel 16.49.)   **81 crimes broad blown** sins in full bloom   **flush** vigorous   **82 audit** account   **save** except for   **83 in . . . thought** as we see it from our mortal perspective   **86 seasoned** matured, readied   **88 know . . . hent** await to be grasped by me on a more horrid occasion. (*Hent* means "act of seizing.")   **89 drunk . . . rage** dead drunk, or in a fit of sexual passion   **91 game** gambling   **92 relish** trace, savor   **95 stays** awaits (me)   **96 physic** purging (by prayer), or, Hamlet's postponement of the killing   **3.4 Location:** The Queen's private chamber.
**1 lay home** reprove him soundly   **2 broad** unrestrained   **4 Much heat** i.e., the King's anger   **I'll silence me** I'll quietly conceal myself. (Ironic, since it is his crying out at line 24 that leads to his death. Some editors emend *silence* to "sconce." The First Quarto's reading, "shroud," is attractive.)   **5 round** blunt

HAMLET (*within*)  Mother, mother, mother!
QUEEN   I'll warrant you, fear me not.
     Withdraw, I hear him coming.

     [*Polonius hides behind the arras.*]

     *Enter Hamlet.*

HAMLET   Now, mother, what's the matter?
QUEEN
     Hamlet, thou hast thy father much offended.          10
HAMLET
     Mother, you have my father much offended.
QUEEN
     Come, come, you answer with an idle tongue.          12
HAMLET
     Go, go, you question with a wicked tongue.
QUEEN
     Why, how now, Hamlet?
HAMLET                          What's the matter now?
QUEEN
     Have you forgot me?
HAMLET                          No, by the rood, not so:    15
     You are the Queen, your husband's brother's wife,
     And—would it were not so!—you are my mother.
QUEEN
     Nay, then, I'll set those to you that can speak.      18
HAMLET
     Come, come, and sit you down; you shall not budge.
     You go not till I set you up a glass
     Where you may see the inmost part of you.
QUEEN
     What wilt thou do? Thou wilt not murder me?
     Help, ho!
POLONIUS [*behind the arras*]   What ho! Help!
HAMLET [*drawing*]
     How now? A rat? Dead for a ducat, dead!              25
               [*He thrusts his rapier through the arras.*]
POLONIUS [*behind the arras*]
     Oh, I am slain!            [*He falls and dies.*]
QUEEN               Oh, me, what hast thou done?
HAMLET   Nay, I know not. Is it the King?
QUEEN
     Oh, what a rash and bloody deed is this!
HAMLET
     A bloody deed—almost as bad, good mother,
     As kill a king, and marry with his brother.

---

**10 thy father** i.e., your stepfather, Claudius   **12 idle** foolish   **15 forgot me** i.e., forgotten
that I am your mother   **rood** cross of Christ   **18 speak** i.e., speak to someone so rude
**25 Dead for a ducat** i.e., I bet a ducat he's dead; or, a ducat is his life's fee.

QUEEN
    As kill a king!
HAMLET        Ay, lady, it was my word.
              *[He parts the arras and discovers Polonius.]*
    Thou wretched, rash, intruding fool, farewell!
    I took thee for thy better. Take thy fortune.
    Thou find'st to be too busy is some danger.—     34
    Leave wringing of your hands. Peace, sit you down,
    And let me wring your heart, for so I shall,
    If it be made of penetrable stuff,
    If damnèd custom have not brazed it so      38
    That it be proof and bulwark against sense.     39
QUEEN
    What have I done, that thou dar'st wag thy tongue
    In noise so rude against me?
HAMLET             Such an act
    That blurs the grace and blush of modesty,
    Calls virtue hypocrite, takes off the rose
    From the fair forehead of an innocent love
    And sets a blister there, makes marriage vows     45
    As false as dicers' oaths. Oh, such a deed
    As from the body of contraction plucks     47
    The very soul, and sweet religion makes     48
    A rhapsody of words. Heaven's face does glow     49
    O'er this solidity and compound mass     50
    With tristful visage, as against the doom,     51
    Is thought-sick at the act.
QUEEN             Ay me, what act,     52
    That roars so loud and thunders in the index?     53
HAMLET *[showing her two likenesses]*
    Look here upon this picture, and on this,
    The counterfeit presentment of two brothers.     55
    See what a grace was seated on this brow:
    Hyperion's curls, the front of Jove himself,     57
    An eye like Mars to threaten and command,     58
    A station like the herald Mercury     59
    New-lighted on a heaven-kissing hill—     60
    A combination and a form indeed
    Where every god did seem to set his seal     62

---

**34 busy** nosey   **38 damnèd custom** habitual wickedness   **brazed** brazened, hardened
**39 proof** impenetrable, like *proof* or tested armor   **sense** feeling   **45 sets a blister** i.e.,
brands as a harlot   **47 contraction** the marriage contract   **48 sweet religion makes** i.e.,
makes marriage vows   **49 rhapsody** senseless string   **49–52 Heaven's . . . act** Heaven's
face blushes at this solid world compounded of the various elements, with sorrowful face
as though the day of doom were near, and is sick with horror at the deed (i.e., Gertrude's
marriage).   **53 index** table of contents, prelude or preface   **55 counterfeit presentment**
representation in portraiture   **57 Hyperion's** the sun-god's   **front** brow   **58 Mars** god
of war   **59 station** manner of standing   **Mercury** winged messenger of the gods
**60 New-lighted** newly alighted   **heaven-kissing** reaching to the sky   **62 set his seal** i.e.,
affix his approval

To give the world assurance of a man.
This was your husband. Look you now what follows:
Here is your husband, like a mildewed ear, 65
Blasting his wholesome brother. Have you eyes? 66
Could you on this fair mountain leave to feed 67
And batten on this moor? Ha, have you eyes? 68
You cannot call it love, for at your age
The heyday in the blood is tame, it's humble, 70
And waits upon the judgment, and what judgment
Would step from this to this? Sense, sure, you have, 72
Else could you not have motion, but sure that sense
Is apoplexed, for madness would not err, 74
Nor sense to ecstasy was ne'er so thralled, 75
But it reserved some quantity of choice 76
To serve in such a difference. What devil was't 77
That thus hath cozened you at hoodman-blind? 78
Eyes without feeling, feeling without sight,
Ears without hands or eyes, smelling sans all, 80
Or but a sickly part of one true sense
Could not so mope. O shame, where is thy blush? 82
Rebellious hell,
If thou canst mutine in a matron's bones, 84
To flaming youth let virtue be as wax 85
And melt in her own fire. Proclaim no shame 86
When the compulsive ardor gives the charge, 87
Since frost itself as actively doth burn, 88
And reason panders will. 89
QUEEN        Oh, Hamlet, speak no more!
Thou turn'st mine eyes into my very soul,
And there I see such black and grainèd spots 92
As will not leave their tinct.
HAMLET                        Nay, but to live 93
In the rank sweat of an enseamèd bed, 94

---

65 ear i.e., of grain   66 Blasting blighting   67 leave cease   68 batten gorge   moor
barren or marshy ground (suggesting also "dark-skinned")   70 The heyday . . . blood
(The blood was thought to be the source of sexual desire.)   72 Sense Perception
through the five senses (the functions of the middle or sensible soul)   74 apoplexed par-
alyzed   err so err   75–77 Nor . . . difference nor could your physical senses ever have
been so enthralled to *ecstasy* or lunacy that they could not distinguish to some degree
between Hamlet Senior and Claudius.   78 cozened cheated   hoodman-blind blind-
man's buff. (In this game, says Hamlet, the devil must have pushed Claudius toward
Gertrude while she was blindfolded.)   80 sans without   82 mope be dazed, act aim-
lessly   84 mutine mutiny   85–86 To . . . fire when it comes to sexually passionate
youth, let virtue melt like a candle or stick of sealing wax held over a candle flame.
(There's no point in hoping for self-restraint among young people when matronly
women set such a bad example.)   86–89 Proclaim . . . will Call it no shameful business
when the compelling ardor of youth delivers the attack, i.e., commits lechery, since the
*frost* of advanced age burns with as active a fire of lust and reason perverts itself by
fomenting lust rather than restraining it.   92 grainèd ingrained, indelible   93 leave
their tinct surrender their dark stain   94 enseamèd saturated in the grease and filth
of passionate lovemaking

Stewed in corruption, honeying and making love                    95
Over the nasty sty!                                               96
QUEEN    Oh, speak to me no more!
These words like daggers enter in my ears.
No more, sweet Hamlet!
HAMLET                            A murderer and a villain,
A slave that is not twentieth part the tithe                     100
Of your precedent lord, a vice of kings,                         101
A cutpurse of the empire and the rule,
That from a shelf the precious diadem stole
And put it in his pocket!
QUEEN    No more!                                                 105

        *Enter Ghost [in his nightgown].*

HAMLET    A king of shreds and patches—                          106
Save me, and hover o'er me with your wings,
You heavenly guards! What would your gracious
    figure?
QUEEN · Alas, he's mad!
HAMLET
Do you not come your tardy son to chide,
That, lapsed in time and passion, lets go by                     111
Th'important acting of your dread command?                       112
Oh, say!
GHOST
Do not forget. This visitation
Is but to whet thy almost blunted purpose.                       115
But look, amazement on thy mother sits.                          116
Oh, step between her and her fighting soul!
Conceit in weakest bodies strongest works.                       118
Speak to her, Hamlet.
HAMLET                            How is it with you, lady?
QUEEN    Alas, how is't with you,
That you do bend your eye on vacancy,
And with th'incorporal air do hold discourse?                    122
Forth at your eyes your spirits wildly peep,
And, as the sleeping soldiers in th'alarm,                       124
Your bedded hair, like life in excrements,                       125
Start up and stand on end. O gentle son,

95 **Stewed** soaked, bathed (with a suggestion of "stew," brothel)   96 **Over . . . sty**
(like barnyard animals)   100 **tithe** tenth part   101 **precedent lord** former husband
**vice** (from the morality plays, a model of iniquity and a buffoon)   105.1 s.d. *nightgown*
a robe for indoor wear   106 **A king . . . patches** i.e., a king whose splendor is all sham; a
clown or fool dressed in motley   111 **lapsed . . . passion** having let time and passion slip
away   112 **Th'important** the importunate, urgent   115 **whet** sharpen   116 **amazement**
distraction   118 **Conceit** Imagination   122 **th'incorporal** the immaterial   124 **as . . .
th'alarm** like soldiers called out of sleep by an alarum   125 **bedded** laid flat   **like life in
excrements** i.e., as though hair, an outgrowth of the body, had a life of its own. (Hair
was thought to be lifeless because it lacks sensation, and so its standing on end would be
unnatural and ominous.)

*V. S. p. 335.*          *Lud. Du Guernier inv. et Sculp. 20*

"Hamlet and the Ghost in Gertrude's Chamber." This eighteenth-century depiction of the scene in which Hamlet sees his father's ghost in full armor in Gertrude's chamber illustrates her confusion at Hamlet's apparent madness. Because the ghost is invisible to her, she can only exclaim: "Alas, how is't with you, / That you do bend your eye on vacancy" (3.4.120–121). (J. Tonson, *The Works of Shakespeare*, vol. VIII [London, 1728]. By permission of the Folger Shakespeare Library.)

Upon the heat and flame of thy distemper                127
Sprinkle cool patience. Whereon do you look?
HAMLET
On him, on him! Look you how pale he glares!
His form and cause conjoined, preaching to stones,      130
Would make them capable.—Do not look upon me,          131
Lest with this piteous action you convert              132
My stern effects. Then what I have to do               133
Will want true color—tears perchance for blood.        134
QUEEN    To whom do you speak this?
HAMLET    Do you see nothing there?
QUEEN
Nothing at all, yet all that is I see.
HAMLET    Nor did you nothing hear?
QUEEN    No, nothing but ourselves.
HAMLET
Why, look you there, look how it steals away!
My father, in his habit as he lived!                   141
Look where he goes even now out at the portal!

                                        *Exit Ghost.*

QUEEN
This is the very coinage of your brain.                143
This bodiless creation ecstasy                         144
Is very cunning in.                                    145
HAMLET    Ecstasy?
My pulse as yours doth temperately keep time,
And makes as healthful music. It is not madness
That I have uttered. Bring me to the test,
And I the matter will reword, which madness            150
Would gambol from. Mother, for love of grace,          151
Lay not that flattering unction to your soul           152
That not your trespass but my madness speaks.
It will but skin and film the ulcerous place,          154
Whiles rank corruption, mining all within,             155
Infects unseen. Confess yourself to heaven,
Repent what's past, avoid what is to come,
And do not spread the compost on the weeds             158
To make them ranker. Forgive me this my virtue;        159
For in the fatness of these pursy times                160

---

127 **distemper** disorder    130 **His . . . conjoined** His appearance joined to his cause for speaking    131 **capable** capable of feeling, receptive    132–133 **convert . . . effects** divert me from my stern duty    134 **want . . . blood** lack plausibility so that (with a play on the normal sense of *color*) I shall shed colorless tears instead of blood    141 **habit** clothes as as when    143 **very** mere    144–145 **This . . . in** Madness is skillful in creating this kind of hallucination.    150 **reword** repeat word for word    151 **gambol** skip away    152 **unction** ointment    154 **skin** grow a skin over    155 **mining** working under the surface    158 **compost** manure    159 **this my virtue** my virtuous talk in reproving you    160 **fatness** grossness    **pursy** flabby, out of shape

Virtue itself of vice must pardon beg,
Yea, curb and woo for leave to do him good.                    162

QUEEN
Oh, Hamlet, thou hast cleft my heart in twain.

HAMLET
Oh, throw away the worser part of it,
And live the purer with the other half.
Good night. But go not to my uncle's bed;
Assume a virtue, if you have it not.
That monster, custom, who all sense doth eat,                  168
Of habits devil, is angel yet in this,                         169
That to the use of actions fair and good
He likewise gives a frock or livery                            171
That aptly is put on. Refrain tonight,                         172
And that shall lend a kind of easiness
To the next abstinence; the next more easy;
For use almost can change the stamp of nature,                 175
And either . . . the devil, or throw him out                   176
With wondrous potency. Once more, good night;
And when you are desirous to be blest,                         178
I'll blessing beg of you. For this same lord,                 179

                              [*pointing to Polonius*]

I do repent; but heaven hath pleased it so
To punish me with this, and this with me,                      181
That I must be their scourge and minister.                     182
I will bestow him, and will answer well                        183
The death I gave him. So, again, good night.
I must be cruel only to be kind.
This bad begins, and worse remains behind.                     186
One word more, good lady.

QUEEN                           What shall I do?

HAMLET
Not this by no means that I bid you do:
Let the bloat king tempt you again to bed,                     189
Pinch wanton on your cheek, call you his mouse,                190
And let him, for a pair of reechy kisses,                      191
Or paddling in your neck with his damned fingers,              192

---

**162 curb** bow, bend the knee   **leave** permission   **168 who . . . eat** which consumes and
overwhelms the physical senses   **169 Of habits devil** devil-like in prompting evil habits
**171 livery** an outer appearance, a customary garb (and hence a predisposition easily assumed in time of stress)   **172 aptly** readily   **175 use** habit   **the stamp of nature** our in-
born traits   **176 And either** (a defective line, often emended by inserting the word "master" after *either*, following the Third Quarto and early editors, or some other word such
as "shame," "lodge," "curb," or "house")   **178–179 when . . . you** i.e., when you are
ready to be penitent and seek God's blessing, I will beg your blessing as a dutiful son
should.   **181 To punish . . . with me** to seek retribution from me for killing Polonius,
and from him through my means   **182 their scourge and minister** i.e., agent of heavenly
retribution   **183 bestow** stow, dispose of   **answer** account or pay for   **186 This** i.e.,
The killing of Polonius   **behind** to come   **189 bloat** bloated   **190 Pinch wanton** i.e.,
leave his love pinches on your cheeks, branding you as wanton   **191 reechy** dirty, filthy
**192 paddling** fingering amorously

Make you to ravel all this matter out                                    193
That I essentially am not in madness,
But mad in craft. 'Twere good you let him know,                          195
For who that's but a queen, fair, sober, wise,
Would from a paddock, from a bat, a gib,                                 197
Such dear concernings hide? Who would do so?                            198
No, in despite of sense and secrecy,                                    199
Unpeg the basket on the house's top,                                    200
Let the birds fly, and like the famous ape,                             201
To try conclusions, in the basket creep                                 202
And break your own neck down.                                           203

QUEEN
Be thou assured, if words be made of breath,
And breath of life, I have no life to breathe
What thou hast said to me.

HAMLET
I must to England. You know that?

QUEEN                                        Alack,
I had forgot. 'Tis so concluded on.

HAMLET
There's letters sealed, and my two schoolfellows,
Whom I will trust as I will adders fanged,
They bear the mandate; they must sweep my way                           211
And marshal me to knavery. Let it work.                                 212
For 'tis the sport to have the engineer                                 213
Hoist with his own petard, and 't shall go hard                         214
But I will delve one yard below their mines                             215
And blow them at the moon. Oh, 'tis most sweet
When in one line two crafts directly meet.                              217
This man shall set me packing.                                          218
I'll lug the guts into the neighbor room.
Mother, good night indeed. This counselor
Is now most still, most secret, and most grave,
Who was in life a foolish prating knave.—

---

193 **ravel . . . out** unravel, disclose   195 **in craft** by cunning   **good** (said sarcastically; also the following eight lines)   197 **paddock** toad   **gib** tomcat   198 **dear concernings** important affairs   199 **sense and secrecy** secrecy that common sense requires   200 **Unpeg the basket** open the cage, i.e., let out the secret   201 **famous ape** (in a story now lost)   202 **try conclusions** test the outcome (in which the ape apparently enters a cage from which birds have been released and then tries to fly out of the cage as they have done, falling to its death)   203 **down** in the fall   211–212 **sweep . . . knavery** sweep a path before me and conduct me to some *knavery* or treachery prepared for me   212 **work** proceed   213 **engineer** maker of *engines* of war   214 **Hoist with** blown up by   **petard** an explosive used to blow in a door or make a breach   214–215 **'t shall . . . will** unless luck is against me, I will   215 **mines** tunnels used in warfare to undermine the enemy's emplacements; Hamlet will countermine by going under their mines.
217 **in one line** i.e., mines and countermines on a collision course, or the countermines directly below the mines   **crafts** acts of guile, plots   218 **set me packing** set me to making schemes, and set me to lugging (him), and, also, send me off in a hurry.

Come, sir, to draw toward an end with you.—                    223
Good night, mother.
                    *Exeunt [separately, Hamlet dragging in Polonius].*

❧

# [4.1]

*Enter King and Queen, with Rosencrantz and
Guildenstern.*

KING
There's matter in these sighs, these profound heaves.                    1
You must translate; 'tis fit we understand them.
Where is your son?
QUEEN
Bestow this place on us a little while.
                    *[Exeunt Rosencrantz and Guildenstern.]*
Ah, mine own lord, what have I seen tonight!
KING
What, Gertrude? How does Hamlet?
QUEEN
Mad as the sea and wind when both contend
Which is the mightier. In his lawless fit,
Behind the arras hearing something stir,
Whips out his rapier, cries, "A rat, a rat!"
And in this brainish apprehension kills                    11
The unseen good old man.
KING                    Oh, heavy deed!                    12
It had been so with us, had we been there.                    13
His liberty is full of threats to all—
To you yourself, to us, to everyone.
Alas, how shall this bloody deed be answered?                    16
It will be laid to us, whose providence                    17
Should have kept short, restrained, and out of haunt                    18
This mad young man. But so much was our love,
We would not understand what was most fit,

---

223 **draw . . . end** finish up (with a pun on *draw,* "pull")
**4.1 Location:** The castle.
**0.1 s.d.** *Enter . . . Queen* (Some editors argue that Gertrude does not in fact exit at the
end of 3.4 and that the scene is continuous here. It is true that the Folio ends 3.4 with
"*Exit Hamlet tugging in Polonius,*" not naming Gertrude, and opens 4.1 with "*Enter
King.*" Yet the Second Quarto concludes 3.4 with a simple "*Exit,*" which often stands
ambiguously for a single exit or an exeunt in early modern texts, and then starts 4.1 with
"*Enter King, and Queene, with Rosencraus and Guyldensterne.*" The King's opening lines
in 4.1 suggest that he has had time, during a brief intervening pause, to become aware of
Gertrude's highly wrought emotional state. In line 35, the King refers to Gertrude's *closet*
as though it were elsewhere. The differences between the Second Quarto and the Folio offer an alternative staging. In either case, 4.1 follows swiftly upon 3.4.)    **1 matter** significance    **heaves** heavy sighs    **11 brainish apprehension** frenzied misapprehension
**12 heavy** grievous    **13 us** i.e., me (the royal "we"; also in line 15)    **16 answered** explained    **17 providence** foresight    **18 short** i.e., on a short tether    **out of haunt** secluded

But, like the owner of a foul disease,
To keep it from divulging, let it feed                           22
Even on the pith of life. Where is he gone?
QUEEN
To draw apart the body he hath killed,
O'er whom his very madness, like some ore                       25
Among a mineral of metals base,                                 26
Shows itself pure: 'a weeps for what is done.
KING   Oh, Gertrude, come away!
The sun no sooner shall the mountains touch
But we will ship him hence, and this vile deed
We must with all our majesty and skill
Both countenance and excuse.—Ho, Guildenstern!                 32

   *Enter Rosencrantz and Guildenstern.*

Friends both, go join you with some further aid.
Hamlet in madness hath Polonius slain,
And from his mother's closet hath he dragged him.
Go seek him out, speak fair, and bring the body                36
Into the chapel. I pray you, haste in this.
   *[Exeunt Rosencrantz and Guildenstern.]*
Come, Gertrude, we'll call up our wisest friends
And let them know both what we mean to do
And what's untimely done . . . . . . .                          40
Whose whisper o'er the world's diameter,                        41
As level as the cannon to his blank,                            42
Transports his poisoned shot, may miss our name
And hit the woundless air. Oh, come away!                       44
My soul is full of discord and dismay.          *Exeunt.*

❖

# [4.2]

   *Enter Hamlet.*

HAMLET   Safely stowed.
ROSENCRANTZ, GUILDENSTERN (*within*)   Hamlet! Lord
   Hamlet!
HAMLET   But soft, what noise? Who calls on Hamlet? Oh,
   here they come.

   *Enter Rosencrantz and Guildenstern.*

---

22 **from divulging** from becoming publicly known   25 **ore** vein of gold   26 **mineral**
mine   32 **countenance** put the best face on   36 **fair** gently, courteously   40 **And . . .**
done (A defective line; conjectures as to the missing words include "So, haply, slander"
[Capell and others]; "For, haply, slander" [Theobald and others]; and "So envious slander" [Jenkins].)   41 **diameter** extent from side to side   42 **As level** with as direct aim
**his blank** its target at point-blank range   44 **woundless** invulnerable
**4.2 Location:** The castle.

ROSENCRANTZ
What have you done, my lord, with the dead body?

HAMLET
Compounded it with dust, whereto 'tis kin.

ROSENCRANTZ
Tell us where 'tis, that we may take it thence
And bear it to the chapel.

HAMLET   Do not believe it.

ROSENCRANTZ   Believe what?

HAMLET   That I can keep your counsel and not mine   12
own. Besides, to be demanded of a sponge, what   13
replication should be made by the son of a king?   14

ROSENCRANTZ   Take you me for a sponge, my lord?

HAMLET   Ay, sir, that soaks up the King's countenance,   16
his rewards, his authorities. But such officers do the   17
King best service in the end. He keeps them, like an
ape, an apple, in the corner of his jaw, first mouthed
to be last swallowed. When he needs what you have
gleaned, it is but squeezing you, and, sponge, you
shall be dry again.

ROSENCRANTZ   I understand you not, my lord.

HAMLET   I am glad of it. A knavish speech sleeps in a   24
foolish ear.

ROSENCRANTZ   My lord, you must tell us where the
body is and go with us to the King.

HAMLET   The body is with the King, but the King is not   28
with the body. The King is a thing—   29

GUILDENSTERN   A thing, my lord?

HAMLET   Of nothing. Bring me to him. Hide fox, and all   31
after!                                     *Exeunt [running].*   32

❖

# [4.3]

*Enter King, and two or three.*

KING
I have sent to seek him, and to find the body.
How dangerous is it that this man goes loose!

---

12–13 **That . . . own** i.e., Don't expect me to do as you bid me and not follow my own
counsel.   13 **demanded of** questioned by   14 **replication** reply   16 **countenance** favor
17 **authorities** delegated power, influence   24 **sleeps in** has no meaning to   28–29 **The . . .
body** (Perhaps alludes to the legal commonplace of "the king's two bodies," which drew a
distinction between the sacred office of kingship and the particular mortal who possessed it
at any given time. Hence, although Claudius's body is necessarily a part of him, true kingship is not contained in it. Similarly, Claudius will have Polonius's body when it is found,
but there is no kingship in this business either.)   31 **Of nothing** (1) of no account (2) lacking the essence of kingship, as in lines 28–29 and note   31–32 **Hide . . . after** (an old signal
cry in the game of hide-and-seek, suggesting that Hamlet now runs away from them)
**4.3 Location: The castle.**

Yet must not we put the strong law on him.
He's loved of the distracted multitude, 4
Who like not in their judgment, but their eyes, 5
And where 'tis so, th'offender's scourge is weighed, 6
But never the offense. To bear all smooth and even, 7
This sudden sending him away must seem
Deliberate pause. Diseases desperate grown 9
By desperate appliance are relieved, 10
Or not at all.

*Enter Rosencrantz, [Guildenstern,] and all the rest.*

How now, what hath befall'n?

ROSENCRANTZ
Where the dead body is bestowed, my lord,
We cannot get from him.

KING                    But where is he?

ROSENCRANTZ
Without, my lord; guarded, to know your pleasure. 14

KING
Bring him before us.

ROSENCRANTZ [*calling*]   Ho! Bring in the lord.

*They enter [with Hamlet].*

KING   Now, Hamlet, where's Polonius?

HAMLET   At supper.

KING   At supper? Where?

HAMLET   Not where he eats, but where 'a is eaten. A
certain convocation of politic worms are e'en at him. 20
Your worm is your only emperor for diet. We fat all 21
creatures else to fat us, and we fat ourselves for
maggots. Your fat king and your lean beggar is but
variable service—two dishes, but to one table. That's 24
the end.

KING   Alas, alas!

HAMLET   A man may fish with the worm that hath eat 27
of a king, and eat of the fish that hath fed of that
worm.

KING   What dost thou mean by this?

---

4 of by   distracted fickle, unstable   5 Who . . . eyes who choose not by judgment but
by appearance   6–7 th'offender's . . . offense i.e., the populace often takes umbrage at
the severity of a punishment without taking into account the gravity of the crime.
7 To . . . even To manage the business in an unprovocative way   9 Deliberate pause
carefully considered action   10 appliance remedies   14 Without Outside   20 politic
worms crafty worms (suited to a master spy like Polonius)   e'en even now   21 Your
worm Your average worm. (Compare *your fat king and your lean beggar* in line 23.)
diet food, eating (with a punning reference to the Diet of Worms, a famous *convocation*
held in 1521)   24 service food served at table. (Worms feed on kings and beggars alike.)
27 eat eaten (pronounced *et*)

HAMLET  Nothing but to show you how a king may go
a progress through the guts of a beggar.                          32
KING  Where is Polonius?
HAMLET  In heaven. Send thither to see. If your messenger
find him not there, seek him i'th'other place yourself.
But if indeed you find him not within this month,
you shall nose him as you go up the stairs into the              37
lobby.
KING [*to some attendants*]  Go seek him there.
HAMLET  'A will stay till you come. [*Exeunt attendants.*]
KING
  Hamlet, this deed, for thine especial safety—
  Which we do tender, as we dearly grieve                        42
  For that which thou hast done—must send thee hence
  With fiery quickness. Therefore prepare thyself.
  The bark is ready, and the wind at help,                       45
  Th'associates tend, and everything is bent                     46
  For England.
HAMLET  For England!
KING  Ay, Hamlet.
HAMLET  Good.
KING
  So is it, if thou knew'st our purposes.
HAMLET  I see a cherub that sees them. But come, for            52
England! Farewell, dear mother.
KING  Thy loving father, Hamlet.
HAMLET  My mother. Father and mother is man and
wife, man and wife is one flesh, and so, my mother.
Come, for England!                             *Exit.*
KING
  Follow him at foot; tempt him with speed aboard.               58
  Delay it not. I'll have him hence tonight.
  Away! For everything is sealed and done
  That else leans on th'affair. Pray you, make haste.            61
                              [*Exeunt all but the King.*]
  And, England, if my love thou hold'st at aught—                62
  As my great power thereof may give thee sense,                 63
  Since yet thy cicatrice looks raw and red                      64
  After the Danish sword, and thy free awe                       65
  Pays homage to us—thou mayst not coldly set                    66
  Our sovereign process, which imports at full,                  67

32 **progress** royal journey of state   37 **nose** smell   42 **tender** regard, hold dear   **dearly** intensely   45 **bark** sailing vessel   46 **tend** wait   **bent** in readiness   52 **cherub** (Cherubim are angels of knowledge. Hamlet hints that both he and heaven are onto Claudius's tricks.)   58 **at foot** close behind, at heel   61 **leans on** bears upon, is related to 62 **England** i.e., King of England   **at aught** at any value   63 **As . . . sense** for so my great power may give you a just appreciation of the importance of valuing my love 64 **cicatrice** scar   65 **free awe** unconstrained show of respect   66 **coldly set** regard with indifference   67 **process** command   **imports at full** conveys specific directions for

By letters congruing to that effect,        68
The present death of Hamlet. Do it, England,        69
For like the hectic in my blood he rages,        70
And thou must cure me. Till I know 'tis done,
Howe'er my haps, my joys were ne'er begun.   *Exit.*   72

❖

# [4.4]

*Enter Fortinbras with his army over the stage.*

FORTINBRAS
Go, Captain, from me greet the Danish king.
Tell him that by his license Fortinbras        2
Craves the conveyance of a promised march        3
Over his kingdom. You know the rendezvous.
If that His Majesty would aught with us,
We shall express our duty in his eye;        6
And let him know so.
CAPTAIN   I will do't, my lord.
FORTINBRAS   Go softly on. [*Exeunt all but the Captain.*]   9

*Enter Hamlet, Rosencrantz, [Guildenstern,] etc.*

HAMLET   Good sir, whose powers are these?        10
CAPTAIN   They are of Norway, sir.
HAMLET   How purposed, sir, I pray you?
CAPTAIN   Against some part of Poland.
HAMLET   Who commands them, sir?
CAPTAIN
The nephew to old Norway, Fortinbras.
HAMLET
Goes it against the main of Poland, sir,        16
Or for some frontier?
CAPTAIN
Truly to speak, and with no addition,        18
We go to gain a little patch of ground
That hath in it no profit but the name.
To pay five ducats, five, I would not farm it;    21
Nor will it yield to Norway or the Pole
A ranker rate, should it be sold in fee.        23
HAMLET
Why, then the Polack never will defend it.

---

68 **congruing** agreeing  **69 present** immediate  **70 hectic** persistent fever
72 **Howe'er . . . begun** whatever else happens, I cannot begin to be happy.
**4.4 Location: The coast of Denmark.**
2 **license** permission  3 **conveyance** unhindered passage  6 **We . . . eye** I will come pay
my respects in person  9 **softly** slowly, circumspectly  10 **powers** forces  16 **main** main
part  18 **addition** exaggeration  21 **To pay** i.e., For a yearly rental of  **farm it** take a
lease of it  23 **ranker** higher  **in fee** fee simple, outright

CAPTAIN
Yes, it is already garrisoned.

HAMLET
Two thousand souls and twenty thousand ducats
Will not debate the question of this straw. 27
This is th'impostume of much wealth and peace, 28
That inward breaks, and shows no cause without 29
Why the man dies. I humbly thank you, sir.

CAPTAIN
God b'wi'you, sir. [*Exit.*]

ROSENCRANTZ    Will't please you go, my lord?

HAMLET
I'll be with you straight. Go a little before.
[*Exeunt all except Hamlet.*]
How all occasions do inform against me 33
And spur my dull revenge! What is a man,
If his chief good and market of his time 35
Be but to sleep and feed? A beast, no more.
Sure he that made us with such large discourse, 37
Looking before and after, gave us not 38
That capability and godlike reason
To fust in us unused. Now, whether it be 40
Bestial oblivion, or some craven scruple 41
Of thinking too precisely on th'event— 42
A thought which, quartered, hath but one part
    wisdom
And ever three parts coward—I do not know
Why yet I live to say "This thing's to do,"
Sith I have cause, and will, and strength, and means 46
To do't. Examples gross as earth exhort me: 47
Witness this army of such mass and charge, 48
Led by a delicate and tender prince, 49
Whose spirit with divine ambition puffed
Makes mouths at the invisible event, 51
Exposing what is mortal and unsure
To all that fortune, death, and danger dare, 53
Even for an eggshell. Rightly to be great 54
Is not to stir without great argument, 55
But greatly to find quarrel in a straw 56
When honor's at the stake. How stand I, then, 57

---

27 debate . . . straw argue about this trifling matter    28 th'impostume the abscess
29 inward breaks festers within    without externally    33 inform against denounce; take
shape against    35 market of profit of    37 discourse power of reasoning    38 Looking
before and after able to review past events and anticipate the future    40 fust grow moldy
41 oblivion forgetfulness    craven cowardly    42 precisely scrupulously    th'event the outcome    46 Sith since    47 gross obvious    48 charge expense    49 delicate and tender of
fine and youthful qualities    51 Makes mouths makes scornful faces    invisible event un-
foreseeable outcome    53 dare could do (to him)    54–57 Rightly . . . stake True greatness
is not a matter of being moved to action solely by a great cause; rather, it is to respond
greatly to an apparently trivial cause when honor is at the stake.

That have a father killed, a mother stained,
Excitements of my reason and my blood,                    59
And let all sleep, while to my shame I see
The imminent death of twenty thousand men
That for a fantasy and trick of fame                      62
Go to their graves like beds, fight for a plot            63
Whereon the numbers cannot try the cause,                 64
Which is not tomb enough and continent                    65
To hide the slain? Oh, from this time forth
My thoughts be bloody or be nothing worth!     *Exit.*

❖

## [4.5]

> *Enter Horatio, [Queen] Gertrude, and a Gentle-*
> *man.*

QUEEN
I will not speak with her.
GENTLEMAN                      She is importunate,
Indeed distract. Her mood will needs be pitied.           2
QUEEN   What would she have?
GENTLEMAN
She speaks much of her father, says she hears
There's tricks i'th' world, and hems, and beats her
  heart,                                                  5
Spurns enviously at straws, speaks things in doubt        6
That carry but half sense. Her speech is nothing,
Yet the unshapèd use of it doth move                      8
The hearers to collection; they yawn at it,               9
And botch the words up fit to their own thoughts,         10
Which, as her winks and nods and gestures yield
  them,                                                   11
Indeed would make one think there might be thought,       12
Though nothing sure, yet much unhappily.                  13
HORATIO
'Twere good she were spoken with, for she may strew
Dangerous conjectures in ill-breeding minds.              15

---

59 **blood** (the supposed seat of the passions)   62 **fantasy** fanciful caprice, illusion
**trick** trifle, deceit   63 **plot** plot of ground   64 **Whereon . . . cause** on which there is
insufficient room for the soldiers needed to fight for it   65 **continent** receptacle,
container
4.5 **Location:** The castle.
2 **distract** out of her mind   5 **tricks** deceptions   **hems** clears her throat, makes "hmm"
sounds   **heart** i.e., breast   6 **Spurns . . . straws** kicks spitefully, takes offense at trifles
**in doubt** of obscure meaning   8 **unshapèd use** incoherent manner   9 **collection** infer-
ence, a guess at some sort of meaning   **yawn** gape, wonder; grasp. (The Folio reading,
"aim," is possible.)   10 **botch** patch   11 **Which** which words   **yield** deliver, represent
12–13 **there might . . . unhappily** that a great deal could be guessed at of a most unfortunate nature, even if one couldn't be at all sure   15 **ill-breeding** prone to suspect the
worst and to make mischief

QUEEN  Let her come in.  [*Exit Gentleman.*]
[*Aside*] To my sick soul, as sin's true nature is,
Each toy seems prologue to some great amiss.                18
So full of artless jealousy is guilt,                       19
It spills itself in fearing to be spilt.                    20

    *Enter Ophelia [distracted].*

OPHELIA
Where is the beauteous majesty of Denmark?
QUEEN  How now, Ophelia?
OPHELIA (*she sings*)
    "How should I your true love know
      From another one?
    By his cockle hat and staff,                        25
    And his sandal shoon."                              26
QUEEN  Alas, sweet lady, what imports this song?
OPHELIA  Say you? Nay, pray you, mark.
    "He is dead and gone, lady,        (*Song.*)
      He is dead and gone;
    At his head a grass-green turf,
      At his heels a stone."
Oho!                                                        33
QUEEN  Nay, but Ophelia—
OPHELIA  Pray you, mark.
[*Sings*] "White his shroud as the mountain snow"—

    *Enter King.*

QUEEN  Alas, look here, my lord.
OPHELIA
    "Larded with sweet flowers;         (*Song.*)         38
    Which bewept to the ground did not go
      With true-love showers."                         40
KING  How do you, pretty lady?
OPHELIA  Well, God 'ild you! They say the owl was a          42
baker's daughter. Lord, we know what we are, but
know not what we may be. God be at your table!
KING  Conceit upon her father.                               45
OPHELIA  Pray let's have no words of this; but when
they ask you what it means, say you this:
    "Tomorrow is Saint Valentine's day,   (*Song.*)
    All in the morning betime,                           49

---

**18 toy** trifle  **amiss** calamity  **19–20 So . . . spilt** Guilt is so burdened with conscience
and guileless fear of detection that it reveals itself through apprehension of disaster.
**20.1 s.d. *Enter Ophelia*** (In the First Quarto, Ophelia enters, "*playing on a lute, and her
hair down, singing.*")  **25 cockle hat** hat with cockleshell stuck in it as a sign that the
wearer had been a pilgrim to the shrine of Saint James of Compostella in Spain  **26 shoon**
shoes  **33 Oho!** (perhaps a sigh)  **38 Larded** Strewn, bedecked  **40 showers** i.e., tears
**42 God 'ild** God yield or reward  **owl** (refers to a legend about a baker's daughter who
was turned into an owl for being ungenerous when Jesus begged a loaf of bread)
**45 Conceit** Fancy, brooding  **49 betime** early

And I a maid at your window,
    To be your Valentine.
Then up he rose, and donned his clothes,
    And dupped the chamber door,                              53
Let in the maid, that out a maid
    Never departed more."
KING Pretty Ophelia—
OPHELIA  Indeed, la, without an oath, I'll make an end
on't:
[*Sings*] "By Gis and by Saint Charity,                        59
    Alack, and fie for shame!
Young men will do't, if they come to't;
    By Cock, they are to blame.                               62
Quoth she, 'Before you tumbled me,
    You promised me to wed.'"
He answers:
    "'So would I ha' done, by yonder sun,
    An thou hadst not come to my bed.'"                       67
KING How long hath she been thus?
OPHELIA  I hope all will be well. We must be patient,
but I cannot choose but weep to think they would lay
him i'th' cold ground. My brother shall know of it.
And so I thank you for your good counsel. Come, my
coach! Good night, ladies, good night, sweet ladies,
good night, good night.                          [*Exit.*]
KING [*to Horatio*]
Follow her close. Give her good watch, I pray you.
                                            [*Exit Horatio.*]
Oh, this is the poison of deep grief; it springs
All from her father's death—and now behold!
Oh, Gertrude, Gertrude,
When sorrows come, they come not single spies,                79
But in battalions. First, her father slain;
Next, your son gone, and he most violent author
Of his own just remove; the people muddied,                   82
Thick and unwholesome in their thoughts and
    whispers
For good Polonius' death—and we have done but
    greenly,                                                   84
In hugger-mugger to inter him; poor Ophelia                    85
Divided from herself and her fair judgment,
Without the which we are pictures or mere beasts;
Last, and as much containing as all these,                     88
Her brother is in secret come from France,

---

**53 dupped** did up, opened   **59 Gis** Jesus   **62 Cock** (a perversion of "God" in oaths;
here also with a quibble on the slang word for penis)   **67 An** if   **79 spies** scouts sent
in advance of the main force   **82 remove** removal   **muddied** stirred up, confused
**84 greenly** foolishly   **85 hugger-mugger** secret haste   **88 as much containing** as full
of serious matter

Feeds on this wonder, keeps himself in clouds,                    90
And wants not buzzers to infect his ear                          91
With pestilent speeches of his father's death,
Wherein necessity, of matter beggared,                           93
Will nothing stick our person to arraign                         94
In ear and ear. Oh, my dear Gertrude, this,                      95
Like to a murd'ring piece, in many places                        96
Gives me superfluous death.                    *A noise within.*  97
QUEEN    Alack, what noise is this?
KING    Attend!                                                  99
Where is my Switzers? Let them guard the door.                   100

*Enter a Messenger.*

What is the matter?
MESSENGER                 Save yourself, my lord!
The ocean, overpeering of his list,                             102
Eats not the flats with more impetuous haste                    103
Than young Laertes, in a riotous head,                          104
O'erbears your officers. The rabble call him lord,
And, as the world were now but to begin,                        106
Antiquity forgot, custom not known,                             107
The ratifiers and props of every word,                          108
They cry, "Choose we! Laertes shall be king!"
Caps, hands, and tongues applaud it to the clouds,              110
"Laertes shall be king, Laertes king!"
QUEEN
How cheerfully on the false trail they cry!
                                               *A noise within.*
Oh, this is counter, you false Danish dogs!                     113

*Enter Laertes with others.*

KING    The doors are broke.
LAERTES
Where is this King?—Sirs, stand you all without.
ALL    No, let's come in.
LAERTES    I pray you, give me leave.

---

90 **Feeds . . . clouds** feeds his resentment on this whole shocking turn of events, keeps himself aloof and mysterious   91 **wants** lacks   **buzzers** gossipers, informers
93 **necessity** i.e., the need to invent some plausible explanation   **of matter beggared** unprovided with facts   94–95 **Will . . . ear** will not hesitate to accuse my (royal) person in everybody's ears   96 **murd'ring piece** cannon loaded so as to scatter its shot
97 **Gives . . . death** kills me over and over   99 **Attend!** Guard me!   100 **Switzers** Swiss guards, mercenaries   102 **overpeering of his list** overflowing its shore, boundary
103 **flats** i.e., flatlands near shore   **impetuous** violent (perhaps also with the meaning of *impiteous* ["impitious," Q2], "pitiless")   104 **riotous head** insurrectionary advance
106–108 **And . . . word** and, as if the world were to be started all over afresh, utterly setting aside all ancient traditional customs that should confirm and underprop our every word and promise   110 **Caps** (The caps are thrown in the air.)   113 **counter** (a hunting term, meaning to follow the trail in a direction opposite to that which the game has taken)

ALL    We will, we will.
LAERTES    I thank you. Keep the door. [*Exeunt followers.*]
                                                Oh, thou vile king,
    Give me my father!
QUEEN [*restraining him*]    Calmly, good Laertes.
LAERTES
    That drop of blood that's calm proclaims me bastard,
    Cries cuckold to my father, brands the harlot
    Even here between the chaste unsmirchèd brow            123
    Of my true mother.
KING                    What is the cause, Laertes,
    That thy rebellion looks so giantlike?                  125
    Let him go, Gertrude. Do not fear our person.           126
    There's such divinity doth hedge a king                 127
    That treason can but peep to what it would,             128
    Acts little of his will. Tell me, Laertes,              129
    Why thou art thus incensed. Let him go, Gertrude.
    Speak, man.
LAERTES            Where is my father?
KING                              Dead.
QUEEN
    But not by him.
KING                    Let him demand his fill.
LAERTES
    How came he dead? I'll not be juggled with.            133
    To hell, allegiance! Vows, to the blackest devil!
    Conscience and grace, to the profoundest pit!
    I dare damnation. To this point I stand,               136
    That both the worlds I give to negligence,             137
    Let come what comes, only I'll be revenged
    Most throughly for my father.                          139
KING    Who shall stay you?
LAERTES    My will, not all the world's.                   141
    And for my means, I'll husband them so well            142
    They shall go far with little.
KING                    Good Laertes,
    If you desire to know the certainty
    Of your dear father, is't writ in your revenge
    That, swoopstake, you will draw both friend and foe,   146
    Winner and loser?

123 **between** amidst    125 **giantlike** (recalling the rising of the giants of Greek mythology against Olympus)    126 **fear our** fear for my    127 **hedge** protect, as with a surrounding barrier    128 **can . . . would** can only peep furtively, as through a barrier, at what it would intend    129 **Acts . . . will** (but) performs little of what it intends.
133 **juggled with** cheated, deceived    136 **To . . . stand** I am resolved in this
137 **both . . . negligence** i.e., both this world and the next are of no consequence to me
139 **throughly** thoroughly    141 **My will . . . world's** I'll stop (*stay*) when my will is accomplished, not for anyone else's.    142 **for** as for    146 **swoopstake** i.e., indiscriminately. (Literally, taking all stakes on the gambling table at once. *Draw* is also a gambling term, meaning "take from.")

LAERTES  None but his enemies.

KING  Will you know them, then?

LAERTES
To his good friends thus wide I'll ope my arms,
And like the kind life-rendering pelican                           151
Repast them with my blood.

KING                              Why, now you speak           152
Like a good child and a true gentleman.
That I am guiltless of your father's death,
And am most sensibly in grief for it,                             155
It shall as level to your judgment 'pear                          156
As day does to your eye.          *A noise within.*

LAERTES
How now, what noise is that?

*Enter Ophelia.*

KING                              Let her come in.

LAERTES
O heat, dry up my brains! Tears seven times salt
Burn out the sense and virtue of mine eye!                       160
By heaven, thy madness shall be paid with weight                 161
Till our scale turn the beam. O rose of May!                     162
Dear maid, kind sister, sweet Ophelia!
O heavens, is't possible a young maid's wits
Should be as mortal as an old man's life?
Nature is fine in love, and where 'tis fine                      166
It sends some precious instance of itself                        167
After the thing it loves.                                        168

OPHELIA
"They bore him barefaced on the bier,        *(Song.)*
    Hey non nonny, nonny, hey nonny,
    And in his grave rained many a tear—"
Fare you well, my dove!

LAERTES
Hadst thou thy wits and didst persuade revenge,
It could not move thus.

OPHELIA  You must sing "A-down a-down," and you                 175
"call him a-down-a." Oh, how the wheel becomes it! It           176
is the false steward that stole his master's daughter.          177

---

**151 pelican** (refers to the belief that the female pelican fed its young with its own
blood)  **152 Repast** feed  **155 sensibly** feelingly  **156 level** plain  **160 virtue** faculty,
power  **161 paid with weight** repaid, avenged equally or more  **162 beam** crossbar of a
balance  **166–168 Nature . . . loves** Human nature is exquisitely sensitive in matters of
love, and in cases of sudden loss it sends some precious part of itself after the lost object
of that love. (In this case, Ophelia's sanity deserts her out of sorrow for her lost father
and perhaps too out of her love for Hamlet.)  **175–176 You . . . a-down-a** (Ophelia
assigns the singing of refrains, like her own "Hey non nonny," to others present.)
**176 wheel** spinning wheel as accompaniment to the song, or refrain  **177 false steward**
(The story is unknown.)

LAERTES   This nothing's more than matter.                                178
OPHELIA   There's rosemary, that's for remembrance;                       179
pray you, love, remember. And there is pansies; that's                    180
for thoughts.
LAERTES   A document in madness, thoughts and                             182
remembrance fitted.
OPHELIA   There's fennel for you, and columbines.                         184
There's rue for you, and here's some for me; we may                       185
call it herb of grace o' Sundays. You must wear your
rue with a difference. There's a daisy. I would give                      187
you some violets, but they withered all when my                          188
father died. They say 'a made a good end—
[*Sings*] "For bonny sweet Robin is all my joy."
LAERTES
Thought and affliction, passion, hell itself,                            191
She turns to favor and to prettiness.                                    192
OPHELIA
"And will 'a not come again?           (*Song.*)
And will 'a not come again?
No, no, he is dead.
Go to thy deathbed,
He never will come again.

"His beard was as white as snow,
All flaxen was his poll.                                                 199
He is gone, he is gone,
And we cast away moan.
God ha' mercy on his soul!"
And of all Christian souls, I pray God. God b'wi'you.
          [*Exit, followed by Gertrude.*]
LAERTES   Do you see this, O God?
KING
Laertes, I must commune with your grief,
Or you deny me right. Go but apart,
Make choice of whom your wisest friends you will,                        207
And they shall hear and judge twixt you and me.

---

**178 This . . . matter** This seeming nonsense is more eloquent than sane utterance.
**179 rosemary** (used as a symbol of remembrance both at weddings and at funerals)
**180 pansies** (emblems of love and courtship; perhaps from French *pensées*, "thoughts")
**182 document** instruction, lesson   **184 There's fennel . . . columbines** (*Fennel* betokens
flattery; *columbines*, unchastity or ingratitude. Throughout, Ophelia addresses her various listeners, giving one flower to one and another to another, perhaps with particular
symbolic significance in each case.)   **185 rue** (emblem of repentance—a signification
that is evident in its popular name, *herb of grace*)   **187 with a difference** (A device
used in heraldry to distinguish one family from another on the coat of arms, here
suggesting that Ophelia and the others have different causes of sorrow and repentance;
perhaps with a play on *rue* in the sense of "ruth," "pity.")   **daisy** (emblem of love's
victims and of faithlessness)   **188 violets** (emblems of faithfulness)   **191 Thought**
Melancholy   **passion** suffering   **192 favor** grace, beauty   **199 poll** head
**207 whom** whichever of

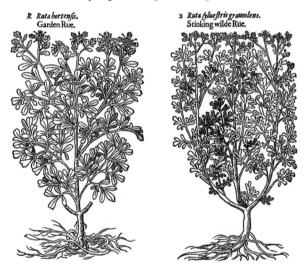

1070 · THE SECOND BOOKE OF THE

✳ *The place.*

*Pena* reporteth that *Dentillaria* groweth about Rome, nigh the hedges and corne fieldes : it like-wise groweth in my garden in great plenty.

✳ *The time.*

It flowreth in Iuly and Auguſt.

✳ *The names.*

Leadwoort is called *Molybdæna, Plumbago Plinij, & Dentillaria Rondeletij* : in Italian *Crepanella,* the Romaines *Herba S. Antonij* : in Illyria *Cucurida* : in Engliſh Leadwoort.

✳ *The temperature.*

*Dentillaria* is of a cauſticke qualitie.

✳ *The vertues.*

A It helpeth the toothach, eſpecially if it be holden in the hand ſome ſmall while.

### Of Rue, or herbe Grace. *Chap.511.*

R *Ruta hortenſis.*
Garden Rue.

2 *Ruta ſylueſtris graueolens.*
Stinking wilde Rue.

✳ *The deſcription.*

GArden Rue or planted Rue, is a ſhrub full of branches, now and then a yard high, or higher: the ſtalkes whereof are couered with a whitiſh barke , the branches are more greene : the leaues heereof conſiſt of diuers parts, and be diuided into wings, about which are certaine little ones, of an odde number, ſomething broad, more long then round, ſmooth and ſomwhat fat, of a graie colour, or greeniſh blue: the flowers in the tops of the branches are of a pale yellow, con-ſiſting of fower little leaues, ſomething hollow : in the middle of which ſtandeth vp a little head or button

According to John Gerard, the leading herbalist of his day, "Rue, or herbe of Grace," is a medicinal drug that "provoketh urine, bringeth downe the sicknes, expellethe the dead childe and afterbirth, being inwardly taken or the decoction drunke...." It is the only flower that Ophelia not only gives away but also reserves for herself: "There's rue for you, and here's some for me" (4.5.185). (John Gerard, *The Herbal or General Historie of Plants* [London, 1597]. By permission of the Folger Shakespeare Library.)

If by direct or by collateral hand                                    209
They find us touched, we will our kingdom give,                       210
Our crown, our life, and all that we call ours
To you in satisfaction; but if not,
Be you content to lend your patience to us,
And we shall jointly labor with your soul
To give it due content.
LAERTES                        Let this be so.
His means of death, his obscure funeral—
No trophy, sword, nor hatchment o'er his bones,                       217
No noble rite, nor formal ostentation—                               218
Cry to be heard, as 'twere from heaven to earth,
That I must call't in question.
KING                           So you shall,                          220
And where th'offense is, let the great ax fall.
I pray you, go with me.                    *Exeunt.*

❖

# [4.6]

*Enter Horatio and others.*

HORATIO
What are they that would speak with me?
GENTLEMAN    Seafaring men, sir. They say they have
    letters for you.                                                    3
HORATIO    Let them come in.        [*Exit Gentleman.*]
I do not know from what part of the world
I should be greeted, if not from Lord Hamlet.

*Enter Sailors.*

FIRST SAILOR    God bless you, sir.
HORATIO    Let him bless thee too.
FIRST SAILOR    'A shall, sir, an't please him. There's a             9
    letter for you, sir—it came from th'ambassador that              10
    was bound for England—if your name be Horatio, as
    I am let to know it is.            [*He gives a letter.*]
HORATIO [*reads*] "Horatio, when thou shalt have overlooked           13
    this, give these fellows some means to the King;                  14
    they have letters for him. Ere we were two days old at
    sea, a pirate of very warlike appointment gave us                 16

---

209 **collateral hand** indirect agency    210 **us touched** me implicated    217 **trophy**
memorial    **hatchment** tablet displaying the armorial bearings of a deceased person
218 **ostentation** ceremony    220 **That** so that    **call't in question** demand an
explanation
4.6 **Location:** The castle.
3 **letters** a letter    9 **an't** if it    10 **th'ambassador** (Hamlet's ostensible role;
see 3.2.172–173.)    13 **overlooked** looked over    14 **means** means of access
16 **appointment** equipage

chase. Finding ourselves too slow of sail, we put on a
compelled valor, and in the grapple I boarded them.
On the instant they got clear of our ship, so I alone
became their prisoner. They have dealt with me like
thieves of mercy, but they knew what they did: I am to                21
do a good turn for them. Let the King have the letters
I have sent, and repair thou to me with as much speed               23
as thou wouldest fly death. I have words to speak in
thine ear will make thee dumb, yet are they much too
light for the bore of the matter. These good fellows will           26
bring thee where I am. Rosencrantz and Guildenstern
hold their course for England. Of them I have much to
tell thee. Farewell.
> He that thou knowest thine, Hamlet."

Come, I will give you way for these your letters,                   31
And do't the speedier that you may direct me
To him from whom you brought them.        *Exeunt.*

## [4.7]

> *Enter King and Laertes.*

KING
Now must your conscience my acquittance seal,                        1
And you must put me in your heart for friend,
Sith you have heard, and with a knowing ear,                         3
That he which hath your noble father slain
Pursued my life.
LAERTES            It well appears. But tell me
Why you proceeded not against these feats                            6
So crimeful and so capital in nature,                                7
As by your safety, greatness, wisdom, all things else,
You mainly were stirred up.                                          9
KING     Oh, for two special reasons,
Which may to you perhaps seem much unsinewed,                        11
But yet to me they're strong. The Queen his mother
Lives almost by his looks, and for myself—
My virtue or my plague, be it either which—
She is so conjunctive to my life and soul                            15
That, as the star moves not but in his sphere,                       16

---

21 **thieves of mercy** merciful thieves   23 **repair** come   26 **bore** caliber, i.e., importance
31 **way** means of access
**4.7 Location: The castle.**
1 **my acquittance seal** confirm or acknowledge my innocence   3 **Sith** since   6 **feats**
acts   7 **capital** punishable by death   9 **mainly** greatly   11 **unsinewed** weak   15 **conjunctive** closely united (an astronomical metaphor)   16 **his** its   **sphere** one of the hollow spheres in which, according to Ptolemaic astronomy, the planets were supposed to
move

I could not but by her. The other motive
Why to a public count I might not go                          18
Is the great love the general gender bear him,                19
Who, dipping all his faults in their affection,
Work like the spring that turneth wood to stone,             21
Convert his gyves to graces, so that my arrows,              22
Too slightly timbered for so loud a wind,                    23
Would have reverted to my bow again
But not where I had aimed them.

LAERTES
And so have I a noble father lost,
A sister driven into desp'rate terms,                        27
Whose worth, if praises may go back again,                   28
Stood challenger on mount of all the age                     29
For her perfections. But my revenge will come.

KING
Break not your sleeps for that. You must not think
That we are made of stuff so flat and dull
That we can let our beard be shook with danger
And think it pastime. You shortly shall hear more.
I loved your father, and we love ourself;
And that, I hope, will teach you to imagine—

*Enter a Messenger with letters.*

How now? What news?

MESSENGER                    Letters, my lord, from Hamlet:
This to Your Majesty, this to the Queen.

*[He gives letters.]*

KING    From Hamlet? Who brought them?

MESSENGER
Sailors, my lord, they say. I saw them not.
They were given me by Claudio. He received them
Of him that brought them.

KING                        Laertes, you shall hear them.—
Leave us.                   *[Exit Messenger.]*
*[He reads.]* "High and mighty, you shall know I am set
naked on your kingdom. Tomorrow shall I beg leave           45
to see your kingly eyes, when I shall, first asking your
pardon, thereunto recount the occasion of my sudden         47
and more strange return.                Hamlet."
What should this mean? Are all the rest come back?
Or is it some abuse, and no such thing?                     50

---

18 **count** account, reckoning, indictment   19 **general gender** common people   21 **Work**
operate, act   **spring** i.e., a spring with such a concentration of lime that it coats a piece
of wood with limestone, in effect gilding and petrifying it   22 **gyves** fetters (which,
gilded by the people's praise, would look like badges of honor)   23 **Too ... wind** with
too light a shaft for so powerful a gust (of popular sentiment)   27 **terms** state, condition
28 **go back** recall what she was   29 **on mount** set up on high   45 **naked** destitute, un-
armed, without following   47 **pardon** (for returning without authorization)   50 **abuse**
deceit   **no such thing** not what the letter says

LAERTES
Know you the hand?
KING          'Tis Hamlet's character. "Naked!"      51
And in a postscript here he says "alone."
Can you devise me?      53
LAERTES
I am lost in it, my lord. But let him come.
It warms the very sickness in my heart
That I shall live and tell him to his teeth,
"Thus didst thou."
KING          If it be so, Laertes—      57
As how should it be so? How otherwise?—      58
Will you be ruled by me?
LAERTES          Ay, my lord,
So you will not o'errule me to a peace.      60
KING
To thine own peace. If he be now returned,
As checking at his voyage, and that he means      62
No more to undertake it, I will work him
To an exploit, now ripe in my device,      64
Under the which he shall not choose but fall;
And for his death no wind of blame shall breathe,
But even his mother shall uncharge the practice      67
And call it accident.
LAERTES          My lord, I will be ruled,
The rather if you could devise it so
That I might be the organ.
KING          It falls right.      70
You have been talked of since your travel much,
And that in Hamlet's hearing, for a quality
Wherein they say you shine. Your sum of parts      73
Did not together pluck such envy from him
As did that one, and that, in my regard,
Of the unworthiest siege.      76
LAERTES    What part is that, my lord?
KING
A very ribbon in the cap of youth,
Yet needful too, for youth no less becomes      79
The light and careless livery that it wears
Than settled age his sables and his weeds      81
Importing health and graveness. Two months since      82

---

51 **character** handwriting    53 **devise** explain to    57 **Thus didst thou** i.e., Here's for what you did to my father.    58 **As . . . otherwise?** how can this (Hamlet's return) be true? Yet how otherwise than true (since we have the evidence of his letter)?    60 **So** provided that    62 **checking at** i.e., turning aside from (like a falcon leaving the quarry to fly at a chance bird)    **that if**    64 **device** devising, invention    67 **uncharge the practice** acquit the stratagem of being a plot    70 **organ** agent, instrument    73 **Your . . . parts** All your other virtues    76 **unworthiest siege** least important rank    79 **no less becomes** is no less adorned by    81–82 **his sables . . . graveness** its rich robes furred with sable and its garments denoting dignified well-being and seriousness

Here was a gentleman of Normandy.
I have seen myself, and served against, the French,
And they can well on horseback, but this gallant                    85
Had witchcraft in't; he grew unto his seat,
And to such wondrous doing brought his horse
As had he been incorpsed and demi-natured                          88
With the brave beast. So far he topped my thought                  89
That I in forgery of shapes and tricks                             90
Come short of what he did.
LAERTES                              A Norman was't?
KING   A Norman.
LAERTES
Upon my life, Lamord.
KING                            The very same.
LAERTES
I know him well. He is the brooch indeed                           94
And gem of all the nation.
KING   He made confession of you,                                  96
And gave you such a masterly report
For art and exercise in your defense,                              98
And for your rapier most especial,
That he cried out 'twould be a sight indeed
If one could match you. Th'escrimers of their nation,              101
He swore, had neither motion, guard, nor eye
If you opposed them. Sir, this report of his
Did Hamlet so envenom with his envy
That he could nothing do but wish and beg
Your sudden coming o'er, to play with you.                         106
Now, out of this—
LAERTES                          What out of this, my lord?
KING
Laertes, was your father dear to you?
Or are you like the painting of a sorrow,
A face without a heart?
LAERTES                          Why ask you this?
KING
Not that I think you did not love your father,
But that I know love is begun by time,                             112
And that I see, in passages of proof,                              113
Time qualifies the spark and fire of it.                           114
There lives within the very flame of love

---

85 **can well** are skilled   88–89 **As . . . beast** as if, centaurlike, he had been made
into one body with the horse, possessing half its nature   89 **topped** surpassed
90 **forgery** fabrication   94 **brooch** ornament   96 **confession** testimonial, admission
of superiority   98 **For . . . defense** with respect to your skill and practice with your
weapon   101 **Th'escrimers** The fencers   106 **sudden** immediate   **play** fence
112 **begun by time** i.e., created by the right circumstance and hence subject to change
113 **passages of proof** actual well-attested instances   114 **qualifies** weakens,
moderates

A kind of wick or snuff that will abate it,     116
And nothing is at a like goodness still,     117
For goodness, growing to a pleurisy,     118
Dies in his own too much. That we would do,     119
We should do when we would; for this "would"
   changes
And hath abatements and delays as many     121
As there are tongues, are hands, are accidents,     122
And then this "should" is like a spendthrift sigh,     123
That hurts by easing. But, to the quick o'th'ulcer:     124
Hamlet comes back. What would you undertake
To show yourself in deed your father's son
More than in words?
LAERTES         To cut his throat i'th' church.
KING
No place, indeed, should murder sanctuarize;     128
Revenge should have no bounds. But good Laertes,
Will you do this, keep close within your chamber.     130
Hamlet returned shall know you are come home.
We'll put on those shall praise your excellence     132
And set a double varnish on the fame
The Frenchman gave you, bring you in fine together,     134
And wager on your heads. He, being remiss,     135
Most generous, and free from all contriving,     136
Will not peruse the foils, so that with ease,
Or with a little shuffling, you may choose
A sword unbated, and in a pass of practice     139
Requite him for your father.
LAERTES         I will do't,
And for that purpose I'll anoint my sword.
I bought an unction of a mountebank     142
So mortal that, but dip a knife in it,
Where it draws blood no cataplasm so rare,     144
Collected from all simples that have virtue     145
Under the moon, can save the thing from death     146

---

**116 snuff** the charred part of a candlewick   **117 nothing . . . still** nothing remains at a constant level of perfection   **118 pleurisy** excess, plethora (literally, a chest inflammation)   **119 in . . . much** of its own excess   **That** That which   **121 abatements** diminutions   **122 As . . . accidents** as there are tongues to dissuade, hands to prevent, and chance events to intervene   **123 spendthrift sigh** (an allusion to the belief that sighs draw blood from the heart)   **124 hurts by easing** i.e., costs the heart blood and wastes precious opportunity even while it affords emotional relief   **quick o'th'ulcer** i.e., heart of the matter   **128 sanctuarize** protect from punishment (alludes to the right of sanctuary with which certain religious places were invested)   **130 Will you do this** if you wish to do this   **132 put on those shall** arrange for some to   **134 in fine** finally   **135 remiss** negligently unsuspicious   **136 generous** noble-minded   **139 unbated** not blunted, having no button   **pass of practice** treacherous thrust in an arranged bout   **142 unction** ointment   **mountebank** quack doctor   **144 cataplasm** plaster or poultice   **145 simples** herbs   **virtue** potency   **146 Under the moon** i.e., anywhere (with reference perhaps to the belief that herbs gathered at night had a special power)

That is but scratched withal. I'll touch my point
With this contagion, that if I gall him slightly,     148
It may be death.

KING                 Let's further think of this,
Weigh what convenience both of time and means
May fit us to our shape. If this should fail,     151
And that our drift look through our bad performance,     152
'Twere better not assayed. Therefore this project
Should have a back or second, that might hold
If this did blast in proof. Soft, let me see.     155
We'll make a solemn wager on your cunnings—     156
I ha 't!
When in your motion you are hot and dry—
As make your bouts more violent to that end—     159
And that he calls for drink, I'll have prepared him
A chalice for the nonce, whereon but sipping,     161
If he by chance escape your venomed stuck,     162
Our purpose may hold there. [*A cry within.*] But stay,
what noise?

    *Enter Queen.*

QUEEN
One woe doth tread upon another's heel,
So fast they follow. Your sister's drowned, Laertes.
LAERTES   Drowned! Oh, where?
QUEEN
There is a willow grows askant the brook,     167
That shows his hoar leaves in the glassy stream;     168
Therewith fantastic garlands did she make
Of crowflowers, nettles, daisies, and long purples,     170
That liberal shepherds give a grosser name,     171
But our cold maids do dead men's fingers call them.     172
There on the pendent boughs her crownet weeds     173
Clamb'ring to hang, an envious sliver broke,     174
When down her weedy trophies and herself     175
Fell in the weeping brook. Her clothes spread wide,
And mermaidlike awhile they bore her up,
Which time she chanted snatches of old lauds,     178
As one incapable of her own distress,     179

---

148 **gall** graze, wound  151 **shape** part we propose to act  152 **drift . . . performance**
intention should be made visible by our bungling  155 **blast in proof** come to grief when
put to the test  156 **cunnings** respective skills  159 **As** i.e., and you should  161 **nonce**
occasion  162 **stuck** thrust (from *stoccado,* a fencing term)  167 **askant** aslant
168 **hoar leaves** white or gray undersides of the leaves  170 **long purples** early purple
orchids  171 **liberal** free-spoken  **a grosser name** (The testicle-resembling tubers of the
orchid, which also in some cases resemble *dead men's fingers,* have earned various slang
names like "dogstones" and "cullions.")  172 **cold** chaste  173 **pendent** overhanging
**crownet** made into a chaplet or coronet  174 **envious sliver** malicious branch
175 **weedy** i.e., of plants  178 **lauds** hymns  179 **incapable of** lacking capacity to
apprehend

Or like a creature native and endued                                    180
Unto that element. But long it could not be
Till that her garments, heavy with their drink,
Pulled the poor wretch from her melodious lay                          183
To muddy death.

LAERTES                    Alas, then she is drowned?

QUEEN    Drowned, drowned.

LAERTES
Too much of water hast thou, poor Ophelia,
And therefore I forbid my tears. But yet
It is our trick; nature her custom holds,                              188
Let shame say what it will. [*He weeps.*] When these
    are gone,                                                         189
The woman will be out. Adieu, my lord.                                190
I have a speech of fire that fain would blaze,
But that this folly douts it.            *Exit.*

KING                       Let's follow, Gertrude.                    192
How much I had to do to calm his rage!
Now fear I this will give it start again;
Therefore let's follow.                   *Exeunt.*

❧

# [5.1]

*Enter two Clowns [with spades and mattocks].*

FIRST CLOWN    Is she to be buried in Christian burial,
    when she willfully seeks her own salvation?                        2

SECOND CLOWN    I tell thee she is; therefore make her
    grave straight. The crowner hath sat on her, and finds            4
    it Christian burial.                                              5

FIRST CLOWN    How can that be, unless she drowned
    herself in her own defense?

SECOND CLOWN    Why, 'tis found so.                                   8

FIRST CLOWN    It must be *se offendendo*, it cannot be else.         9
    For here lies the point: if I drown myself wittingly,
    it argues an act, and an act hath three branches—it is

---

180 **endued** adapted by nature    183 **lay** ballad, song    188 **It is our trick** i.e., weeping
is our natural way (when sad)    189–190 **When . . . out** When my tears are all shed, the
woman in me will be expended, satisfied.    192 **douts** extinguishes. (The Second Quarto
reads "drownes.")
**5.1 Location: A churchyard.**
0.1 s.d. **Clowns** rustics    2 **salvation** (a blunder for "damnation," or perhaps a suggestion that Ophelia was taking her own shortcut to heaven)    4 **straight** straightway, immediately (but with a pun on *strait*, "narrow")    **crowner** coroner    **sat on her** conducted an
inquest on her case    4–5 **finds it** gives his official verdict that her means of death was
consistent with    8 **found so** determined so in the coroner's verdict    9 *se offendendo* (a
comic mistake for *se defendendo*, a term used in verdicts of self-defense)

to act, to do, and to perform. Argal, she drowned                    12
herself wittingly.
SECOND CLOWN   Nay, but hear you, goodman delve—                      14
FIRST CLOWN   Give me leave. Here lies the water; good.
Here stands the man; good. If the man go to this
water and drown himself, it is, will he, nill he, he                 17
goes, mark you that. But if the water come to him and
drown him, he drowns not himself. Argal, he that is
not guilty of his own death shortens not his own life.
SECOND CLOWN   But is this law?
FIRST CLOWN   Ay, marry, is't—crowner's quest law.                   22
SECOND CLOWN   Will you ha' the truth on't? If this had
not been a gentlewoman, she should have been
buried out o' Christian burial.
FIRST CLOWN   Why, there thou say'st. And the more                   26
pity that great folk should have countenance in this                 27
world to drown or hang themselves, more than their
even-Christian. Come, my spade. There is no ancient                  29
gentlemen but gardeners, ditchers, and grave makers.
They hold up Adam's profession.                                      31
SECOND CLOWN   Was he a gentleman?
FIRST CLOWN   'A was the first that ever bore arms.                  33
SECOND CLOWN   Why, he had none.
FIRST CLOWN   What, art a heathen? How dost thou
understand the Scripture? The Scripture says Adam
digged. Could he dig without arms? I'll put another                  37
question to thee. If thou answerest me not to the
purpose, confess thyself—                                            39
SECOND CLOWN   Go to.
FIRST CLOWN   What is he that builds stronger than
either the mason, the shipwright, or the carpenter?
SECOND CLOWN   The gallows maker, for that frame                     43
outlives a thousand tenants.
FIRST CLOWN   I like thy wit well, in good faith. The
gallows does well. But how does it well? It does well to             46
those that do ill. Now thou dost ill to say the gallows
is built stronger than the church. Argal, the gallows
may do well to thee. To't again, come.
SECOND CLOWN   "Who builds stronger than a mason, a
shipwright, or a carpenter?"

---

**12 Argal** (corruption of *ergo,* "therefore")   **14 goodman** (an honorific title often used
with the name of a profession or craft)   **17 will he, nill he** whether he will or no, willy-
nilly   **22 quest** inquest   **26 there thou say'st** i.e., that's right   **27 countenance** privilege
**29 even-Christian** fellow Christians   **ancient** going back to ancient times   **31 hold up**
maintain   **33 bore arms** (To be entitled to bear a coat of arms would make Adam a gentleman, but as one who bore a spade, our common ancestor was an ordinary delver in
the earth.)   **37 arms** i.e., the arms of the body   **39 confess thyself** (The saying continues,
"and be hanged.")   **43 frame** (1) gallows (2) structure   **46 does well** (1) is an apt answer (2) does a good turn

FIRST CLOWN   Ay, tell me that, and unyoke.                                    52
SECOND CLOWN   Marry, now I can tell.
FIRST CLOWN   To't.
SECOND CLOWN   Mass, I cannot tell.                                            55

*Enter Hamlet and Horatio [at a distance].*

FIRST CLOWN   Cudgel thy brains no more about it, for
your dull ass will not mend his pace with beating; and
when you are asked this question next, say "a grave
maker." The houses he makes lasts till doomsday. Go
get thee in and fetch me a stoup of liquor.                                    60
                     [*Exit Second Clown. First Clown digs.*]
                                                            *Song.*
"In youth, when I did love, did love,                                          61
      Methought it was very sweet,
   To contract—oh—the time for—a—my behove,                                   63
   Oh, methought there—a—was nothing—a—
         meet."                                                                64
HAMLET   Has this fellow no feeling of his business, 'a                        65
sings in grave-making?
HORATIO   Custom hath made it in him a property of                             67
easiness.                                                                      68
HAMLET   'Tis e'en so. The hand of little employment
hath the daintier sense.                                                       70
FIRST CLOWN                               *Song.*
   "But age with his stealing steps
      Hath clawed me in his clutch,
   And hath shipped me into the land,                                          73
      As if I had never been such."
                              [*He throws up a skull.*]
HAMLET   That skull had a tongue in it and could sing
once. How the knave jowls it to the ground, as if                             76
'twere Cain's jawbone, that did the first murder! This
might be the pate of a politician, which this ass now                         78
o'erreaches, one that would circumvent God, might                             79
it not?
HORATIO   It might, my lord.
HAMLET   Or of a courtier, which could say, "Good
morrow, sweet lord! How dost thou, sweet lord?"

---

**52 unyoke** i.e., after this great effort, you may unharness the team of your wits.
**55 Mass** By the Mass   **60 stoup** two-quart measure   **61 In . . . love** (This and the two
following stanzas, with nonsensical variations, are from a poem attributed to Lord Vaux
and printed in *Tottel's Miscellany,* 1557. The *oh* and *a* [for "ah"] seemingly are the
grunts of the digger.)   **63 To contract . . . behove** i.e., to shorten the time for my own
advantage. (Perhaps he means to *prolong* it.)   **64 meet** suitable, i.e., more suitable
**65 'a** that he   **67–68 property of easiness** something he can do easily and indifferently
**70 daintier sense** more delicate sense of feeling   **73 into the land** i.e., toward my grave
(?) (But note the lack of rhyme in *steps, land.*)   **76 jowls** dashes (with a pun on *jowl,*
"jawbone")   **78 politician** schemer, plotter   **79 o'erreaches** circumvents, gets the
better of

This might be my Lord Such-a-one, that praised my
Lord Such-a-one's horse when 'a meant to beg it,
might it not?
HORATIO    Ay, my lord.
HAMLET    Why, e'en so, and now my Lady Worm's,
chapless, and knocked about the mazard with a                        89
sexton's spade. Here's fine revolution, an we had the trick          90
to see't. Did these bones cost no more the breeding                  91
but to play at loggets with them? Mine ache to think                 92
on't.
FIRST CLOWN                              *Song.*
    "A pickax and a spade, a spade,
        For and a shrouding sheet;                                   95
    Oh, a pit of clay for to be made
        For such a guest is meet."
                            [*He throws up another skull.*]
HAMLET    There's another. Why may not that be the skull
of a lawyer? Where be his quiddities now, his quillities,            99
his cases, his tenures, and his tricks? Why does                     100
he suffer this mad knave now to knock him about the
sconce with a dirty shovel, and will not tell him of his            102
action of battery? Hum, this fellow might be in 's time             103
a great buyer of land, with his statutes, his recognizances,        104
his fines, his double vouchers, his recoveries.                     105
Is this the fine of his fines and the recovery of his               106
recoveries, to have his fine pate full of fine dirt? Will           107
his vouchers vouch him no more of his purchases, and                108
double ones too, than the length and breadth of a                   109
pair of indentures? The very conveyances of his lands              110
will scarcely lie in this box, and must th'inheritor                111
himself have no more, ha?
HORATIO    Not a jot more, my lord.

**89 chapless** having no lower jaw    **mazard** i.e., head (literally, a drinking vessel)
**90 revolution** turn of Fortune's wheel, change.    **trick** knack    **91–92 cost . . . but** involve
so little expense and care in upbringing that we may    **92 loggets** a game in which pieces
of hard wood shaped like Indian clubs or bowling pins are thrown to lie as near as possible to a stake    **95 For and** and moreover    **99 his quiddities . . . quillities** his subtleties,
his legal niceties    **100 tenures** the holding of a piece of property or office, or the conditions or period of such holding    **102 sconce** head    **103 action of battery** lawsuit about
physical assault    **104 his statutes** his legal documents acknowledging obligation of a
debt    **104 recognizances** bonds undertaking to repay debts    **105 fines** procedures for
converting entailed estates into "fee simple" or freehold    **double vouchers** vouchers
signed by two signatories guaranteeing the legality of real estate titles    **recoveries** suits to
obtain the authority of a court judgment for the holding of land    **106–107 Is this . . .
dirt?** Is this the end of his legal maneuvers and profitable land deals, to have the skull of
his elegant head filled full of minutely sifted dirt? (With multiple wordplay on *fine* and
*fines*.)    **107–110 Will . . . indentures?** Will his vouchers, even double ones, guarantee
him no more land than is needed to bury him in, being no bigger than the deed of conveyance? (An *indenture* is literally a legal document drawn up in duplicate on a single
sheet and then cut apart on a zigzag line so that each pair was uniquely matched.)
**111 box** (1) deed box (2) coffin    **th'inheritor** the acquirer, owner

HAMLET    Is not parchment made of sheepskins?
HORATIO    Ay, my lord, and of calves' skins too.
HAMLET    They are sheep and calves which seek out assurance    116
in that. I will speak to this fellow.—Whose    117
grave's this, sirrah?    118
FIRST CLOWN    Mine, sir.
[*Sings*] "Oh, pit of clay for to be made
For such a guest is meet."
HAMLET    I think it be thine, indeed, for thou liest in't.
FIRST CLOWN    You lie out on't, sir, and therefore 'tis
not yours. For my part, I do not lie in't, yet it is mine.
HAMLET    Thou dost lie in't, to be in't and say it is
thine. 'Tis for the dead, not for the quick; therefore    126
thou liest.
FIRST CLOWN    'Tis a quick lie, sir; 'twill away again
from me to you.
HAMLET    What man dost thou dig it for?
FIRST CLOWN    For no man, sir.
HAMLET    What woman, then?
FIRST CLOWN    For none, neither.
HAMLET    Who is to be buried in't?
FIRST CLOWN    One that was a woman, sir, but, rest her
soul, she's dead.
HAMLET    How absolute the knave is! We must speak by    137
the card, or equivocation will undo us. By the Lord,    138
Horatio, this three years I have took note of it: the age    139
is grown so picked that the toe of the peasant comes so    140
near the heel of the courtier he galls his kibe.—How    141
long hast thou been grave maker?
FIRST CLOWN    Of all the days i'th' year, I came to't that
day that our last king Hamlet overcame Fortinbras.
HAMLET    How long is that since?
FIRST CLOWN    Cannot you tell that? Every fool can tell
that. It was that very day that young Hamlet was
born—he that is mad and sent into England.
HAMLET    Ay, marry, why was he sent into England?
FIRST CLOWN    Why, because 'a was mad. 'A shall
recover his wits there, or if 'a do not, 'tis no great
matter there.
HAMLET    Why?
FIRST CLOWN    'Twill not be seen in him there. There the
men are as mad as he.
HAMLET    How came he mad?

116–17 **assurance in that** safety in legal parchments    118 **sirrah** (a term of address to inferiors)    126 **quick** living    137 **absolute** strict, precise    137–138 **by the card** i.e., with precision (literally, by the mariner's compass-card, on which the points of the compass were marked)    138 **equivocation** ambiguity in the use of terms    139 **took** taken    139–141 **the age . . . kibe** i.e., the age has grown so finical and mannered that the lower classes ape their social betters, chafing at their heels. (*Kibes* are chilblains on the heels.)

FIRST CLOWN   Very strangely, they say.
HAMLET   How strangely?
FIRST CLOWN   Faith, e'en with losing his wits.
HAMLET   Upon what ground?                                          160
FIRST CLOWN   Why, here in Denmark. I have been
sexton here, man and boy, thirty years.
HAMLET   How long will a man lie i'th'earth ere he rot?
FIRST CLOWN   Faith, if 'a be not rotten before 'a die—as
we have many pocky corpses nowadays, that will         165
scarce hold the laying in—'a will last you some eight    166
year or nine year. A tanner will last you nine year.
HAMLET   Why he more than another?
FIRST CLOWN   Why, sir, his hide is so tanned with his
trade that 'a will keep out water a great while, and
your water is a sore decayer of your whoreson dead         ·        171
body. [He picks up a skull.] Here's a skull now hath
lien you i'th'earth three-and-twenty years.                173
HAMLET   Whose was it?
FIRST CLOWN   A whoreson mad fellow's it was. Whose
do you think it was?
HAMLET   Nay, I know not.
FIRST CLOWN   A pestilence on him for a mad rogue! 'A
poured a flagon of Rhenish on my head once. This          179
same skull, sir, was, sir, Yorick's skull, the King's jester.
HAMLET   This?
FIRST CLOWN   E'en that.
HAMLET   Let me see. [He takes the skull.] Alas, poor
Yorick! I knew him, Horatio, a fellow of infinite jest, of
most excellent fancy. He hath bore me on his back a      185
thousand times, and now how abhorred in my
imagination it is! My gorge rises at it. Here hung those   187
lips that I have kissed I know not how oft. Where be
your gibes now? Your gambols, your songs, your            189
flashes of merriment that were wont to set the table on
a roar? Not one now, to mock your own grinning?
Quite chopfallen? Now get you to my lady's chamber    192
and tell her, let her paint an inch thick, to this favor     193
she must come. Make her laugh at that. Prithee,
Horatio, tell me one thing.
HORATIO   What's that, my lord?

---

160 **ground** cause. (But, in the next line, the gravedigger takes the word in the sense of
"land," "country.")   165 **pocky** rotten, diseased (literally, with the pox, or syphilis)
166 **hold the laying in** hold together long enough to be interred   **last you** last. (*You* is
used colloquially here and in the following lines.)   171 **sore** keen, veritable   **whoreson**
(an expression of contemptuous familiarity)   173 **lien you** lain. (See the note at line
166.)   179 **Rhenish** Rhine wine   185 **bore** borne   187 **My gorge rises** i.e., I feel nause-
ated   189 **gibes** taunts   192 **chopfallen** (1) lacking the lower jaw (2) dejected
193 **favor** aspect, appearance

HAMLET    Dost thou think Alexander looked o' this
fashion i'th'earth?
HORATIO    E'en so.
HAMLET    And smelt so? Pah! [*He throws down the skull.*]
HORATIO    E'en so, my lord.
HAMLET    To what base uses we may return, Horatio!
Why may not imagination trace the noble dust of
Alexander till 'a find it stopping a bunghole?                   204
HORATIO    'Twere to consider too curiously to consider        205
so.
HAMLET    No, faith, not a jot, but to follow him thither
with modesty enough, and likelihood to lead it. As             208
thus: Alexander died, Alexander was buried, Alexander
returneth to dust, the dust is earth, of earth we
make loam, and why of that loam whereto he was                 211
converted might they not stop a beer barrel?
Imperious Caesar, dead and turned to clay,                     213
Might stop a hole to keep the wind away.
Oh, that that earth which kept the world in awe
Should patch a wall t'expel the winter's flaw!                 216

*Enter King, Queen, Laertes, and the corpse [of
Ophelia, in procession, with Priest, lords, etc.].*

But soft, but soft awhile! Here comes the King,                217
The Queen, the courtiers. Who is this they follow?
And with such maimèd rites? This doth betoken                  219
The corpse they follow did with desperate hand
Fordo it own life. 'Twas of some estate.                       221
Couch we awhile and mark.                                      222
                    [*He and Horatio conceal themselves.
                    Ophelia's body is taken to the grave.*]
LAERTES    What ceremony else?
HAMLET    [*to Horatio*]
That is Laertes, a very noble youth. Mark.
LAERTES    What ceremony else?
PRIEST
Her obsequies have been as far enlarged
As we have warranty. Her death was doubtful,                   227
And but that great command o'ersways the order                 228
She should in ground unsanctified been lodged                  229
Till the last trumpet. For charitable prayers,                 230
Shards, flints, and pebbles should be thrown on her.           231

204 **bunghole** hole for filling or emptying a cask    205 **curiously** minutely    208 **with . . .
lead it** with moderation and plausibility    211 **loam** a mixture of clay, straw, sand, etc.
used to mold bricks, or, in this case, bungs for a beer barrel    213 **Imperious** Imperial
216 **flaw** gust of wind    217 **soft** i.e., wait, be careful    219 **maimèd** mutilated,
incomplete    221 **Fordo it** destroy its    **estate** rank    222 **Couch we** Let's hide, lie low
227 **warranty** i.e., ecclesiastical authority    228 **order** (1) prescribed practice (2) religious
order of clerics    229 **She should . . . lodged** she should have been buried in unsanctified
ground    230 **For** In place of    231 **Shards** broken bits of pottery

Yet here she is allowed her virgin crants,                                    232
Her maiden strewments, and the bringing home                                  233
Of bell and burial.                                                           234

LAERTES
Must there no more be done?

PRIEST                              No more be done.
We should profane the service of the dead
To sing a requiem and such rest to her                                        237
As to peace-parted souls.

LAERTES                             Lay her i'th'earth,                        238
And from her fair and unpolluted flesh
May violets spring! I tell thee, churlish priest,                             240
A ministering angel shall my sister be
When thou liest howling.

HAMLET [to Horatio]          What, the fair Ophelia!                          242

QUEEN [scattering flowers]    Sweets to the sweet! Farewell.
I hoped thou shouldst have been my Hamlet's wife.
I thought thy bride-bed to have decked, sweet maid,
And not t' have strewed thy grave.

LAERTES                             Oh, treble woe
Fall ten times treble on that cursèd head
Whose wicked deed thy most ingenious sense                                    248
Deprived thee of! Hold off the earth awhile,
Till I have caught her once more in mine arms.
                    [He leaps into the grave and embraces Ophelia.]
Now pile your dust upon the quick and dead,
Till of this flat a mountain you have made
T' o'ertop old Pelion or the skyish head                                      253
Of blue Olympus.

HAMLET [coming forward]    What is he whose grief
Bears such an emphasis, whose phrase of sorrow                                255
Conjures the wandering stars and makes them stand                            256
Like wonder-wounded hearers? This is I,                                       257
Hamlet the Dane.                                                              258

LAERTES [grappling with him]    The devil take thy soul!                      259

---

232 **crants** garlands betokening maidenhood    233 **strewments** flowers strewn on a coffin
233–234 **bringing . . . burial** laying the body to rest, to the sound of the bell    237 **such
rest** i.e., to pray for such rest    238 **peace-parted souls** those who have died at peace with
God    240 **violets** (See 4.5.188 and note.)    242 **howling** i.e., in hell    248 **ingenious
sense** a mind that is quick, alert, of fine qualities    253 **Pelion** a mountain in northern
Thessaly; compare *Olympus* and *Ossa* in lines 254 and 286. (In their rebellion against
the Olympian gods, the giants attempted to heap Ossa on Pelion in order to scale Olympus.)    255 **emphasis** i.e., rhetorical and florid emphasis. (*Phrase* has a similar rhetorical
connotation.)    256 **wandering stars** planets    257 **wonder-wounded** struck with
amazement    258 **the Dane** (This title normally signifies the King; see 1.1.17 and note.)
259 **s.d. grappling with him** The testimony of the First Quarto that *"Hamlet leaps in after Laertes"* and of the ballad "Elegy on Burbage," published in *Gentleman's Magazine*
in 1825 ("Oft have I seen him leap into a grave") seem to indicate one way in which this
fight was staged; however, the difficulty of fitting two contenders and Ophelia's body
into a confined space (probably the trapdoor) suggests to many editors the alternative,
that Laertes jumps out of the grave to attack Hamlet.)

HAMLET   Thou pray'st not well.
I prithee, take thy fingers from my throat,
For though I am not splenitive and rash,                                   262
Yet have I in me something dangerous,
Which let thy wisdom fear. Hold off thy hand.
KING   Pluck them asunder.
QUEEN   Hamlet, Hamlet!
ALL   Gentlemen!
HORATIO   Good my lord, be quiet.
                                        [*Hamlet and Laertes are parted.*]
HAMLET
Why, I will fight with him upon this theme
Until my eyelids will no longer wag.                                        270
QUEEN   Oh, my son, what theme?
HAMLET
I loved Ophelia. Forty thousand brothers
Could not with all their quantity of love
Make up my sum. What wilt thou do for her?
KING   Oh, he is mad, Laertes.
QUEEN   For love of God, forbear him.                                       276
HAMLET
'Swounds, show me what thou'lt do.                                          277
Woo't weep? Woo't fight? Woo't fast? Woo't tear
   thyself?                                                                 278
Woo't drink up eisel? Eat a crocodile?                                     279
I'll do't. Dost come here to whine?
To outface me with leaping in her grave?
Be buried quick with her, and so will I.                                   282
And if thou prate of mountains, let them throw
Millions of acres on us, till our ground,
Singeing his pate against the burning zone,                               285
Make Ossa like a wart! Nay, an thou'lt mouth,                              286
I'll rant as well as thou.
QUEEN                        This is mere madness,                         287
And thus awhile the fit will work on him;
Anon, as patient as the female dove
When that her golden couplets are disclosed,                              290
His silence will sit drooping.
HAMLET                        Hear you, sir.
What is the reason that you use me thus?

---

262 **splenitive** quick-tempered   270 **wag** move. (A fluttering eyelid is a conventional sign
that life has not yet gone.)   276 **forbear him** leave him alone   277 **'Swounds** By His
(Christ's) wounds   278 **Woo't** Wilt thou   279 **Woo't . . . eisel?** Will you drink up
a whole draft of vinegar? (An extremely self-punishing task as a way of expressing grief.)
**crocodile** (Crocodiles were tough and dangerous, and were supposed to shed crocodile
tears.)   282 **quick** alive   285 **his pate** its head, i.e., top   **burning zone** zone in the celestial sphere containing the sun's orbit, between the tropics of Cancer and Capricorn
286 **Ossa** (See 253n.)   **an thou'lt mouth** if you want to rant   287 **mere** utter
290 **golden couplets** two baby pigeons, covered with yellow down   **disclosed** hatched

I loved you ever. But it is no matter.
Let Hercules himself do what he may,                                    294
The cat will mew, and dog will have his day.                            295

*Exit Hamlet.*

KING

I pray thee, good Horatio, wait upon him.

*[Exit] Horatio.*

[*To Laertes*] Strengthen your patience in our last
   night's speech;                                                      297
We'll put the matter to the present push.—                             298
Good Gertrude, set some watch over your son.—
This grave shall have a living monument.                                300
An hour of quiet shortly shall we see;                                  301
Till then, in patience our proceeding be.        *Exeunt.*

❖

# [5.2]

*Enter Hamlet and Horatio.*

HAMLET

So much for this, sir; now shall you see the other.                    1
You do remember all the circumstance?
HORATIO   Remember it, my lord!
HAMLET

Sir, in my heart there was a kind of fighting
That would not let me sleep. Methought I lay
Worse than the mutines in the bilboes. Rashly,                         6
And praised be rashness for it—let us know                             7
Our indiscretion sometime serves us well                               8
When our deep plots do pall, and that should learn us                  9
There's a divinity that shapes our ends,
Rough-hew them how we will—
HORATIO                              That is most certain.              11
HAMLET   Up from my cabin,
My sea-gown scarfed about me, in the dark                              13
Groped I to find out them, had my desire,                              14

---

**294–295 Let . . . day** i.e., (1) Even Hercules couldn't stop Laertes's theatrical rant (2) I, too, will have my turn; i.e., despite any blustering attempts at interference, every person will sooner or later do what he or she must do.   **297 in** i.e., by recalling   **298 present push** immediate test   **300 living** lasting. (For Laertes' private understanding, Claudius also hints that Hamlet's death will serve as such a monument.)   **301 hour of quiet** time free of conflict
**5.2 Location:** The castle.
**1 see the other** hear the other news. (See 4.6.24–26.)   **6 mutines** mutineers   **bilboes** shackles   **Rashly** On impulse. (This adverb goes with lines 12 ff.)   **7 know** acknowledge
**8 indiscretion** lack of foresight and judgment (not an indiscreet act)   **9 pall** fail, falter, go stale   **learn** teach   **11 Rough-hew** shape roughly   **13 sea-gown** seaman's coat
**scarfed** loosely wrapped   **14 them** i.e., Rosencrantz and Guildenstern

Fingered their packet, and in fine withdrew                    15
To mine own room again, making so bold,
My fears forgetting manners, to unseal
Their grand commission; where I found, Horatio—
Ah, royal knavery!—an exact command,
Larded with many several sorts of reasons                     20
Importing Denmark's health and England's too,                 21
With, ho! such bugs and goblins in my life,                   22
That on the supervise, no leisure bated,                      23
No, not to stay the grinding of the ax,                       24
My head should be struck off.
HORATIO                          Is't possible?
HAMLET [*giving a document*]
Here's the commission. Read it at more leisure.
But wilt thou hear now how I did proceed?
HORATIO    I beseech you.

HAMLET
Being thus benetted round with villainies—
Ere I could make a prologue to my brains,                     30
They had begun the play—I sat me down,                        31
Devised a new commission, wrote it fair.                      32
I once did hold it, as our statists do,                       33
A baseness to write fair, and labored much                    34
How to forget that learning, but, sir, now
It did me yeoman's service. Wilt thou know
Th'effect of what I wrote?
HORATIO                          Ay, good my lord.

HAMLET
An earnest conjuration from the King,                         38
As England was his faithful tributary,
As love between them like the palm might flourish,            40
As peace should still her wheaten garland wear                41
And stand a comma 'tween their amities,                       42
And many suchlike "as"es of great charge,                     43
That on the view and knowing of these contents,
Without debatement further more or less,
He should those bearers put to sudden death,
Not shriving time allowed.
HORATIO                          How was this sealed?         47

---

**15 Fingered** pilfered, pinched  **in fine** finally, in conclusion   **20 Larded** garnished
**several** different   **21 Importing** relating to   **22 With . . . life** i.e., with all sorts of warnings
of imaginary dangers if I were allowed to continue living. (*Bugs* are bugbears, hobgoblins.)
**23 That . . . bated** that on the reading of this commission, no delay being allowed   **24 stay**
await   **30–31 Ere . . . play** before I could consciously turn my brain to the matter, it had
started working on a plan   **32 fair** in a clear hand   **33 statists** politicians, men of public
affairs   **34 A baseness** beneath my dignity   **38 conjuration** entreaty   **40 palm** (An image
of health; see Psalm 92.12.)   **41 still** always   **wheaten garland** (symbolic of fruitful agri-
culture, of peace and plenty)   **42 comma** (indicating continuity, link)   **43 "as"es** (1) the
"whereases" of a formal document (2) asses   **charge** (1) import (2) burden (appropriate to
asses)   **47 shriving time** time for confession and absolution

HAMLET
Why, even in that was heaven ordinant.                                    48
I had my father's signet in my purse,                                    49
Which was the model of that Danish seal;                                 50
Folded the writ up in the form of th'other,                             51
Subscribed it, gave't th'impression, placed it safely,                  52
The changeling never known. Now, the next day                           53
Was our sea fight, and what to this was sequent                         54
Thou knowest already.
HORATIO
So Guildenstern and Rosencrantz go to't.
HAMLET
Why, man, they did make love to this employment.
They are not near my conscience. Their defeat                           58
Does by their own insinuation grow.                                     59
'Tis dangerous when the baser nature comes                              60
Between the pass and fell incensèd points                               61
Of mighty opposites.
HORATIO                         Why, what a king is this!                62
HAMLET
Does it not, think thee, stand me now upon—                             63
He that hath killed my king and whored my mother,
Popped in between th'election and my hopes,                             65
Thrown out his angle for my proper life,                                66
And with such coz'nage—is't not perfect conscience                      67
To quit him with this arm? And is't not to be damned                    68
To let this canker of our nature come                                   69
In further evil?                                                        70
HORATIO
It must be shortly known to him from England
What is the issue of the business there.
HAMLET
It will be short. The interim is mine,
And a man's life's no more than to say "one."                           74
But I am very sorry, good Horatio,
That to Laertes I forgot myself,
For by the image of my cause I see
The portraiture of his. I'll court his favors.

---

48 ordinant directing   49 signet small seal   50 model replica   51 writ writing
52 Subscribed signed (with forged signature)   impression i.e., with a wax seal
53 changeling i.e., substituted letter (literally, a fairy child substituted for a human one)
54 was sequent followed   58 defeat destruction   59 insinuation intrusive intervention,
sticking their noses in my business   60 baser of lower social station   61 pass thrust
fell fierce   62 opposites antagonists   63 stand me now upon become incumbent
on me now   65 th'election (The Danish monarch was "elected" by a small number
of high-ranking electors.)   66 angle fishhook   proper very   67 coz'nage trickery
68 quit requite, pay back   69 canker ulcer   69–70 come In grow into   74 a man's . . .
"one" one's whole life occupies such a short time, only as long as it takes to count
to 1.

But, sure, the bravery of his grief did put me 79
Into a tow'ring passion.
HORATIO                   Peace, who comes here?

*Enter a Courtier [Osric].*

OSRIC   Your Lordship is right welcome back to Denmark.
HAMLET   I humbly thank you, sir. [*To Horatio*] Dost
know this water fly?
HORATIO   No, my good lord.
HAMLET   Thy state is the more gracious, for 'tis a vice to
know him. He hath much land, and fertile. Let a beast 86
be lord of beasts, and his crib shall stand at the King's 87
mess. 'Tis a chuff, but, as I say, spacious in the 88
possession of dirt.
OSRIC   Sweet lord, if Your Lordship were at leisure, I
should impart a thing to you from His Majesty.
HAMLET   I will receive it, sir, with all diligence of spirit.
Put your bonnet to his right use; 'tis for the head. 93
OSRIC   I thank Your Lordship, it is very hot.
HAMLET   No, believe me, 'tis very cold. The wind is
northerly.
OSRIC   It is indifferent cold, my lord, indeed. 97
HAMLET   But yet methinks it is very sultry and hot for
my complexion. 99
OSRIC   Exceedingly, my lord. It is very sultry, as
'twere—I cannot tell how. My lord, His Majesty bade
me signify to you that 'a has laid a great wager on your
head. Sir, this is the matter—
HAMLET   I beseech you, remember.
                   [*Hamlet moves him to put on his hat.*]
OSRIC   Nay, good my lord; for my ease, in good faith. 105
Sir, here is newly come to court Laertes—believe me,
an absolute gentleman, full of most excellent differences, 107
of very soft society and great showing. Indeed, 108
to speak feelingly of him, he is the card or calendar of 109
gentry, for you shall find in him the continent of what 110
part a gentleman would see. 111

---

79 **bravery** bravado   86–88 **Let . . . mess** i.e., If a man, no matter how beastlike, is as
rich in livestock and possessions as Osric, he may eat at the King's table.   87 **crib**
manger   88 **chuff** boor, churl. (The Second Quarto spelling, "chough," is a variant
spelling that also suggests the meaning here of "chattering jackdaw.")   93 **bonnet**
any kind of cap or hat   **his** its   97 **indifferent** somewhat   99 **complexion** constitution   105 **for my ease** (a conventional reply declining the invitation to put the hat
back on)   107 **absolute** perfect   **differences** special qualities   108 **soft society**
agreeable manners   **great showing** distinguished appearance   109 **feelingly** with just
perception   109–110 **the card . . . gentry** the model or paradigm (literally, a chart
or directory) of good breeding   110–111 **the continent . . . see** one who contains in
himself all the qualities a gentleman would like to see. (A *continent* is that which
contains.)

HAMLET   Sir, his definement suffers no perdition in                      112
you, though I know to divide him inventorially would                      113
dozy th'arithmetic of memory, and yet but yaw                             114
neither in respect of his quick sail. But, in the verity of               115
extolment, I take him to be a soul of great article, and                  116
his infusion of such dearth and rareness as, to make                      117
true diction of him, his semblable is his mirror and                      118
who else would trace him his umbrage, nothing                             119
more.                                                                     120
OSRIC   Your Lordship speaks most infallibly of him.
HAMLET   The concernancy, sir? Why do we wrap the                         122
gentleman in our more rawer breath?                                       123
OSRIC   Sir?
HORATIO   Is't not possible to understand in another                      125
tongue? You will do't, sir, really.                                       126
HAMLET   What imports the nomination of this                              127
gentleman?
OSRIC   Of Laertes?
HORATIO   [*to Hamlet*]   His purse is empty already; all 's
golden words are spent.
HAMLET   Of him, sir.
OSRIC   I know you are not ignorant—
HAMLET   I would you did, sir. Yet in faith if you did,                   134
it would not much approve me. Well, sir?                                  135
OSRIC   You are not ignorant of what excellence Laertes
is—
HAMLET   I dare not confess that, lest I should compare                   138
with him in excellence. But to know a man well were                       139
to know himself.                                                          140

---

**112–115 his definement . . . sail** the task of defining Laertes's excellences suffers
no diminution in your description of him, though I know that to enumerate all his
graces would stupify one's powers of memory, and even so could do no more than
veer unsteadily off course in a vain attempt to keep up with his rapid forward motion. (Hamlet mocks Osric by parodying his jargon-filled speeches.)   **115–120 But . . .
more** But, in true praise of him, I take him to be a person of remarkable value, and
his essence of such rarity and excellence as, to speak truly of him, none can compare
with him other than his own mirror; anyone following in his footsteps can only hope
to be the shadow to his substance, nothing more.   **122 concernancy** import, rele-
vance   **123 rawer breath** unrefined speech that can only come short in praising him
**125–126 Is't . . . tongue?** i.e., Is it not possible for you, Osric, to understand and
communicate in any other tongue than the overblown rhetoric you have used?
(Alternatively, Horatio could be asking Hamlet to speak more plainly.)
**126 You will do't** i.e., You can if you try, or, you may well have to try (to speak
plainly).   **127 nomination** naming   **134–135 I would . . . approve me** (Responding
to Osric's incompleted sentence as though it were a complete statement, Hamlet says,
with mock politeness, "I wish you did know me to be not ignorant [i.e., to be knowl-
edgeable] about matters," and then turns this into an insult: "But if you did, your
recommendation of me would be of little value in any case.")   **138–140 I dare . . .
himself** I dare not boast of knowing Laertes's excellence lest I seem to imply a comparable excellence in myself. Certainly, to know another person well, one must
know oneself.

OSRIC    I mean, sir, for his weapon; but in the imputation    141
laid on him by them, in his meed he's unfellowed.    142
HAMLET    What's his weapon?
OSRIC    Rapier and dagger.
HAMLET    That's two of his weapons—but well.    145
OSRIC    The King, sir, hath wagered with him six Barbary
horses, against the which he has impawned, as I take    147
it, six French rapiers and poniards, with their assigns,    148
as girdle, hangers, and so. Three of the carriages, in    149
faith, are very dear to fancy, very responsive to the    150
hilts, most delicate carriages, and of very liberal    151
conceit.    152
HAMLET    What call you the carriages?    153
HORATIO [*to Hamlet*]    I knew you must be edified by
the margent ere you had done.    155
OSRIC    The carriages, sir, are the hangers.
HAMLET    The phrase would be more germane to the
matter if we could carry a cannon by our sides; I would
it might be hangers till then. But, on: six Barbary horses
against six French swords, their assigns, and three liberal-
conceited carriages; that's the French bet against
the Danish. Why is this impawned, as you call it?
OSRIC    The King, sir, hath laid, sir, that in a dozen    163
passes between yourself and him, he shall not exceed    164
you three hits. He hath laid on twelve for nine, and it
would come to immediate trial, if Your Lordship would
vouchsafe the answer.    167
HAMLET    How if I answer no?
OSRIC    I mean, my lord, the opposition of your person
in trial.
HAMLET    Sir, I will walk here in the hall. If it please His
Majesty, it is the breathing time of day with me. Let    172
the foils be brought, the gentleman willing, and the
King hold his purpose, I will win for him an I can; if
not, I will gain nothing but my shame and the odd
hits.

---

**141–142 I mean . . . unfellowed** I mean his excellence with his rapier, not his general
excellence; in the reputation he enjoys for use of his weapons, his merit is unequaled.
**145 but well** but never mind    **147 he** i.e., Laertes    **impawned** staked, wagered
**148 poniards** daggers    **assigns** appurtenances    **149 hangers** straps on the sword belt
(*girdle*), from which the sword hung    **and so** and so on.    **149–152 Three . . . conceit**
Three of the hangers, truly, are very pleasing to the fancy, decoratively matched with
the hilts, delicate in workmanship, and made with elaborate ingenuity.    **153 What call
you** What do you refer to when you say    **155 margent** margin of a book, place for ex-
planatory notes    **163 laid** wagered    **164 passes** bouts. (The odds of the betting are
hard to explain. Possibly the King bets that Hamlet will win at least five out of twelve,
at which point Laertes raises the odds against himself by betting he will win nine.)
**167 vouchsafe the answer** be so good as to accept the challenge. (Hamlet deliberately
takes the phrase in its literal sense of replying.)    **172 breathing time** exercise period
**Let** i.e., If

OSRIC   Shall I deliver you so?                                             177
HAMLET   To this effect, sir—after what flourish your
  nature will.
OSRIC   I commend my duty to Your Lordship.                                 180
HAMLET   Yours, yours.                           [*Exit Osric.*]
  'A does well to commend it himself; there are no tongues
  else for 's turn.                                                         183
HORATIO   This lapwing runs away with the shell on his                      184
  head.
HAMLET   'A did comply with his dug before 'a sucked                        186
  it. Thus has he—and many more of the same breed                          187
  that I know the drossy age dotes on—only got the                         188
  tune of the time, and, out of an habit of encounter, a                   189
  kind of yeasty collection, which carries them through                    190
  and through the most fanned and winnowed opinions;                       191
  and do but blow them to their trial, the bubbles                         192
  are out.                                                                  193

  *Enter a Lord.*

LORD   My lord, His Majesty commended him to you by
  young Osric, who brings back to him that you attend
  him in the hall. He sends to know if your pleasure
  hold to play with Laertes, or that you will take longer                  197
  time.
HAMLET   I am constant to my purposes; they follow the
  King's pleasure. If his fitness speaks, mine is ready;                   200
  now or whensoever, provided I be so able as now.
LORD   The King and Queen and all are coming down.
HAMLET   In happy time.                                                     203
LORD   The Queen desires you to use some gentle                            204
  entertainment to Laertes before you fall to play.                        205
HAMLET   She well instructs me.                 [*Exit Lord.*]
HORATIO   You will lose, my lord.
HAMLET   I do not think so. Since he went into France, I
  have been in continual practice; I shall win at the odds.

---

**177 deliver you** report what you say   **180 commend** commit to your favor. (A conventional salutation, but Hamlet wryly uses a more literal meaning, "recommend," "praise," in line 182.)   **183 for 's turn** for his purposes, i.e., to do it for him.   **184 lapwing** (A proverbial type of youthful forwardness. Also, a bird that draws intruders away from its nest and was thought to run about with its head in the shell when newly hatched; a seeming reference to Osric's hat.)   **186 comply . . . dug** observe ceremonious formality toward his nurse's or mother's teat   **187–193 Thus . . . are out** Thus has he—and many like him of the sort our frivolous age dotes on—acquired the trendy manner of speech of the time, and, out of habitual conversation with courtiers of their own kind, have collected together a kind of frothy medley of current phrases, which enables such gallants to hold their own among persons of the most select and well-sifted views; and yet do but test them by merely blowing on them, and their bubbles burst.   **197 play** fence   **that** if   **200 If . . . ready** If he declares his readiness, my convenience waits on his   **203 In happy time** (a phrase of courtesy indicating that the time is convenient)   **205 entertainment** greeting

But thou wouldst not think how ill all's here about my
heart; but it is no matter.
HORATIO  Nay, good my lord—
HAMLET  It is but foolery, but it is such a kind of          213
gaingiving as would perhaps trouble a woman.              214
HORATIO  If your mind dislike anything, obey it. I will
forestall their repair hither and say you are not fit.     216
HAMLET  Not a whit, we defy augury. There is special       217
providence in the fall of a sparrow. If it be now, 'tis
not to come; if it be not to come, it will be now; if it
be not now; yet it will come. The readiness is all. Since  220
no man of aught he leaves knows, what is't to leave        221
betimes? Let be.                                            222

    *A table prepared.* [*Enter*] *trumpets, drums, and*
    *officers with cushions; King, Queen,* [*Osric,*] *and*
    *all the state; foils, daggers,* [*and wine borne in;*]
    *and Laertes.*

KING
Come, Hamlet, come and take this hand from me.
      [*The King puts Laertes's hand into Hamlet's.*]
HAMLET [*to Laertes*]
Give me your pardon, sir. I have done you wrong,
But pardon't as you are a gentleman.
This presence knows,                                        226
And you must needs have heard, how I am punished            227
With a sore distraction. What I have done
That might your nature, honor, and exception                229
Roughly awake, I here proclaim was madness.
Was't Hamlet wronged Laertes? Never Hamlet.
If Hamlet from himself be ta'en away,
And when he's not himself does wrong Laertes,
Then Hamlet does it not, Hamlet denies it.
Who does it, then? His madness. If't be so,
Hamlet is of the faction that is wronged;                   236
His madness is poor Hamlet's enemy.
Sir, in this audience
Let my disclaiming from a purposed evil
Free me so far in your most generous thoughts
That I have shot my arrow o'er the house
And hurt my brother.

---

214 **gaingiving** misgiving  216 **repair** coming  217 **augury** the attempt to read signs of
future events in order to avoid predicted trouble  220–222 **Since . . . Let be** Since no one
has knowledge of what he is leaving behind, what does an early death matter after all?
Enough; forbear.  222.1 s.d. **trumpets, drums** trumpeters, drummers  222.3 s.d. **all the
state** the entire court  226 **presence** royal assembly  227 **punished** afflicted
229 **exception** disapproval  236 **faction** party

LAERTES          I am satisfied in nature,     242
Whose motive in this case should stir me most     243
To my revenge. But in my terms of honor
I stand aloof, and will no reconcilement
Till by some elder masters of known honor
I have a voice and precedent of peace     247
To keep my name ungored. But till that time     248
I do receive your offered love like love,
And will not wrong it.
HAMLET          I embrace it freely,
And will this brothers' wager frankly play.—     251
Give us the foils. Come on.
LAERTES          Come, one for me.
HAMLET
I'll be your foil, Laertes. In mine ignorance     253
Your skill shall, like a star i'th' darkest night,
Stick fiery off indeed.
LAERTES          You mock me, sir.     255
HAMLET    No, by this hand.
KING
Give them the foils, young Osric. Cousin Hamlet,
You know the wager?
HAMLET          Very well, my lord.
Your Grace has laid the odds o'th' weaker side.     259
KING
I do not fear it; I have seen you both.
But since he is bettered, we have therefore odds.     261
LAERTES
This is too heavy. Let me see another.
*[He exchanges his foil for another.]*
HAMLET
This likes me well. These foils have all a length?     263
*[They prepare to fence.]*
OSRIC    Ay, my good lord.
KING
Set me the stoups of wine upon that table.
If Hamlet give the first or second hit,
Or quit in answer of the third exchange,     267
Let all the battlements their ordnance fire.
The King shall drink to Hamlet's better breath,     269

---

242 **in nature** i.e., as to my personal feelings   243 **motive** prompting   247 **voice** authoritative pronouncement   **of peace** for reconciliation   248 **name ungored** reputation un-
wounded   251 **frankly** without ill feeling or the burden of rancor   253 **foil** thin metal
background which sets a jewel off (with pun on the blunted rapier for fencing)
255 **Stick fiery off** stand out brilliantly   259 **laid . . . side** backed the weaker side
261 **is bettered** is the odds-on favorite. (Laertes's handicap is the "three hits" specified
in line 165.)   263 **likes** pleases   267 **Or . . . exchange** or draws even with Laertes by
winning the third exchange   269 **better breath** improved vigor

*Vincentio Sauiolo his Practise.*

# THE THYRDE DAYES
### *Discourse, of* Rapier *and* Dagger.

*Luk̄.*

I Know not certainly, whether it hath been my earneft defire to encounter you, that raifde me earlier this morning than my accuftomed houre, or to be affertained of fome doubtfull queftions, which yefter-night were propofed by fome gentlemen and my felfe, in difcourfe

Vincentio Saviolo, *His practise* (1595). Hamlet supposes that he and Laertes duel with "foils," rapiers (or long swords) whose pointed ends have been blunted by placing a knob or button over them. He wants to know that these weapons are matched and give neither player an advantage. He asks: "These foils have all a length?" (5.2.263). Duels were sometimes fought with a second weapon, a dagger (or short sword), as in this illustration. (By permission of the Folger Shakespeare Library.)

And in the cup an union shall he throw                                                    270
Richer than that which four successive kings
In Denmark's crown have worn. Give me the cups,
And let the kettle to the trumpet speak,                                                  273
The trumpet to the cannoneer without,
The cannons to the heavens, the heaven to earth,
"Now the King drinks to Hamlet." Come, begin.
                                                          *Trumpets the while.*
And you, the judges, bear a wary eye.

HAMLET   Come on, sir.
LAERTES  Come, my lord. [*They fence. Hamlet scores a hit.*]
HAMLET   One.
LAERTES  No.
HAMLET   Judgment.
OSRIC                    A hit, a very palpable hit.                                       282
                             *Drum, trumpets, and shot. Flourish.*
                             *A piece goes off.*
LAERTES  Well, again.
KING
Stay, give me drink. Hamlet, this pearl is thine.
                   [*He drinks, and throws a pearl in Hamlet's cup.*]
Here's to thy health. Give him the cup.
HAMLET
I'll play this bout first. Set it by awhile.
Come. [*They fence.*] Another hit; what say you?
LAERTES  A touch, a touch, I do confess't.
KING
Our son shall win.
QUEEN                    He's fat and scant of breath.                                     289
Here, Hamlet, take my napkin, rub thy brows.                                              290
The Queen carouses to thy fortune, Hamlet.                                                291
HAMLET   Good madam!
KING     Gertrude, do not drink.
QUEEN
I will, my lord, I pray you pardon me.                    [*She drinks.*]
KING [*aside*]
It is the poisoned cup. It is too late.
HAMLET
I dare not drink yet, madam; by and by.
QUEEN    Come, let me wipe thy face.
LAERTES [*aside to the King*]
My lord, I'll hit him now.
KING                              I do not think't.
LAERTES [*aside*]
And yet it is almost against my conscience.

---

270 **union** pearl. (So called, according to Pliny's *Natural History*, 9, because pearls are
*unique*, never identical.)   273 **kettle** kettledrum   282.2 **s.d.** *A piece* A cannon   289 **fat**
not physically fit, out of training   290 **napkin** handkerchief   291 **carouses** drinks a toast

HAMLET
Come, for the third, Laertes. You do but dally.
I pray you, pass with your best violence;                                    301
I am afeard you make a wanton of me.                                        302
LAERTES   Say you so? Come on.                                   [*They fence.*]
OSRIC   Nothing neither way.
LAERTES
Have at you now!                                                               305
                    [*Laertes wounds Hamlet; then, in scuffling,
                    they change rapiers, and Hamlet wounds Laertes.*]
KING                         Part them! They are incensed.
HAMLET
Nay, come, again.                                           [*The Queen falls.*]
OSRIC                       Look to the Queen there, ho!
HORATIO
They bleed on both sides. How is it, my lord?
OSRIC   How is't, Laertes?
LAERTES
Why, as a woodcock to mine own springe, Osric;                          309
I am justly killed with mine own treachery.
HAMLET
How does the Queen?
KING                       She swoons to see them bleed.
QUEEN
No, no, the drink, the drink—Oh, my dear Hamlet—
The drink, the drink! I am poisoned.                             [*She dies.*]
HAMLET
Oh, villainy! Ho, let the door be locked!
Treachery! Seek it out.                           [*Laertes falls. Exit Osric.*]
LAERTES
It is here, Hamlet. Hamlet, thou art slain.
No med'cine in the world can do thee good;
In thee there is not half an hour's life.
The treacherous instrument is in thy hand,
Unbated and envenomed. The foul practice                               320
Hath turned itself on me. Lo, here I lie,
Never to rise again. Thy mother's poisoned.
I can no more. The King, the King's to blame.
HAMLET
The point envenomed too? Then, venom, to thy work.
                                                         [*He stabs the King.*]
ALL   Treason! Treason!

---

301 **pass** thrust   302 **make . . . me** i.e., treat me like a spoiled child, trifle with me
305.1–2 s.d. *in scuffling, they change rapiers* (This stage direction occurs in the Folio.
According to a widespread stage tradition, Hamlet receives a scratch, realizes that
Laertes's sword is unbated, and accordingly forces an exchange.)   309 **woodcock** a bird,
a type of stupidity or as a decoy   **springe** trap, snare   320 **Unbated** not blunted with a
button   **practice** plot

KING
  Oh, yet defend me, friends! I am but hurt.
HAMLET [*forcing the King to drink*]
  Here, thou incestuous, murderous, damnèd Dane,
  Drink off this potion. Is thy union here?                        328
  Follow my mother.                          [*The King dies.*]
LAERTES                   He is justly served.
  It is a poison tempered by himself.                             330
  Exchange forgiveness with me, noble Hamlet.
  Mine and my father's death come not upon thee,
  Nor thine on me!                              [*He dies.*]
HAMLET
  Heaven make thee free of it! I follow thee.
  I am dead, Horatio. Wretched Queen, adieu!
  You that look pale and tremble at this chance,                  336
  That are but mutes or audience to this act,                     337
  Had I but time—as this fell sergeant, Death,                    338
  Is strict in his arrest—oh, I could tell you—                   339
  But let it be. Horatio, I am dead;
  Thou livest. Report me and my cause aright
  To the unsatisfied.
HORATIO                   Never believe it.
  I am more an antique Roman than a Dane.                         343
  Here's yet some liquor left.
                    [*He attempts to drink from the poisoned cup.
                                        Hamlet prevents him.*]
HAMLET                   As thou'rt a man,
  Give me the cup! Let go! By heaven, I'll ha 't.
  Oh, God, Horatio, what a wounded name,
  Things standing thus unknown, shall I leave behind
      me!
  If thou didst ever hold me in thy heart,
  Absent thee from felicity awhile,
  And in this harsh world draw thy breath in pain
  To tell my story. *A march afar off* [*and a volley within*].
  What warlike noise is this?

          *Enter Osric.*

OSRIC
  Young Fortinbras, with conquest come from Poland,
  To th'ambassadors of England gives
  This warlike volley.

---

328 **union** pearl. (See line 270; with grim puns on the word's other meanings: marriage,
shared death.)    330 **tempered** mixed    336 **chance** mischance    337 **mutes** silent
observers (literally, actors with nonspeaking parts)    338 **fell sergeant** remorseless
arresting officer    339 **strict** (1) severely just (2) unavoidable    **arrest** (1) taking into
custody (2) stopping my speech    343 **Roman** (Suicide was an honorable choice for
many Romans as an alternative to a dishonorable life.)

HAMLET              Oh, I die, Horatio!
The potent poison quite o'ercrows my spirit.          355
I cannot live to hear the news from England,
But I do prophesy th'election lights
On Fortinbras. He has my dying voice.          358
So tell him, with th'occurrents more and less      359
Which have solicited. The rest is silence.     [*He dies.*]  360
HORATIO
Now cracks a noble heart. Good night, sweet prince,
And flights of angels sing thee to thy rest!
                        [*March within.*]
Why does the drum come hither?

    *Enter Fortinbras, with the [English] Ambassadors*
    [*with drum, colors, and attendants*].

FORTINBRAS
Where is this sight?
HORATIO             What is it you would see?
If aught of woe or wonder, cease your search.
FORTINBRAS
This quarry cries on havoc. O proud Death,     366
What feast is toward in thine eternal cell,     367
That thou so many princes at a shot
So bloodily hast struck?
FIRST AMBASSADOR       The sight is dismal,
And our affairs from England come too late.
The ears are senseless that should give us hearing,
To tell him his commandment is fulfilled,
That Rosencrantz and Guildenstern are dead.
Where should we have our thanks?
HORATIO                Not from his mouth,  374
Had it th'ability of life to thank you.
He never gave commandment for their death.
But since, so jump upon this bloody question,  377
You from the Polack wars and you from England
Are here arrived, give order that these bodies
High on a stage be placèd to the view,     380
And let me speak to th' yet unknowing world
How these things came about. So shall you hear
Of carnal, bloody, and unnatural acts,
Of accidental judgments, casual slaughters,    384

---

355 **o'ercrows** triumphs over (like the winner in a cockfight)   358 **voice** vote
359 **th'occurrents** the events, incidents   360 **solicited** moved, urged. (Hamlet doesn't
finish saying what the events have prompted—presumably, his acts of vengeance, or his
reporting of those events to Fortinbras.)   366 **This . . . havoc** This heap of dead bodies
loudly proclaims a general slaughter.   367 **feast** i.e., Death feasting on those who have
fallen   **toward** in preparation   374 **his** Claudius's   377 **so jump . . . question** so hard
on the heels of this bloody business   380 **stage** platform   384 **judgments** retributions
**casual** occurring by chance

Of deaths put on by cunning and forced cause,                385
And, in this upshot, purposes mistook
Fall'n on th'inventors' heads. All this can I
Truly deliver.
FORTINBRAS      Let us haste to hear it,
And call the noblest to the audience.
For me, with sorrow I embrace my fortune.
I have some rights of memory in this kingdom,              391
Which now to claim my vantage doth invite me.             392
HORATIO
Of that I shall have also cause to speak,
And from his mouth whose voice will draw on more.         394
But let this same be presently performed,                 395
Even while men's minds are wild, lest more
      mischance
On plots and errors happen.
FORTINBRAS                      Let four captains          397
Bear Hamlet, like a soldier, to the stage,
For he was likely, had he been put on,                    399
To have proved most royal; and for his passage,           400
The soldiers' music and the rite of war
Speak loudly for him.                                     402
Take up the bodies. Such a sight as this
Becomes the field, but here shows much amiss.             404
Go bid the soldiers shoot.
              *Exeunt [marching, bearing off the dead bodies;*
                     *a peal of ordnance is shot off].*

# Notes

Copy text: the Second Quarto of 1604–1605 [Q2]. The First
Folio text also represents an independently authoritative text;
although seemingly not the correct choice for copy text, the Folio text is considerably less marred by typographical errors
than is Q2. The adopted readings in these notes are from F unless otherwise indicated; [eds.] means that the adopted reading
was first proposed by some editor since the time of F. Some
readings are also supplied from the First Quarto of 1603 [Q1].
Act and scene divisions are missing in Quartos 1–2; the Folio
provides such markings only through 1.3 and at Act 2.

385 **put on** instigated   **forced cause** contrivance   391 **of memory** traditional, remembered, unforgotten   392 **vantage** favorable opportunity   394 **voice . . . more** vote will
influence still others   395 **presently** immediately   397 **On** on top of   399 **put on** i.e.,
invested in royal office and so put to the test   400 **for his passage** to mark his passing
402 **Speak** (let them) speak   404 **Becomes the field** suits the field of battle

Abbreviations used:
F       The First Folio
Q       Quarto
s.d.    stage direction
s.p.    speech prefix

**1.1 1 Who's** Whose   **19 soldier** [F, Q1] souldiers   **44 off** [Q1] of
**48 harrows** horrowes   **67 sledded Polacks** [eds.] sleaded pollax
**77 why** [F, Q1] with **cast** cost   **91 heraldry** [F, Q1] heraldy   **92 those**
[F, Q1] these   **95 returned** returne   **97 cov'nant** comart   **98 designed**
[eds.] desseigne   **112 e'en so** [eds.] enso   **116 mote** [eds.] moth
**119 tenantless** tennatlesse   **125 feared** [eds.] feare   **142 you** [F, Q1]
your   **144 at it** it   **181 conveniently** [F, Q1] conuenient

**1.2. 0.2** [and elsewhere] *Gertrude* Gertrad   **1 KING** *Claud.*   **67 so** so
much   **77 good** coold   **82 shapes** [Q3] chapes   **83 denote** deuote
**96 a** or   **105 corpse** [eds.] course   **112 you. For** you for   **114 retrograde**
retrogard   **129 sullied** [eds.] sallied [Q2] solid [F]   **132 self** seale
**133 weary** wary   **137 to this** thus   **140 satyr** [F4] satire   **143 would** [F,
Q1] should   **149 even she** [F; not in Q2]   **174 to drink deep** [F, Q1] for
to drinke   **178 to see** [F, Q1] to   **199 waste** [F2] wast [Q2, F]   **206 jelly
with . . . fear,** gelly, with . . . feare   **210 Where, as** [Q5] Whereas
**225 Indeed, indeed** [F, Q1] Indeede   **241 Very like, very like** [F, Q1]
Very like   **242 hundred** hundreth   **243 MARCELLUS, BERNARDO**
[eds.] *Both*   **247 tonight** to nigh   **256 fare** farre **257 eleven** a leauen
**259.1** *Exeunt* [at line 258 in Q2]   **262 Foul** [F, Q1] fonde

**1.3. 3 convoy is** conuay, in   **12 bulk** bulkes   **18** [F; not in Q2]   **29 weigh**
way   **49 like a** a a   **74 Are** Or   **75 be** boy   **76 loan** loue   **110 Running**
[eds.] Wrong [Q2] Roaming [F]   **116 springes** springs   **126 tether** tider
**130 implorators** imploratotors   **131 bawds** [eds.] bonds   **132 beguile**
beguide

**1.4. 2 is a** is   **6.1 go off** [eds.] *goes of*   **17 revel** [Q3] reueale
**19 clepe** clip   **36 evil** [eds.] eale [Q2] ease [Q3]   **37 often dout** [eds.]
of a doubt   **49 inurned** interr'd [Q2, Q1]   **61, 79 wafts** waues
**80 off** of   **82 artery** arture   **86.1** *Exeunt Exit*   **87 imagination**
[F, Q1] imagion

**1.5. 1 Whither** [eds.] Whether   **20 on** [eds.] an   **21 fretful porcupine** [F,
Q1] fearfull Porpentine   **44 wit** [eds.] wits   **48 what a** what   **56 lust**
[F, Q1] but **angel** Angel   **57 sate** [F] sort   **59 scent** [eds.] sent   **68 alleys** [eds.] allies   **69 posset** possesse   **96 stiffly** swiftly   **119 bird** and
**128 HORATIO, MARCELLUS** *Booth* [also at line 151] **heaven, my
lord** heauen   **138 Look you, I'll** I will   **158 s.d.** *cries Ghost cries*
**179 some'er** so mere   **185 Well** well, well [Q1, Q2]

**2.1. 0.1** *man* [eds.] *man or two*   **3 marvelous** meruiles   **29 Faith, no**
Fayth   **41 warrant** wit   **42 sullies** sallies   **43 wi'th'** with   **60 o'ertook**

or tooke  64 takes take  76 s.d. *Exit Reynaldo. Enter Ophelia* [after line 75 in Q2]  107 passion passions  114 quoted [eds.] coted 2.2.  0.1 [and elsewhere] *Rosencrantz Rosencraus*  57 o'erhasty hastie 73 three [F, Q1] threescore  90 since brevity breuitie  125 This [Q2 has a speech prefix: *Pol.* This]  126 above about  137 winking working  143 his her  148 watch wath  149 to a to  151 'tis [F, Q1; not in Q2]  170.1. *Exeunt* [eds.] *Exit*  210 sanity sanctity  212–213 and suddenly . . . him [F; not in Q2]  213 honorable lord Lord  214 most humbly take take  215 cannot, sir cannot  216 more not more 224 excellent extent  228–229 overhappy. / On [at line 169 in Q2] euer happy on  229 cap lap  240–270 Let . . . attended [F; not in Q2] 267 ROSENCRANTZ, GUILDENSTERN *Both* [F]  273 even euer 288 could can  292 off of  304 What a What  306–307 admirable, in action how . . . angel, in [F, subst.] admirable in action, how . . . Angell in  310 no, nor nor  314 you yee  321 of on  324–325 the clown . . . sear [F; not in Q2] tickle [eds.] tickled [F]  326 blank black 337–362 How . . . too [F; not in Q2]  342 berattle [eds.] beratled [F] 349 most like [eds.] like most [F]  373 lest my let me  381 too to 398–399 tragical-historical, tragical-comical-historical-pastoral [F; not in Q2]  401 light . . . these [eds.] light for the lawe of writ, and the liberty: these  425 By'r by  429 e'en to 't ento't French falconers friendly Fankners  433 [and elsewhere] FIRST PLAYER *Player* 436–437 caviare cauiary  443 affectation affection  446 tale [F, Q1] talke  456 heraldry [F, Q1] heraldy dismal. Head dismall head 474 Then senseless Ilium [F; not in Q2]  481 And, like Like  495 fellies [F4] follies [Q2] Fallies [F]  504 "Moblèd queen" is good [F; not in Q2; F reads "Inobled']  506 bisson *Bison*  514 husband's [F, Q1] husband  519 whe'er where  540 a [F; not in Q2]  541 or [F, Q1] lines, or  546 s.d. *Exeunt players* [see textual note at line 548]  547 till tell 548.1 *Exeunt* [F; Q2 has "*Exeunt Pol. and Players*" after line 547] 554 his the  556 and an  559 to Hecuba [F, Q1] to her  561 the cue that  582 O, vengeance [F; not in Q2]  584 father [Q1, Q3, Q4; not in Q2, F]  588 scullion [F] stallyon [Q2] scalion [Q1]  600 the devil a deale the devil the deale 3.1.  1 And An  28 too two  32 lawful espials [F; not in Q2]  33 Will Wee'le  46 loneliness lowliness to too  56 Let's withdraw with-draw 56.2 *Enter Hamlet* [after line 55 in Q2]  65 wished. To wisht to 73 disprized despiz'd  84 of us all [F, Q1; not in Q2]  86 sicklied sickled  93 well, well, well well  100 the these  108 your honesty you 119 inoculate euocutat  122 to a a  130 knaves all knaues  144 paintings too [Q1] paintings  146 jig, you amble gig & amble  147 lips list 148 your ignorance [F, Q1] ignorance  155 Th'expectancy Th'expectation  159 music musickt  160 that what  161 tune time  162 feature stature  164 [Q2 has "*Exit*" at the end of this line]  191 unwatched vnmatcht

**3.2. 10 tatters** totters split [F, Q1] spleet **27 of the** of **29 praise** praysd
**37 sir** [F; not in Q2] **45.1 Enter** ... *Rosencrantz* [after line 47
in Q2] **88 detecting** detected **96 now. My lord, now my Lord.**
**107 [and elsewhere] QUEEN** *Ger.* **108 metal** mettle **112–113** [F; not
in Q2] **127 devil** deule [Q2] Diuel [F] **133.1 sound** [eds.] *sounds*
**133.7 s.d. Anon Comes** *anon come* **135 miching** [F, Q1] munching
**140 keep counsel** [F, Q1] keepe **153 [and throughout scene] PLAYER
KING** *King* **154 orbèd** orb'd the **159 [and throughout scene]
PLAYER QUEEN** *Quee.* **162 your** our **164** [Q2 follows here with
an extraneous unrhymed line: "For women feare too much, euen as
they loue"] **165 For** And **166 In** Eyther none, in **167 love** Lord
**179 Wormwood, wormwood** That's wormwood **180 PLAYER
QUEEN** [not in Q2] **188 like** the **197 joys** joy **217 An** And
**221 a widow** [F, Q1] I be a widow be [F] be a **226.1 Exit** [F, Q1]
*Exeunt* **240 wince** [Q1] winch [Q2, F] **241.1** [after line 242 in Q2]
**254 Confederate** [F, Q1] Considerat **256 infected** [F, Q1, Q4]
inuected **258 usurp** vsurps **264** [F; not in Q2] **274 with two**
with **288.1** [F; after line 293 in Q2] **308 start** stare **317 of my** of
**343.1** [after line 341 in Q2] **357 thumb** the vmber **366 to the top**
of to **370 can fret me** [F] fret me not [Q2] can fret me, yet [Q1]
**371.1** [after line 372 in Q2] **385 POLONIUS** [F; not in Q2]
**386 Leave me, friends** [so F; Q2 places before "I will say so," and
assigns both to Hamlet] **388 breathes** breakes **390 bitter** ... day
business as the bitter day **395 daggers** [F, Q1] dagger
**3.3. 19 huge** hough **22 ruin** raine **23 but with** but **35.1 Exit** [after "I
know" in F] **50 pardoned** pardon **58 Offense's** [eds.] Offences **shove**
showe **73 pat** ... **a-praying** but now a is a praying **75 revenged**
reuendge **79 hire and salary** base and silly **81 With all** Withall
**3.4. 5–6 with him** ... **Mother, Mother, Mother** [F; not in Q2] **7 warrant** wait **8.1 Enter Hamlet** [at line 5 in Q2] **21 inmost** most
**23 Help, ho!** Helps how **43 off of** of **51 tristful** heated **53** [assigned in
Q2 to Hamlet] **60 heaven-kissing** heaue, a kissing **89 panders** pardons **91 mine** ... **soul** my very eyes into my soule **92 grainèd**
greeued **93 not leave** leaue there **100 tithe** kyth **146 Ecstasy** [F; not
in Q2] **150 I the** the **165 live** leaue **172 Refrain tonight** to refraine
night **193 ravel** rouell **205 to breathe** [eds] to breath **222 a** [F, Q1]
a most **224.1 Exeunt** [eds.] *Exit*
**4.1. 32.1** [at 31 in Q2]
**4.2. 0.1** [Q2: "*Enter Hamlet, Rosencraus, and others.*"] **2–3** [F; not in
Q2; the s.p. in F is "*Gentlemen*"] **4 HAMLET** [not in Q2] **5.1** [F;
not in Q2] **7 Compounded** Compound **18–19 an ape** [not in Q2]
**31–32 Hide** ... **after** [F; not in Q2]
**4.3. 44 With fiery quickness** [F; not in Q2] **56 and so** so **72 were** will
**begun** begin
**4.4. 20–21 name. To** name To

4.5. **16 Let . . . in** [assigned in Q2 to Horatio] **20.1** [after line 16 in Q2]
**38 with** all with **52 clothes** close **57 Indeed, la** Indeede **62 to** too
**83 in their** in **98** [F; not in Q2] **100.1** [below line 97 in Q2]
**103 impetuous** [Q3, F2] impitious [Q2] impittious [F] **109 They** The
**146 swoopstake** [eds.] soopstake [Q1 reads "Swoop-stakelike"]
**158 Let her come in** [assigned in Q2 to Laertes and placed before
"How now, what noyse is that?"] **s.d. Enter Ophelia** [after line 157 in
Q2] **162 Till** Tell **165 an old** [F, Q1] a poore **166–168, 170** [F; not
in Q2] **186 must** [F, Q1] may **191 affliction** [F, Q1] afflictions
**199 All flaxen** Flaxen **203 Christian** [F] Christians **souls, I pray God**
[F, Q1] soules **204 you see** you **217 trophy, sword** trophe sword
4.6. **7, 9 FIRST SAILOR** Say. **9 an't** and **22 good turn** turne **26 bore**
bord **30 He** So **31 will give** will
4.7. **6 proceeded** proceede **7 crimeful** criminall **15 conjunctive** concliue
**22 gyves** Giues **23 loud a wind** loued Arm'd **25 had** haue **37 How**
**. . . Hamlet** [F; not in Q2] **38 This** These **46–47 your pardon** you
pardon **48 and more strange** [F; not in Q2] **Hamlet** [F; not in Q2]
**56 shall live** [F, Q1] live **62 checking** the King **78 ribbon** [eds.] rib-
aud **89 my** me **101 escrimers** [eds.] Scrimures **116 wick** [eds.]
weeke **123 spendthrift** [Q5] spend thirfts **135 on** ore **139 pass** pace
**141 for that** for **151 shape.** If shape if **157 ha't** hate **160 prepared**
prefard **168 hoar** horry **172 cold** cullcold **192 douts** [F "doubts"]
drownes
5.1. **1** [and throughout] **FIRST CLOWN** Clowne **3** [and throughout]
**SECOND CLOWN** Other **9 se offendendo** so offended **12 and to**
to **Argal** or all **34–37 SECOND CLOWN: Why . . . arms?** [F; not
in Q2] **43 that frame** that **55.1** [before line 65 in Q2] **60 stoup**
soope **70 daintier** dintier **85 meant** [F, Q1, Q3] went **89 mazard**
massene **106–107 Is . . . recoveries** [F; not in Q2] **107–108 Will his**
will **109 double ones too** doubles **120 Oh** or **121** [F; not in Q2]
**143 Of all** Of **165 nowadays** [F; not in Q2] **183 Let me see** [F; not
in Q] **192 chamber** [F, Q1] table **208–209 As thus** [F; not in Q2]
**216 winter's** waters **226, 235 PRIEST** Doct. **231 Shards, flints** Flints
**246 t'have** haue **247 trebel** double **262 and rash** rash **288 thus**
this **296.1** [Exit] Horatio and Horatio **301 shortly** thereby
**302 Till** Tell
5.2. **5 Methought** my thought **6 bilboes** bilbo **9 pall** fall **17 unseal** vn-
fold **19 Ah,** [eds.] A **29 villainies** villaines **30 Ere** Or **43 "as"** es as
sir **52 Subscribed** Subscribe **57, 68–80** [F; not in Q2] **73 interim is**
[eds.] interim's [F] **78 court** [eds.] count [F] **81** [and throughout] **OS-
RIC** Cour. **82 humbly** humble **93 Put your** your **98 sultry** sully **for**
or **107 gentleman** [eds.] gentlemen **109 feelingly** [Q4] fellingly
**114 dozy** [eds.] dazzie yaw [eds.] raw **141 his** [eds.] this **142 him by**
**them,** him, by them **149 hangers** hanger **156 carriages** carriage
**159 might be** be might **162 impawned, as** [eds.] all [Q2] impon'd, as

[F]  174 **purpose, I** purpose; I  181–182 **Yours, yours.** 'A does Yours
doo's  186 **comply** so sir  190 **yeasty** histy  191 **fanned** [eds.] pro-
phane [Q2] fond [F]  **winnowed** trennowed  210 **But thou** thou  218 **be
now** be  220 **will come** well come  238 [F; not in Q2]  248 **To keep**
To till all  252 **foils. Come on** foiles.  255 **off of**  261 **bettered** better
270 **union** Vnice ["Onixe" in some copies]  288 **A touch, a touch, I** I
302 **afeard** sure  316 **Hamlet.** Hamlet *Hamlet*  319 **thy** [F, Q1] my
327 **murderous** [F; not in Q2]  328 **off of thy union** [F, Q1] the Onixe
345 **ha't** [eds.] hate [Q2] have't [F]  366 **proud** prou'd  369 **FIRST
AMBASSADOR** *Embas.*  381 **th' yet** yet  385 **forced** for no  394 **on** no

Passages contained only in F and omitted from Q2 are noted in the
textual notes above. Listed here are the more important instances
in which Q2 contains words, lines, and passages omitted in F.

1.  **112–129** BERNARDO I think . . . countrymen
2.  **58–60** wrung . . . consent
3.  **9** perfume and
4.  **17–38** This heavy-headed . . . scandal  **75–78** The very . . . beneath
2.1.  **122** Come
2.2.  **17** Whether . . . thus  **217** except my life  **363** very  **366** 'Sblood
     (and some other profanity passim)  **371** then  **444–445** as wholesome
     . . . fine  **521–522** of this  **589** Hum
3.2.  **169–170** Where . . . there  **216–217** To . . . scope
3.4.  **72–77** Sense . . . difference  **79–82** Eyes . . . mope  **168–172** That
     monster . . . put on  **174–177** the next . . . potency  **187** One word . . .
     lady  **209–217** There's . . . meet
4.1.  **4** Bestow . . . while  **41–44** Whose . . . air
4.2.  **4** But soft
4.3.  **26–29** KING Alas . . . worm
4.4.  **9–67** *Enter Hamlet* . . . worth
4.5.  **33** Oho
4.7.  **68–82** LAERTES My lord . . . graveness  **101–103** Th' escrimers . . .
     them  **115–124** There . . . ulcer
5.1.  **154** There
5.2.  **106–142** here is . . . unfellowed (replaced in F by "you are not igno-
     rant of what excellence Laertes is at his weapon")  **154–155** HORA-
     TIO [*to Hamlet*] I knew . . . done  **193–207** *Enter a Lord* . . . lose, my
     lord (replaced in F by "You will lose this wager, my lord")  **222** Let be

# CONTEXTS

# Spiritual and Mental Life

Shakespeare and his contemporaries entertained the possibility that they were surrounded by a spirit world, for the most part unseen and unheard but still influential. Its influence could be delightful and comforting; it could also provoke terrible torments. When Caliban (the inhabitant of an island in *The Tempest*) reports "the isle is full of noises, / Sounds and sweet airs that give delight and hurt not" (3.2.133–134), he represents the best of such experiences. The worst appears in the terror of the guards on the ramparts of Elsinore and in Hamlet's deep confusion when his father's ghost urges revenge for his "foul and most unnatural murder" (1.5.26). Hamlet is not even sure of the Ghost's true identity: "The spirit that I have seen / May be the devil . . . [who] Abuses me to damn me" (2.2.599–604). Once the existence of a spirit world was granted, it was practically impossible to determine the nature and extent of its effect on human behavior.

Early modern commentary on the spirit world ranges from Timothy Bright's refutation of the claim that spirits cause melancholy, a disease he attributes to an abundance of humors in the brain, to Joseph Hall's defense of the idea that human beings are immersed in a contest between the forces of good and evil, comforting those in distress and terrifying the morally culpable. Between the opinions of the rational Bright and the sensitive Hall were various others which tried to explain extraordinary or even totally mysterious emotional states. Ludwig Lavater (his first name was Anglicized as Lewes) addresses the meaning of ghostly appearances without making a specific determination about their provenance: They might be emanations of a sick brain, or they might be emissaries from purgatory returning to earth to seek the help of the living in reducing the terms of their punishment. Robert Burton, whose *The Anatomy of Melancholy* (1628) is still read today for its observations on illness as well as on the conditions of life common in early modern England, analyzes the symptoms of "melancholy." As a term designating a troubled mental and emotional state, it can refer to a slight and transient disability brought about by some unusual circumstance. If this disability persists, it grows into a "habit," behavior becomes exaggerated and erratic, and fits of terror and grief alternate with periods of jesting and morbid wit.

## Joseph Hall (1574–1656)

*A prolific writer of satire, Bishop Hall is remembered chiefly for his critique of the Catholic Church,* Mundus Alter et Idem, *translated as* The Discovery of a New World *(1608). Of his many treatises on the principles of Protestant practice and theology, those on the unseen spirit world are especially useful in understanding the uncertainty with which Shakespeare's contemporaries faced life's challenges.* Meditations and Vows *assumes the ubiquity of such a spirit world, while* The Invisible World *worries about the deceptiveness of its manifestations. In both, Hall shows a keen regard for what we might call the conflict between immaterial forces of good and evil. He describes a spirit world that is manifest in intensely emotional moments, whether fearful or joyful; he assumes that diabolical or angelic entities affect human behavior. While he is confident that angels are in charge of all of human history, he also conveys the terror provoked by the possibility that one of the faithful might meet with their malevolent counterparts.*

### from *Meditations and Vows*[1]
[Our existence is permeated with the life of spirits]

There is no man, nor place, free from spirits, although they testify their presence by visible effects but in few. Every man is a host to entertain angels, though not in visible shapes, as Abraham, and Lot.[2]

---

[1]Joseph Hall, *Meditations and Vows* and *The Invisible World* in *Works*, 12 vols., London, 1837; vol. 8, pp. 88, 409.

[2]Abraham, the patriarch of the tribes of Israel, was addressed by God on numerous occasions. See Genesis 15–18. Lot was visited by angels. See Genesis 19.1, 2.

The evil ones do nothing but provoke us to sin and plot mischiefs against us by casting into our way dangerous objects, by suggesting sinful motions to our minds, by stirring up enemies against us amongst men, by frighting us with terrors in ourselves, by accusing us to God. On the contrary, the good angels are ever removing our hindrances from good and our occasions of evil, mitigating our temptations, helping us against our enemies, delivering us from dangers, comforting us in sorrows, furthering our good purposes, and, at last, carrying up our souls to heaven. It would affright a weak Christian that knows the power and malice of wicked spirits to consider their presence and number; but when, with the eyes of Elisha's servant,[3] he sees those on his side at present, as diligent, more powerful, he cannot but take heart again; especially if he consider, that neither of them is without God; limiting the one, the bounds of their temptation; directing the other,[4] in the safeguard of his children. Whereupon it is come to pass, that, though there be many legions of devils, and every one more strong than many legions of men and more malicious than strong, yet the little flock of God's church liveth and prospereth. I have everwith me invisible friends and enemies. The consideration of mine enemies shall keep me from security, and make me fearful of doing ought to advantage them. The consideration of my spiritual friends shall comfort me against the terror of the other, shall remedy my solitariness, shall make me wary of doing ought indecently, grieving me rather that I have ever heretofore made them turn away their eyes for shame of that whereof I have not been ashamed, that I have no more enjoyed their society, that I have been no more affected with their presence. What though I see them not? I believe them. I were no Christian, if my faith were not as sure as my sense.

### from *The Invisible World*
[Spirits can take what form they like—a fear Hamlet expresses]

How vain is the observation of those authors who make this the difference between the apparitions of good angels and evil: That the good make choice of the shapes, either of beautiful persons or of those creatures which are clean and hurt less . . . ; whereas the evil put themselves into the forms of deformed men or of harmful and

---

[3]Gehazi, the servant of Elisha who sees his master's spiritual power, although he himself has none; see 2 Kings 4.

[4]The evil spirit and the good spirit.

filthy beasts, as of a goat to the assembly of witches, . . . when we see that the very glory of angels escapes not their counterfeisance.

## Ludwig Lavater (1527–1586)

*A Swiss Protestant theologian, Ludwig Lavater composed a number of works in Latin which were later translated into English and published in London. Testifying to the vital interest of his contemporaries in a spirit world, his treatise on ghosts, De spectris, translated as* Of Ghosts and Spirits Walking by Night, *rehearses various opinions on their provenance, the evidence for their appearance, and the likelihood that they are no more than phantasms produced by melancholy. Even so, Lavater is intrigued by the possibility that ghosts may be the souls of the dead who, although sentenced to a term in purgatory, are allowed to wander for a time on earth—precisely the situation the ghost of Hamlet's father describes. Lavater supposes that the reason such souls return to earth is to thank those living men and women who have made restitution for their sins. This is certainly not the reason the vengeful ghost seeks out his son, Hamlet. Lavater concludes by repudiating the doctrine of purgatory as inconsistent with a godly reading of Scripture, but his lengthy account of this intermediate station between hell and heaven suggests how fascinating its imaginative and emotional appeal might have been even to those who were compelled to reject it on theological grounds.*

### from *Of Ghosts and Spirits Walking by Night*[1]
[How people speak of strange sights]

There have been very many in all ages which have utterly denied that there be any spirits or strange sights. The philosophers of Epicurus's[2] sect did jest and laugh at all those things which were reported of them, and counted them as feigned and counterfeit, by the which only children and fools, and plain simple men were made afraid. When Cassius, who was an Epicurian, understood by Brutus

---

[1]Ludwig Lavater, *Of Ghosts and Spirits Walking by Night*, trans. R.H., London, 1572; pp. 9, 10, 71, 72, 102–104, 109, 114.
[2]Epicurus (341–270 BCE) relied only on evidence from the senses and rejected the idea of a supernatural world.

that he had seen a certain vision, he (as Plutarch doth testify) endeavored to attribute the matter to natural causes.[3] We read in the twenty-third chapter of the Acts of the Apostles that the Sadduceys[4] did not believe there should be any resurrection of the dead, and that they denied there were any spirits of angels. Yea, and at this day, many good and godly men believe those things to be but tales, which are talked of to and fro concerning those imagined visions, partly because in all their life, they never saw any such and partly or rather especially, because in time past men have been so often deceived with apparitions, visions and false miracles done by monks and priests, that now they take things that are true to be as utterly false. Whatsoever the cause is, it may be proved, by witness of many writers and by daily experience also, that spirits and strange sights do sometime appear, and that in very deed many strange and marvelous things do happen. True it is, that many men do falsely persuade themselves that they see or hear ghosts: for that which they imagine they see or hear proceedeth either of melancholy, madness, weakness of the senses, fear, or of some other perturbation; or else when they see or hear beasts, vapors, or some other natural things, then they vainly suppose they have seen sights I wote[5] not what. [ . . . ] There is no doubt but that almost all those things which the common people judge to be wonderful sights are nothing less than so. But in the mean season[6] it cannot be denied but that strange sights and many other such like things are sometimes heard and also seen.

### [How spirits affect people]

[N]o man can deny but that [there are] many honest and credible persons of both kinds, as well men as women of whom some are living and some already departed, which have and do affirm that they

---

[3]Gaius Cassius, one of the assassins of Julius Caesar, committed suicide after losing the battle of Philippi (42 BCE). Marcus Junius Brutus, another of Caesar's assassins, also committed suicide after Philippi. The biographies of the Greek historian Plutarch (d. 120), known as *Parallel Lives*, provided Shakespeare with source material for his Greek and Roman plays. On Brutus's dream, see Shakespeare's *Julius Caesar*, 4.2.326–337.

[4]Sadduceys (or Sadducees) were members of a sect of Jews that flourished c. 200 BCE. They followed only the written law and disputed oral tradition, the existence of demons, and the concept of the Messiah. See Acts 23.6–9.

[5]Know.

[6]The poor season, a time of dearth and desperation.

have sometimes in the day and sometimes in the night seen and heard spirits. Some man walketh alone in his house and behold a spirit appeareth in his sight, yea and sometimes the dogs also perceive them, and fall down at their master's feet, and will by no means depart from them, for they are sore afraid themselves too. Some man goeth to bed, and layeth him down to rest, and by and by there is something pinching him, or pulling off the clothes; sometimes it sitteth on him or lieth down in the bed with him, and many times it walketh up and down in the chamber. . . . Many times in the night season there have been certain spirits heard softly going or spitting or groaning, who, being asked what they were have made answer that they were the souls of this or that man, and that they now endure extreme torments. If by chance any man did ask of them by what means they might be delivered out of those tortures, they have answered that in case a certain number of masses were sung for them, or pilgrimages vowed to some saints, or some other such like deed done for their sake, that then surely they should be delivered. Afterward appearing in great light and glory, they have said that they were delivered and have therefore rendered great thanks to their good benefactors and have in like manner promised that they will make intercession to God and our Lady for them.[7] And thereby it may be well proved that they were not always priests or other bold and wicked men which have feigned themselves to be souls of men deceased, as I have before said, in so much that even in those men's chambers when they have been shut, there have appeared such things, [even] when they have with a candle diligently searched before, whether anything have lurked in some corner or no.

### [Spirits from purgatory]

The papists in former times have publicly both taught and written that those spirits which men sometime see and hear be either good or bad angels or else the souls of those which either live in everlasting bliss, or in purgatory, or in the place of damned persons. And that divers of them are those souls that crave aid and deliverance of men. [ . . . ]

Of this place, to wit, purgatory, popish writers teach marvelous things. Some of them say that purgatory is also under the earth as hell is. Some say that hell and purgatory are both one place, albeit the pains be divers according to the deserts of souls. Furthermore

[7]The benefactors.

they say, that under the earth there are more places of punishment in which the souls of the dead may be purged. For they say that this or that soul hath been seen in this or that mountain, flood, or valley, in which it hath committed offence, and that these are particular purgatories, assigned unto them for some special cause before the day of Judgment, after which time all manner of purgatories as well general as particular shall cease. Some of them say that the pain of purgatory is all one with the punishment of hell and that they differ only in this, that the one hath an end the other no end; and that it is far more easy to endure all the pains of this world which all men since Adam's time have sustained, even unto the day of the last Judgment than to bear one day's space of the least of those two punishments.

Hereunto they add that the spirits as well of the good as the ill do come and are sent unto men living from hell. And that by the common law of justice, all men at the day of Judgment shall come to their trial from hell; and that none before that time can come from thence. Farther they teach, that by God's license and dispensation certain, yea before the day of judgment, are permitted to come out of hell and that not for ever but only for a season, for the instructing and terrifying of the living. Moreover that God doth license souls to return from those two places, partly for the comfort and warning of the living and partly to pray aid of them.

Now touching the suffrages or ways of succor whereby souls are dispatched out of purgatory, popish doctors appoint four means: That is, the healthful offering of the sacrifice in the sacrament of the altar, almsgiving, prayer, fasting. And under these members, they comprise all other, as vowed pilgrimages, visiting of churches, helping of the poor, and the furthering of God's worship and glory, etc. But above all, they extol their mass as a thing of greatest force to redeem souls out of misery, of whose wonderful effect, and of the rest even now recited by us, they allege many strange examples.

Neither only in their writings, but in open pulpit also they have taught, how excellent and noble an act it is for men touched with compassion with these aforesaid works to rid the soul that appeareth unto them and craveth their help out of the pains of purgatory. Or if they cannot so do, yet to ease and assuage their torture. For say they, the souls after their deliverance, cease not in most earnest manner to pray for their benefactors and helpers. On the other side, they teach that it is an horrible and heinous offence if a man give no succor to such as seek it at his hands, especially if it be the soul of his parents, brethren and sisters. For except by them they might conveniently be released of so manifold miseries they would not so earnestly crave their help. Wherefore say they, no man should be so void of natural affection, so cruel and outrageous, that he should at any time deny to bestow some small wealth to benefit those by whom he hath before by divers and sundry ways been pleasured.

If they were not the souls of the dead which crave help and succor but devilish spirits, they would not will them to pray, fast, or give alms for their sakes, for that the devils do hate those as also all other good works.

[Why purgatory is not to be believed in]

Now that the souls neither of the faithful nor of infidels do wander any longer on the earth when they be once severed from the bodies, I will make it plain and evident unto you by these reasons following. First certain it is, that such as depart hence, either die in faith or in unbelief. Touching those that go hence in a right belief, their souls are by and by in possession of life everlasting and they that depart in unbelief do straightway become partakers of eternal damnation. The souls do not vanish away and die with the body, as the Epicures' opinion is, neither yet be in every place, as some do imagine. Touching this matter I will allege pithy and manifold testimonies out of the holy Scripture, out of which alone this question may and ought to be tried and discussed.

## Timothy Bright (1551–1615)

*Timothy Bright, a physician by training, was an early exponent of a rational approach to claims for the existence of a spirit world. Best known as the inventor of shorthand (his* Characterie: An Art of Short Swift and Secret Writing by Characters *[1588] was his first publication), Bright produced two books on the health of the human body (one recommending ways to preserve health, the other to cure disease) before writing his incisive work on melancholy. Bright subscribes to the Galenic theory of medicine, which posited that just as a sound body depended on a salutary balance among the four principal humors— blood, phlegm, bile, and lymph—so a diseased body was brought about by humoral imbalances. He attributes melancholy to the collection of a "gross humor" in the brain which causes fantastic apparitions. The resulting delusions bode permanent mental damage: fantastic apparitions could remain in the memory and distort every aspect of a worldview. By contrast, Bright insists, profound feelings of guilt and unworthiness are not symptomatic of true melancholy, although they can result in moods that resemble those created by the disease. Rather, they are the perfectly understandable reactions of a sinner who is struggling with his past. For Bright's contemporaries, this important distinction between melancholy as a mental disease and spiritual anxiety as a condition of the soul discouraged belief in a spirit world. For Bright, the person who believed he saw spirits was either suffering from the effects of a humoral imbalance or speaking figuratively about his fear of God's wrath.*

### from *A Treatise of Melancholy*[1]
#### [The emotions created by melancholy]

Now let us consider what passions they are that melancholy driveth us unto, and how it doth so diversely distract those that are oppressed therewith. The perturbations of melancholy are for the most part sad and fearful and [also] such as rise of them: as distrust, doubt, diffidence, or despair, sometimes furious, and sometimes merry in appearance, through a kind of Sardonian[2] and false laughter, as the humor is disposed that procureth these diversities. Those which are sad and pensive rise of the melancholic humor which is the grossest part of the blood. [ . . . ] This for the most part is settled in the spleen and with his vapors annoyeth the heart; and, passing up to the brain, counterfeiteth terrible objects to the fantasy; and, polluting both the substance and spirits of the brain, causeth it without external occasion to forge monstrous fictions and terrible to the conceit, which the judgment taking as they are presented by the disordered instrument, deliver over to the heart, which hath no judgment of discretion in itself, but giving credit to the mistaken report of the brain, breaketh out into that inordinate passion, against reason.

This cometh to pass because the instrument of discretion is depraved by these melancholic spirits, and a darkness and clouds of

[1]Timothy Bright, *A Treatise of Melancholy*, London, 1586; sigs. Giii–Giiii verso; Mviii verso.

[2]Sardonic, sarcastic.

melancholy vapors, rising from that puddle of the spleen, obscure the clearness which our spirits are endued with and is requisite to the due discretion of outward objects. This at the first is not so extreme, neither doth it shew so apparently, as in process of time, when the substance of the brain hath plentifully drunk of that splenetic fog,[3] whereby his nature is become of the same quality, and the pure and bright spirits so defiled and eclipsed, that their indifferency alike to all sensible things is now drawn to a partiality and inclination, as by melancholy they are enforced. For where that natural and internal light is darkened, their fancies arise vain, false and void of ground, even as in the external sensible darkness a false illusion will appear unto our imagination, which, the light being brought in, is discerned to be an abuse of fancy.

Now the internal darkness, affecting more nigh by our nature[4] than the outward, is cause of greater fears and more molesteth us with terror than that which taketh from us the sight of sensible things especially,[5] arising not of absence of light only but by a presence of a substantial obscurity, which is possessed with an actual power of operation.[6] This, taking hold of the brain by process of time, giveth it an habit of depraved conceit, whereby it fancieth not according to truth but as the nature of that humor leadeth it, altogether ghastly and fearful. This causeth not only fantastical apparitions wrought by apprehension only of common sense[7]; but [also] fantasy, another part of internal sense, compoundeth and forgeth disguised shapes,[8] which give great terror unto the heart, and cause it with the lively spirit[9] to hide itself as well as it can, by contraction in all parts, from those counterfeit goblins, which the brain dispossessed of right discerning, feigneth unto the heart.

Neither only is common sense and fantasy thus overtaken with delusion [sic], but memory also receiveth a wound therewith, which disableth it both to keep in memory and to record those things whereof it took some custody before this passion, and after

[3]Of the spleen, bitter.
[4]Affecting us more.
[5]The night; physical blindness.
[6]The inner darkness or "substantial obscurity" actually affects what we think we see.
[7]The interpretation of ordinary sense perceptions.
[8]Fantastic images.
[9]The heart and its internal spirit.

therewith are defaced. For as the common sense and fantasy, which do offer [things] unto the memory to lay up, deliver but fables instead of true report—and those tragical that dismay all the sensible frame of our bodies—so either is the memory wholly distracted by importunity of those doubts and fears that it neglecteth the custody of other store[10]; or else it recordeth and apprehendeth only such as by this importunity is thrust thereupon, [that is], nothing but darkness, peril, doubt, frights, and whatsoever the heart of man doth abhor.

### [Melancholy as a misery of the soul]

Of all kinds of miseries that befall unto man, none is so miserable as that which riseth of the sense of God's wrath and revenging hand against the guilty soul of a sinner. Other calamities affect the body and one part only of our nature; this the soul, which carrieth the whole[11] into society of the same misery. Such as are of the body, although they approach nigher the quick[12] than poverty or want of necessaries for maintenance of this life, yet they fail in degree of misery and come short of that which this[13] forceth upon the soul. The other touch those parts where the soul commandeth: poverty, nakedness, sickness and other of that kind are mitigated with a mind resolute in patience or endued with wisdom to ease that [which] grieveth by supply of remedy. [T]his seizeth upon the seat of wisdom itself, and chargeth upon all the excellency of understanding, and grindeth into powder all that standeth firm, and melteth like the dew before the sun whatsoever we reckon of as support of our defects, and subdueth that wherewith all things else are of us subdued. [T]he cause, the guilt, the punishment, the revenge, the ministers of the wrath, all [are] concurring together in more forcible sort (and that against the universal state of our nature, not for a time, but for ever) than in any other kind of calamity whatsoever.

Here the cause is not either wound or surfeit, shipwreck or spoil, infamy or disgrace, but all kinds of misery joined together with a troubled spirit, feeling the beginnings and expecting with

[10]Memory.
[11]The whole person.
[12]What is alive, vital.
[13]Guilt.

desperate fear the eternal consummation of the indignation and fierce wrath of God's vengeance against the violation of his holy commandments; which, although in this life it taketh not away the use of outward benefits, yet doth the internal anguish bereave us of all delight of them and that pleasant relish they are endued with to our comforts; so that manifold better were it [that] the use of them were quite taken away than for us in such sort to enjoy them. Neither is here the guiltiness[14] of breach of human laws (whose punishment extendeth no farther then this present life, which even of itself is full of calamities not much inferior to the pain adjoined unto the transgression of civil laws) but of the law divine and the censure executed with the hand of God, whose fierce wrath prosecuteth the punishment eternally as his displeasure is like to himself, and followeth us into our graves, and receiveth no satisfaction with any punishment, either in regard of continuance or of extremity.[15]

## Robert Burton (1577–1640)

*Robert Burton's popular treatise* The Anatomy of Melancholy *examines all aspects of a disease we would be hard put to identify. But in the seventeenth century, it was a familiar if protean condition: Melancholy could manifest itself as a kind of discouragement with the exigencies of life or (at the opposite extreme) as a radical rejection of all affective relations. Burton's treatise appeared in eight successively more elaborate editions throughout the century. It was widely read well into the nineteenth century.*

*Melancholy, as Burton theorized it, was not a simple condition of the body induced by a humoral imbalance; rather, it was a complex illness implicating mind and body in various ways and degrees. This kind of symptomology would be variously named in later epochs as "demonic possession," "hysteria," or "shell shock." Burton also saw that its manifestations among different persons might be quite variable: While the common sense of one person might be able to withstand the effects of a fairly severe trauma, the*

---

[14]Owing to.

[15]Here Bright explicitly repudiates the doctrine of purgatory.

*emotional disposition of another less capable of moral fortitude could cause him to collapse completely. Especially evocative for Hamlet is Burton's idea that melancholy can begin as a kind of moodiness and become progressively more debilitating—even a permanent disorder. Such a sense of the range of melancholy behavior allows us to speculate on how Hamlet's mental state may be changing during the course of the play. In Act 1, we see that he suffers from deep grief over the death of his father; by Act 3, we sense that he has become obsessively crazed by the news he has heard from the Ghost. Burton also identifies a melancholy peculiar to women, which he attributes to a lack of work and discipline. Its chief victims are "nice gentlewomen [. . .] that fare well in great houses"—a situation like that of Ophelia. Finally, Burton's emphasis on sexual abstinence as a cause of melancholy suggests that Hamlet and Ophelia may share a disability; we can read Hamlet's rejection of Ophelia as a would-be "breeder of sinners" (3.1.123) as an index of his own frustration.*

## from *The Anatomy of Melancholy*[1]
### [A melancholy disposition]

Melancholy, the subject of our present discourse, is either in disposition or habit. In disposition[2] is that transitory melancholy which goes and comes upon every small occasion of sorrow, need, sickness, trouble, fear, grief, passion, or perturbation of the mind, any manner of care, discontent, or thought, which causeth anguish, dullness, heaviness and vexation of spirit, any ways opposite to pleasure, mirth, joy, delight, causing frowardness in us, or a dislike. In which equivocal and improper sense, we call him melancholy that is dull, sad, sour, lumpish, ill-disposed, solitary, any way moved or displeased. And from these melancholy dispositions no man living is free, no Stoic,[3] none so wise, none so happy, none so patient, so generous, so godly, so divine that can vindicate himself, so well-composed, but more or less, some time or other, he feels the smart of it. Melancholy in this sense is the character of mortality.

---

[1]Robert Burton, *The Anatomy of Melancholy*, ed. A. R. Shilleto, 3 vols., London, 1896; vol. 1, pp. 164–166, 471–472, 479–480.

[2]By nature.

[3]Stoic philosophy, initiated by Zeno in the 4th c. BCE, promoted a stringent moral discipline that required indifference to the emotions.

### [Melancholy as a habitual frame of mind]

But forasmuch as so few can embrace this good counsel of his (*St. Paul, 2 Tim.* 2.3[4]), or use it aright, but rather—as so many brute beasts give a way to their passion—voluntarily subject and precipitate themselves into a labyrinth of cares, woes, miseries, and suffer their souls to be overcome by them, [and] cannot arm themselves with that patience as they ought to do, it falleth out oftentimes that these dispositions become habits, and [that] many affects contemned (as Seneca notes *Epist. 96. lib.* 10[5]) make a disease. Even as one distillation not yet grown to custom makes a cough but [one] continual and inveterate causeth a consumption of the lungs, so do these our melancholy provocations; and according as the humor itself is intended or remitted in men, as their temperature of body or rational soul is better able to make resistance, so are they more or less affected. For that which is but a flea-biting to one, causeth insufferable torment to another; and [that] which one by his singular moderation and well-composed carriage can happily overcome, a second is not [one] whit able to sustain. But upon every small occasion of misconceived abuse, injury, grief, disgrace, loss, cross, rumor, etc. (if solitary or idle), [he] yields so far to passion that his complexion is altered, his digestion hindered, his sleep gone, his spirits obscured, and his heart heavy, his hypochondries misaffected.[6] Wind, crudity on a sudden overtake him, and he himself [is] overcome with melancholy. [ . . . ] This melancholy of which we are to treat is an habit [ . . . ] a chronic or continual disease, a settled humor, as Aurelianus[7] and others call it, not errant, but fixed; and as it was long increasing, so, now being (pleasant or painful) grown to an habit, it will hardly be removed.

### [Symptoms of melancholy]

The symptoms of the mind are superfluous and continual cogitations; for, when the head is heated, it scorcheth the blood, and from

---

[4]"Thou therefore endure hardness, as a good soldier of Jesus Christ."

[5]Roman philosopher Seneca (4 BCE–65) wrote primarily in the field of ethics; his *Epistles* (letters) promote a prudent way of life.

[6]His upper abdomen disturbed.

[7]Physician of Sicca in Numidia (fl. 5th c.) who translated works on the passions by Soranus of Ephesus, a physician under the emperors Hadrian and Trajan, 98–137. Soranus's almost twenty books of medicine were widely translated and distributed throughout the late classical period.

thence proceed melancholy fumes, which trouble the mind, *Avicenna.*[8] They are very choleric, and soon hot, solitary, sad, often silent, watchful, discontent, *Montaltus, cap. 24.*[9] If anything trouble them, they cannot sleep, but fret themselves still, till another object mitigate or time wear it out. They have grievous passions and immoderate perturbations of the mind—fear, sorrow, &c.—yet not so continual but that they are sometimes merry, apt to profuse laughter, which is more to be wondered at. . . . [I]f they be ruddy,[10] they are delighted in jests and oftentimes scoffers themselves, conceited and merry, witty, of a pleasant disposition, and yet grievously melancholy anon after.

[Women's melancholy]

[T]he best and surest remedy of all is to see them well placed and married to good husbands in due time; [. . .] this [is] the ready cure, to give them content to their desires. I write not this to patronize any wanton, idle flirt, lascivious or light housewives, which are too forward many times, unruly, and apt to cast away themselves on him that comes next, without all care, counsel, circumspection, and judgment. If religion, good discipline, honest education, wholesome exhortation, fair promises, fame, and loss of good name, cannot inhibit and deter such (which to chaste and sober maids cannot choose but avail much), labor and exercise, strict diet, rigor and threats, may more opportunely be used, and are able of themselves to qualify and divert an ill-disposed temperament. For seldom shall you see a hired servant, a poor handmaid, although ancient, that is kept hard to her work and bodily labor, [or] a coarse country wench troubled in this kind. But rather noble virgins, nice gentlewomen, such as are solitary and idle, live at ease, lead a life out of action and employment, that fare well in great houses and jovial companies, ill-disposed peradventure of themselves, and not willing to make any resistance, discontented otherwise, of weak judgment, able bodies and subject to passions [. . .], such for the most part are misaffected and prone to this disease. I do not so much pity them that may otherwise be eased. But

[8]An 11th c. Arabian philosopher who wrote over 100 treatises on the natural sciences. His medicine was based on Galenic principles.

[9]Portuguese physician Filotea Eliao Montalto (d. 1616) wrote a work on optics.

[10]Of a sanguine humor, cheerful and optimistic.

[in] those alone that out of a strong temperament [and an] innate constitution are violently carried away with this torrent of inward humors [. . .] yet cannot make resistance—these grievances will appear, this malady will take place, and now manifestly show itself, and may not otherwise be helped.

### [The dangers of celibacy]

How odious and abominable are those superstitious and rash vows of popish monasteries to bind and enforce men and women to vow virginity, to lead a single life against the laws of nature, opposite to religion, policy, and humanity, so to starve, to offer violence, to suppress the vigor of youth by rigorous statutes, severe laws, vain persuasions, to debar them of that to which by their innate temperature they are so furiously inclined, urgently carried, and sometimes precipitated, even irresistibly led, to the prejudice of their soul's health and good estate of body and mind! [. . .] Better marry than burn, saith the Apostle,[11] but they are otherwise persuaded. They will by all means quench their neighbor's house if it be on fire, but that fire of lust, which breaks out into such lamentable flames, they will not take notice of; their own bowels oftentimes, flesh and blood, shall so rage and burn, and they will not see it.

[11]Paul; see 1 Corinthians 7.9: "But if they cannot contain, let them marry: for it is better to marry than to burn." By "burn" Paul means either to suffer sexual frustration or indulge in sex out of wedlock and thus burn in sin.

# Purgatory

The Christian doctrine of purgatory is at least as old as the church itself and may even derive from the ancient Jewish belief in prayers for the dead noted in the Apocrypha, the fourteen books appended to the Old Testament and accepted by Catholics as Scripture. In one of these books, Judas asks his host to pray for their comrades killed in battle and sends money to Jerusalem to compensate for their sins (2 Macc. 12.42–44). A rationale for the doctrine is suggested by one of the early church doctors, Clement of Alexandria (150–216?). Asking what can be expected of those who die without having fulfilled the requirement of penance, he answers:

> the believer through discipline divests himself of his passions and passes to the mansion which is better than the former one, passes to the greatest torment, taking with him the characteristic of repentance for the faults he may have committed after baptism. He is tortured then still more, not yet attaining what he sees others have acquired. The greatest torments are assigned unto the believer, for God's righteousness is good, and His goodness righteous [ . . . ]. [T]hose punishments cease in the course of expiation and purification.

The idea that a soul undergoing purgation in this "mansion" can be helped by the prayers of the living is expressed by Ambrose of Alexandria (d. 250) in his funeral oration for the emperor Theodosius: "I loved him, therefore [ . . . ] I will not leave him till by my prayers and lamentations he shall be admitted unto the holy mount of the Lord to which his deserts call him." These concepts—of a place of purgation preparatory to entering heaven and the possibility of a loving communion of the living with those in purgatory— remain definitive for Roman Catholics, involving the belief in salvation through charitable works and in the church as a mystical body transcending the limits of real time and place. The doctrine of purgatory, which allowed for the satisfaction of or retribution for venial (though not mortal) sin, was established as a feature of Catholic theology by the councils of Lyons (1274) and Florence (1439); bishops were required to teach it to the faithful by the Council of Trent (1545–1563).

Protestants rejected the doctrine of purgatory for the very reasons Catholics affirmed it. Denying the necessity of charitable works for salvation and insisting on faith alone, Protestants portrayed purgatory as a deception. Not only did the notion of purgation neglect the significance of Christ's sacrifice but also its social effects were a corruption: The sale of pardons and indulgences in order to buy time out of purgatory sapped charity that should have gone to relieve the poor and needy, and the clergy could not be counted on to spend this revenue wisely. The abuse of pardons and indulgences was protested by Simon Fish, probably a Lollard sympathizer, in *A Supplication for the Beggars* (1529). Scriptural objections to the doctrine of purgatory were detailed in *The Institution of Christian Religion* (1536) by John Calvin, the most prominent sixteenth-century Protestant theologian. John Véron pointed out that monies donated to buy time out of purgatory was a misuse of charity.

English Catholics meanwhile continued to promote "purgatory" both to strengthen the bonds among Catholics and to urge on the faithful the importance of doing penance for sin. Cardinal William Allen's *A Defense and Declaration of the Catholic Church's Doctrine, Touching Purgatory* (1577) stressed the fellowship of Catholics in life as well as in death and through the fires of purgatory, seeing purgatory as an expression of the "natural compassion of the church [that] passeth through every member thereof."

Cardinal Robert Bellarmine, in *The Art of Dying Well* (1622), regarded purgatory as a warning to the living: its pains far exceed those exacted by the penitential acts required of sinners still in this life. The doctrine of purgatory underscored the principal differences between theologies. For a Catholic, moral behavior in this life was a factor in eternal salvation, and purgatory was the means to atone for venial, if not mortal, sins. For a Protestant, Christ's sacrifice was entirely sufficient to save the faithful; to say that a Christian might earn salvation by moral action was to misread Scripture.

In *Hamlet*, it is the ghost of the old king, Hamlet's father, who refers to purgatory as his "prison-house," where for "a certain term" he is "confined to fast in fires, / Till the foul crimes done in my days of nature / Are burned and purged away" (1.5.11–14). His request to his son is not, however, for prayers or the purchase of indulgences, but for revenge on his murderer, the new king Claudius. This is not the kind of request that Catholic doctrine condoned, particularly from a sinful soul in purgatory. Christian precept, natural law, and English law and custom forbad individual acts of revenge; a wrongdoer was to be punished only by the law and according to its provisions. Even so, a vast and rich tradition of fictions, from Greek tragedy to Jacobean drama, was devoted to acts of vengeance and retribution, often validated on the grounds of personal honor. This tradition is illustrated by Laertes, who insists on taking revenge on Hamlet for his father's murder "in my terms of honor," although he is "satisfied in nature" that Hamlet acted in all innocence (5.2.244, 242). The extraordinary nature of the Ghost's request to Hamlet explains some of Hamlet's hesitation throughout the play. Even assuming the Ghost is "honest" and tells no lies, Hamlet risks his own damnation if he commits murder, a mortal sin. Read in light of Christian doctrine, the Ghost is suspect; if he is not a "goblin damn'd," he is also not "a spirit of health" (1.4.40).

## Simon Fish (d. 1531)

*Simon Fish was clearly interested in the new theology proposed by reformers on the continent. Committed to the study of God's word, he sold William Tyndale's translation of the New Testament to persons interested in the reformation of the church in England. On hearing Fish's attack on the doctrine of purgatory and the practice of granting indulgences in his* Supplication for the Beggars *(1529), Henry VIII is said to have responded, "If a man should pull down an old stone wall and begin at the lower part, the upper part thereof might chance to fall upon his head"—an image that warns against challenging clerical practice before the crown acquires supreme control of the church, as it did in 1537.*

## from *A Supplication for the Beggars*[1]
### [Clerical greed and the doctrine of purgatory]

Neither have they any other color[2] to gather these yearly exactions[3] into their hands, but that they say they pray for us to God to deliver our souls out of the pains of purgatory, without whose prayer, they say, or at least without the Pope's pardon, we could never be delivered thence; which if it be true, then is it good reason that we give them all these things, although were it a hundred times as much. But there be many men of great literature and judgment that—for the love they have unto the truth and unto the commonwealth—have not feared to put themselves into the greatest infamy that may be in abjection of[4] all the world, ye, in peril of death, to declare their opinion in this matter; which is that there is no purgatory, but that it is a thing invented by the covetousness of the spirituality,[5] only to translate all kingdoms from other princes unto them, and that there is not one word spoken of it in all Holy Scripture. They say also that if there were a purgatory, and also that if the pope with his pardons for money may deliver one soul thence, he may deliver him as well without money; if he may deliver one, he may deliver a thousand; if he may deliver a thousand, he may deliver them all, and so destroy purgatory. And then is he a cruel tyrant without all charity if he keep them there in prison and in pain till men will give him money. Likewise, say they—of all the whole sort of the spirituality—that if they will not pray for no man but for them that give them money, they are tyrants and lack charity, and suffer those souls to be punished and pained uncharitably for lack of their prayers. These sort of folks they call heretics, these they burn, these they rage against, put to open shame, and make them bear faggots. But whether they be heretics or not, well I wote that this purgatory and the Pope's pardons is [sic] all the cause of translation of your kingdom so fast into their hands,[6] wherefore it is manifest it cannot be of Christ, for he gave more to

---

[1]Simon Fish, *A Supplication for the Beggars,* ed. Frederick J. Furnivall, London, 1871; pp. 10–11.

[2]Justification.

[3]Tithes were collected annually (an indulgence was granted occasionally for a consideration).

[4]In abasement before.

[5]Clergy.

[6]Fish claims that the commonwealth or the property of the people is being transferred to the church by those seeking remission from time in purgatory.

the temporal kingdom, he himself paid tribute to Caesar, he took nothing from him but taught that the high powers should be always obeyed; ye, he himself (although he were most free lord of all and innocent) was obedient unto the high powers unto death.

## John Calvin (1509–1564)

*John Calvin provided the Protestant reformation with its most articulate apologist. Trained in theology and law, he conveyed a vision of human affairs in relation to divine action that comprehended the course of human history from its beginnings in the Fall from Paradise to the Last Judgment and the end of time. Educated to be a Catholic priest, Calvin was given the curacy of the parish of St. Martin de Marteville in 1527 at the age of eighteen. Electing to study law, he then settled in Bourges, where he worked with the great Italian jurist Andrea Alciati. He went on to learn Greek and Hebrew, immersing himself in Scripture, and in 1534, after experiencing a sudden conversion to reformist thinking, he resigned his Catholic offices and began his life's work, The Institution of Christian Religion, a work that went into many editions. This profoundly analytical exposition of Christian doctrine covers its essential elements: law, faith, prayer, sacraments, false sacraments, and Christian liberty. The following excerpts are taken from its chapters on prayer.*

*Calvin reads Scripture with an unfailing commitment to discovering its divine reasonableness: he argues that because God is omnipotent, the shaper of human history, man can have no other part in its drama than as God's instrument. Human nature, determined by its derivation from the fallen Adam and Eve, is inherently sinful, yet it can be inspired by the Holy Spirit. God may impute the righteousness of Christ to the penitent, although the divine choice is inscrutable. Calvin's sharp distinction between divine power and human weakness is the basis of his repudiation of the doctrine of purgatory. Man is not to be saved by works, acts that he may have experienced as willed or chosen; he has to rely on God's saving grace, the scriptural promise of Christ's perfect atonement for human sin. At the time of its publication, Calvin's theology effectively undermined the grand moral and spiritual economy that had sustained the Catholic Church since its beginning.*

*In danger of arrest by French authorities, Calvin lived for a time in Basel and eventually settled in Geneva, where he continued his scholarly and ecclesiastical work by amplifying* The Institution, *writing* A Commentary on the Epistle to Romans *and other works of theology, and establishing that city as a Protestant theocracy. He died in Geneva in 1564.*

## from *The Institution of Christian Religion*[1]
### [The Catholic practice of granting pardons and indulgences]

Out of this doctrine of satisfactions do flow indulgences or pardons. For they say that that which our power wanteth to make satisfaction is supplied by these pardons. And they run so far forth into madness that they define them to be the distribution of the merits of Christ and of the martyrs, which the Pope dealeth abroad by his bulls.[2] But although they have more need of *helleborus*[3] to purge their frantic brain than arguments to answer them, so that it is not much worthy the travail to stand upon confuting such trifling errors, which are already shaken with many battlerams and of themselves grow into decayed age and bend toward falling, yet because a short confutation of them shall be profitable for some that be ignorant, I will not altogether omit it. As for this: that pardons have so long stood safe and have so long been unpunished, having been used with so outrageous and furious licentiousness . . . may serve to teach us in how dark a night of errors men in certain ages past have been drowned. They saw themselves to be openly and uncoloredly scorned of the Pope and his Bullbearers; [they saw themselves as] gainful markets to be made of the salvation of their souls, the price of salvation to be valued at a few pence and nothing set out to be freely given; [they saw] that by this color they be wiped of offerings to be filthily spent upon brothels, bawds and bankerings,[4] that the greatest blowers abroad of pardons are the greatest despisers of them, that this monster doth daily more and more with greater licentiousness overrun the world and grow into outrage, and that there is no end, new lead daily brought and new money gotten. Yet with high reverence they received, they worshipped and bought pardons, and such as among the rest saw somewhat farther,

---

[1]John Calvin, *The Institution of Christian Religion*, trans. Thomas Norton, London, 1587; pp. 218, 219 verso, 220, 220 verso.

[2]An edict, order, or official document from the Pope could grant a formal pardon for sins.

[3]Plant thought to have healing power.

[4]By this device, their offerings would be taken to pay for the luxuries bought by clergy. Bankerings are feasts.

yet thought them to be godly deceits whereby men might be beguiled with some profit. At the length, since the world suffered itself to be somewhat wise, pardons wax cold[5] and by little and little become frozen till they utterly vanish away.

[Why the practice of granting pardons and
indulgences denies the words of the gospel]

Now [. . .] who taught the Pope to enclose in lead and parchment the grace of Jesus Christ, which the Lord willed to be distributed by the word of the Gospel? Truly either the gospel of God must be false, or their pardons false. For, that Christ is offered us in the gospel, with all abundance of heavenly benefits, with all his merits, with all his righteousness, wisdom and grace, without any exception, Paul witnesseth where he saith that the word of reconciliation was delivered to the ministers, whereby they might use this form of message, as it were Christ giving exhortation by them: "we beseech you, be ye so reconciled to God."[6] He hath made him that knew no sin to be made sin for us, that we might be made the righteousness of God in him. And the faithful know of what value is that common partaking of Christ, which (as the same Apostle witnesseth) is offered us to be enjoyed in the Gospel. Contrariwise the pardons do bring out [of] the storehouse of the Pope a certain pittance of grace and fasten it to lead parchment, yea and to a certain place,[7] and sever it from the word of God. If a man should ask whence this abuse took beginning: it seemeth to have proceeded hereof, that when in time past penitents were charged with more rigorous satisfactions than all could bear, they which felt themselves above measure oppressed with penance enjoined them, required of the church a release. The mitigation that was granted to such was called an indulgence or pardon. But when they turned satisfactions from the church to God, and said that they were recompenses whereby men may redeem themselves from the judgment of God, then they therewithal did also draw these indulgences or pardons to be propitiatory remedies to deliver us from deserved punishments. As for these blasphemers that we have recited, they forged them so shamelessly that they can have no color at all.

[5]Become unpopular.
[6]Paul asks that ministers preach salvation by faith alone.
[7]Where the indulgence was issued.

### [Purgatory is a device of Satan]

Now let them no more trouble us with their purgation, because it is with this axe already broken, hewed down, and overthrown from the very foundations. For I do not agree to [sic] some men that think best to dissemble in this point and make no mention at all of purgatory, whereupon (as they say) great contentions do arise, but small edification is gotten. Truly I myself would also think such trifles worthy to be negligently passed over, if they did not account them earnest matters. But forasmuch as purgatory is built of many blasphemies, and is daily upheld with new blasphemies, and raiseth up many and grievous offenses, truly it is not to be winked at. This peradventure might after a sort have been dissembled for a time, that it was invented by curious and bold rashness without the word of God; that men believed of it by I wot[8] not what revelations, feigned by the craft of Satan; that for the confirmation of it certain places of Scripture were fondly wrested. Albeit the Lord giveth not leave to man's presumptuousness so to break into the secret places of his judgments, and hath severely forbidden men to enquire for truth at dead men, neglecting his word, and permitteth not his word to be so unreverently defiled. But let us grant, that all those things might for a while have been borne with as things of no great importance. But when the cleansing of sins is sought elsewhere than in the blood of Christ, when satisfaction is given away to any other thing, then it is most perilous not to speak of it. Therefore we must cry out not only with vehement stretching of our voice, but also of our throat and sides[9]: that purgatory is the damnable device of Satan, that it maketh void the cross of Christ, that it layeth an intolerable slander upon the mercy of God, that it feebleth and overthroweth our faith. For what else is purgatory among them but the satisfaction that the souls of men departed to pay after their death? So that overthrowing the opinion of satisfaction, purgatory is immediately overthrown by the very roots. But if in our former discourse it is more than evident that the blood of Christ is the only satisfaction, propitiatory sacrifice, and cleansing for the sins of the faithful, what remaineth but that purgatory is a mere and horrible blasphemy against Christ? I pass over the robberies of God wherewith

[8]Know.
[9]Lungs.

it is daily defended, the offenses that it breedeth in religion, and other things innumerable, which we see to have come out of the same spring of ungodliness.

## John Véron (d. 1563)

*After studying theology in Orleans, John Véron, a Huguenot clergyman, settled in England in 1536. He was ordained under Edward VI in 1551, was deprived of his benefice under Mary in 1554, and became vicar of St. Sepulchre under Elizabeth in 1560. A staunch supporter of continental reformers, he followed their lead by writing treatises on free will, against justification by works, and on clerical marriage. The* Hunting of Purgatory to Death *follows Calvin's reasons for repudiating the doctrine of purgatory and emphasizes forms of charity particularly enjoined of Protestants: helping the living and serving their "brethren," neighbors, and fellow citizens.*

### from The Hunting of Purgatory to Death[1]
[The greed of the clergy promotes belief in purgatory]

The causes that did move me to write this present book are so manifest and known of all men that I need not in a manner but to open them. First and foremost, we see that if this feigned purgatory and vain opinion of praying for the dead, which be only grounded upon the foolish imaginations and dreams of a sort of superstitious and covetous persons, were once taken away, their abominable and most blasphemous sacrifice of the mass—wherewith they do altogether blaspheme and tread under feet the whole merits of the earth,[2] passion and bloodshedding of our savior Jesus Christ—could never take place again, what alteration or change soever for our ingratitude and unthankfulness ensue and follow. For take away the lucre and gains that the popish priests have had by saying of masses for the dead, and then few or none will they say, so that this popish merchant being once driven away from among Christian men, Mistress Missa[3]

[1] John Véron, *The Hunting of Purgatory to Death*, London, 1561; sigs. Aiiii–Avii.
[2] The body.
[3] The mass.

hath lost the chiefest stay and best friend that she hath in all the world and is never like to recover.

Secondly, by this abominable doctrine of purgatory, the true purgatory of the Christians, which is the most precious blood of the only begotten son of God, our savior Jesus Christ that doth truly purge and cleans us from all our sins, when by the hearing of God's word our hearts are through faith sprinkled with it, is altogether abolished. Yea, Christ himself is made an imperfect and as it were half a savior and of less authority and power than their holy father the pope is. For where as they do attribute unto their Antichrist[4] authority and power to absolve men, *a paena et culpa*,[5] that is to say from the offence and the punishment that is due unto it, they be not ashamed to say that Christ doth only by his death deliver us from the offence, and that we must suffer the pain or punishment that is due unto our sins in the fire of purgatory and there make satisfaction[6] for them; and that if any do escape without going through this roasting fire of theirs, it is because they have done their penance and made full satisfaction for their sins in this life. Who could hear our savior Jesus Christ, the merits of his death and passion, and the efficacy and virtue of his bloodshedding thus horribly to be blasphemed and hold his peace?

## [How to live godly[7] in this world]

Moreover as long as men's minds be possessed with such vain opinion that they can make satisfaction for their sins in the fire of purgatory, and that they may be delivered from thence for a piece of money, who will care to live godly in this world or to make restitution of the goods that he hath wrongfully gotten, sith[8] the paying a little tribute and as it were part of the booty unto the priests, he may be assoiled and acquitted of all his robberies and immediately be delivered from those intolerable pains and torments, or not come into them at all, if he will in his lifetime with a sum of money purchase a general pardon of all his sins, that is to say from the pain

---

[4]"Antichrist" was a Protestant term for the erroneous Christ they claimed was worshipped by the Roman Catholics.

[5]From punishment to blame.

[6]Atone.

[7]For Protestants, "godly" described the behavior and practices of a devout Christian, faithful to the Calvinist principles of predestination and salvation by faith alone.

[8]Since.

and offence at the bishop of Rome's hand? Whereas on the contrary, if men were thoroughly persuaded that there is none other purgatory but the blood of our savior Jesus Christ, taken hold upon through a lively faith working through charity, and that there is no hope of pardon and forgiveness to be obtained at God's hands except we do to the uttermost of our power endeavor ourselves to be reconciled unto our brethren, and to make amends and restitution unto them that we have done wrong and injury unto, and not to a sort of gaping ravens which we never offended, then would they live otherwise than they do, and take better heed how they get their goods. And if they have taken wrongfully away any man's goods, they would seek all manner of means for to agree with their adversary, that is to say, with their neighbor and brother, whom they have offended and wronged, while they be yet in the way and in this present life. They would not tarry to make restitution and to be at unity and peace, both with God and their neighbor.

## Cardinal William Allen (1532–1594)

*The written work of William Allen illustrates how strongly the recusant movement in England (comprising its Roman Catholic subjects) could register its beliefs during the last decades of the sixteenth century. Refusing the Oath of Supremacy, which established that the monarch, Queen Elizabeth, was the head of the English church, Allen left England in 1565, visiting thereafter only on short trips. He founded a college for training English priests at Douai in northern France in 1568, where he and his colleagues began the translation into Latin of a Bible designed especially for Catholics. Having known of Spanish plans for invading England in 1587, he was in no position to continue his influence in England after the defeat of the Armada in 1588. He died in poverty in Rome in 1594.*

*His treatise in defense of the doctrine of purgatory, published in 1577, stresses the responsibility of Catholics to make restitution for their sins within the setting of the mystical church in which "every good work of any one member wonderfully redoundeth to all the rest." On Allen's account, purgatory not only provides a term and a place for the restitution of venial sin after death but also offers the living a way to maintain contact with the dead through acts of charity. Allen envisages a Catholic Church held together in a "unity of love" that has existed from the moment of its foundation. To assert anything else, he states, is to take refuge in a "cloaked paganism."*

## from *A Defense and Declaration of the Catholic Church's Doctrine, Touching Purgatory*[1]

### [One finds salvation within the body of the church]

As it is most true, and the very ground of all Christian comfort, that Christ's death hath paid duly and sufficiently for the sins of all the world, by that abundant price of redemption paid upon the cross, so it is of like credit to all faithful that no man was ever partaker of this singular benefit but in the knot and unity of his body mystical which is the church, to the members whereof the streams of his holy blood and beams of his grace for the remission of sin and sanctification be orderly, through the blessed sacraments as conduits of God's mercy, conveyed. For as in baptism, where man is perfectly renewed, it was seemly to set the offender at this first entrance on clear ground, and make him free for all things done abroad, so it exceedingly setteth forth God's justice and nothing impaireth his mercy to use (as in all commonwealths by nature and God's prescription if practiced) with grace, discipline; with justice, clemency; with favor, correction; and with love, due chastisement of such sins as have by the household children been committed. Now therefore, if after thy free admission to this family of Christ, thou do grievously offend, remission may then be had again, but not commonly without sharp discipline, seeing the father of this our holy household punisheth where he loveth and chastiseth every child whom he receiveth. Whose justice in punishment of sin not only the wicked but also the good must fear.

### [Purgatory]

After the sins of man be pardoned, God oftentimes punisheth the offender, the church punisheth him, and man punisheth himself, ergo there is some pain due after sin be remitted. Secondly, this pain cannot always be discharged in this world, either for lack of space after the remission, as it happeth in repentance at the hour of death, or else when the party liveth in perpetual wealth without care or cogitation of any satisfaction; therefore it must be answered in another place. Thirdly, the common infirmities and the daily trespasses which abase

[1]Cardinal William Allen, *A Defense and Declaration of the Catholic Church's Doctrine, Touching Purgatory,* London, 1577; pp. 31–33, 90, 197, 202, 252–253.

and defile the works even of the virtuous, of their proper condition do deserve pain for a time, as the mortal offence deserveth perpetual. Therefore as the mortal sin, being not here pardoned, must of justice have the reward of everlasting punishment, so it must needs follow that the venial fault, not here forgiven, should have the reward which of nature it requireth: that is to say, temporal pain.

And therefore not only the wicked but the very just also must travail to have their daily infirmities and frailty of their corrupt natures forgiven: crying without ceasing "forgive us our debts." [ . . . ] For no man alive shall be able to stand before the face of God in his own justice or righteousness, and if these light sins should never be imputed, then it were needless to cry for mercy or confess debt, as every man doth, be he never so passing holy. To be brief, this debt of pain for sin, by any way remaining at the departure hence, must of justice be answered: Which, [as this] cannot be without punishment in the next life, then there must a place of judgment for temporal and transitory pains in the other world.

### [The communion of the faithful with the dead]

But now what means may be found to ease our brethren departed of their pain? Or what ways can be acceptable in the sight of God to procure mercy and grace, where the sufferers themselves, being out of the state of deserving and place of well working, cannot help themselves, nor by any motion of mind attain more mercy than their life past did deserve? Where shall we then find ease for them? Surely nowhere else but in the unity and knot of that holy fellowship, in which the benefit of the head pertaineth to all the members and every good work of any one member wonderfully redoundeth to all the rest. This society is called in our creed the communion of saints, that is to say, a blessed brotherhood under Christ the head, by love and religion so wrought and wrapped together that what any one member of this fast body hath, the other lacketh it not; what one wanteth the other supplieth; when one smarteth all feeleth in a manner the life sorrow; when one joyeth, the other rejoyseth withall. [ . . . ] The souls and saints in heaven, the faithful people on earth, the chosen children that suffer chastisement in purgatory, are, by the perfect bond of this unity, as one aboundeth, ready to serve the other; as one lacketh, to crave of the other. The souls happily promoted to the joy of Christ's blessed kingdom in this unity and knot of love, perpetually pray for the doubtful state of their own fellows beneath: the careful condition of the members below, continually crieth for help at their hands in heaven above. [ ... ]

[T]his natural compassion of the church, passeth through every member thereof, and ought to move every man by the law of nature to procure as much help as he may. And so much the more do we owe this natural duty unto them, because they now cannot help themselves, being out of the state of deserving and place of well working, only abiding God's mercy in the sore sufferance of pains intolerable. They themselves, as yet your brethren and a portion of your body, require to be partakers of your benefits. They feel ease of every prayer; your alms quensheth their heat, your fasting releaseth their pain, your sacrifice wipeth their sins and sores; so strong is the communion of saints, that, whatsoever you do that is acceptable, it issueth abundantly down to them.

[How those in purgatory benefit from the prayers of the living]

The benefit bestowed upon the poor is a sovereign ground of God's rewarding. And in thy oblations[2] for the departed, have always the same intent and scope that a father hath practising for the recovery of his sick child, being young and tender, who, for his sick son, bringeth into the church of our Lord God, wax, oil, incense, and with devotion and faith lighteth them in the boy's behalf. For that the child himself, being wholly unskillful of the ordinances of our Christianity, would never go about any such thing, even so must a man think of the deceased person's case, that he may and doth offer (as in another man's person) wax, oil and such like, as commonly for redemption are offered. [ ... ] The reader as he list, may perchance with more leisure, or at least with less injury to other, weigh the wonderful waste that sin and heresy hath wrought in our days of darkness. And when he considereth these things, that be now of most men counted mere madness, to have been liked, allowed, preached, avouched, sent out in solemn works and writings—to the view of the world and the sight of all posterity—from the very heart and spring of the Christian church, [ ... ] shall he not wonder with all wise men at our downfall so deep? Shall he not marvel [that] under one name

---

[2]Prayers.

of Christianity, that goeth yet common to our days with those happy times past, [there is] such diversity of case and conditions that the one under so glorious a name must be nothing else but a cloaked paganism? But yet I would not he should occupy over-much his mind in this consideration, till he see the whole rank of God's holy host and all the blessed band of martyrs and saints stand with us for the full defense of truth and the common church, their mother and ours.

## Cardinal Robert Bellarmine (1542–1621)

*Born a Catholic in Italy, Robert Bellarmine remained a staunch opponent of the reformed religion all his life. Entering the Society of Jesus in 1560 at the age of eighteen, he lectured on theological controversy at the University of Louvain. He was made a cardinal in 1599 and the bishop of Monte Pulciano in 1607. His major work—a three-volume critique of Protestant thought and practice,* Disputationes de Controversiis Christianae Fidei, *or* Disputations on the Controversies of the Christian Faith—*forced his Protestant opponents to answer his objections point by point. In quite a different vein, his simply styled* The Art of Dying Well *stresses for lay readers how strenuous regimes of penance could help avoid the pains of purgatory.*

### from *The Art of Dying Well*[1]

[What is satisfaction?]

There remaineth satisfaction,[2] of which our ancestors, most wise and prudent men, did make far more account then we seem now to do. For they, when seriously they did consider that it was far more easy to make satisfaction unto God on earth, than in purging flames of the next life, did impose most heavy and very long penalties. And as for time, they enjoined penances of seven years, of fifteen, of thirty, and sometimes of their whole life; and as for the quality, they enjoined very frequent fasts and yet more frequent prayers. Again,

---

[1]Robert Bellarmine, *The Art of Dying Well*, St. Omer, France, 1622; pp. 129–131.
[2]Recompense for sins.

they did forbid their penitents to go to the baths[3]; they should not ride, go in coach, or use any bravery[4] in apparel; [ . . . ] they should abstain from plays, from sports, from spectacles in the open theaters; and finally their whole life was consumed as it were in grief and mourning as became true penitents.

Now we are become so weak and tender, forsooth, that a penance imposed of fasting in bread and water for a few days, with the seven psalms and litanies to be rehearsed in the same, and an alms of a little money bestowed on the poor, doth seem severe enough, although it be imposed for cleansing the soul from many great sins and enormities. But that wherein here we favor ourselves, we shall grievously smoke for in purgatory, God's justice requiring full satisfaction, unless in this life our contrition be so great as proceeding from most fervent charity that it be able to obtain of the mercy of God, full remission and pardon of all sin and punishment due unto the same.

[3]The public baths were considered to be places in which indecent or lascivious actions were tolerated.

[4]Ostentation.

# Revenge

To explore the workings of justice in a Christian society, Shakespeare draws on themes and motifs traditionally associated with revenge tragedy. Unlike the popular revenge tragedies of the late Elizabethan and early Stuart theater, however—Marlowe's *Jew of Malta* (1592), Kyd's *The Spanish Tragedy* (1592), Shakespeare's own *Titus Andronicus* (1594), and Middleton's *The Revenger's Tragedy* (1607)—*Hamlet* is thoroughly informed by Christian theology. Like any typical revenge tragedy, it lays out the impulse to revenge, but it also gestures toward the absolute prohibition of revenge in divine and positive law. And while traditional revenge tragedy tends not to invoke providence, *Hamlet* suggests that a providential order inheres in human affairs.

The politics of revenge are not less problematized. As head of state, Claudius, even if tyrannical, wields supreme judicial power. As a regicide (though not quite a usurper—he was elected to the throne of Denmark), he has come by this power illicitly. By 1600, English political thought was divided as to rights of resistance in such cases. Most opinion declared that a wronged subject had no recourse against tyranny but prayer. But Hamlet is not just a wronged subject; he is also a prince and prospective heir to the throne. Do Claudius's crime and therefore his illicit rule put Hamlet in a privileged position? Indeed, do they go some way toward making Hamlet de facto king of Denmark, one who, by rightfully punishing his uncle, transforms an act of revenge into one of an exemplary justice? Such is the implication of the Ghost's request to Hamlet to revenge his murder. But would a soul in purgatory make such a request? The action of the play raises these questions without answering them. The Biblical prohibition against revenge was absolute, but commentary on relevant passages in Scripture varied. William Dickinson stressed the function of positive law in maintaining justice throughout the realm, Thomas Beard reflected on providential punishments, and Francis Bacon considered situations in which revenge might be justified.

## The Bible

*In Shakespeare's day, English men and women believed that Scripture was the Word of God and the equivalent of divine law. Like natural law, comprised in the unwritten primal codes of conduct shared by all people, divine law was thought to provide positive law, decided by the courts and made by statute in Parliament, with its immutable foundations. Cain's mark and God's words on vengeance announced in both Old and New Testaments (Leviticus, Deuteronomy, Hebrews, and Romans) not only illustrated a universal prohibition against vengeful murder but also implied the law administered by the state and sanctioned by God. Persons harmed by particular injuries had to seek satisfaction in courts of justice. Claudius identifies himself as "Cain" when he speaks of his "offence" as one that has "the primal eldest curse upon it" (3.3.37) and so calls into question any right to revenge that Hamlet, a Christian, might claim. When urged to revenge by his beloved father, Hamlet confronts a hideous dilemma: either he fails to honor his father or he damns himself with the sin of murder.*

### from Genesis 4.9–15[1]

Then the Lord said unto Cain, Where is Abel thy brother? Who answered, I cannot tell. Am I my brother's keeper? Again he said, What hast thou done? the voice of thy brother's blood crieth unto me from the ground. Now therefore thou art cursed from the earth which hath opened her mouth to receive thy brother's blood from thine hand. When thou shalt till the ground, it shall not henceforth yield unto thee her strength: a vagabond and a renegade shalt thou be in the earth. Then Cain said to the Lord, My punishment is greater than I can bear. Behold, thou hast cast me out this day from the earth, and from thy face shall I be hid,

---

[1]The Bible and Holy Scriptures, Geneva, 1560. This translation into English of the Hebrew and Greek bibles remained the standard text for English Protestants who leaned toward Puritanism. It was followed by the less popular (and less "godly") Bishops' Bible, published in London in 1568.

and shall be a vagabond and a renegade in the earth, and whosoever findeth me shall slay me. Then the Lord said unto him, Doubtless whosoever slayeth Cain, he shall be punished sevenfold. And the Lord set a mark upon Cain lest any man finding him should kill him.

### from Romans 12.19

Dearly beloved, avenge not yourselves, but give place unto wrath: for it is written, Vengeance is mine: I will repay, saith the Lord.

## William Dickinson (b. 1585)

*Endorsing divine right theory, William Dickinson asserts the absolute right of kings to assume judicial power and to assign it to their magistrates as required. Stressing positive law's derivation from the Word of God, Dickinson declares that it prohibits an individual person from taking vengeful action on his own and insists that the monarch's subjects adhere to prescribed legal procedures.*

### from *The King's Right*[1]

[The subject's place; the sovereign's power]

[L]et every one, whether he be a vessel of honor or dishonor, content himself with his place and submit his will to the obedience of those laws which his maker hath set down to be observed. And of all creatures men have most cause to yield their obedience unto God as the judge, not only because *Quia fecit*, he made them, *Sed donavit* too, he hath bestowed on them those honors and privileges which may justly challenge this acknowledgement from them, that he is the judge. [ . . . ] [I]t hath pleased God even from the beginning to rule and judge by men. Some power he hath put over and deputed to such amongst us as he knoweth fittest for so high a calling. [ . . . ]

[N]ot only our goods and bodies but our lives also ought to be subject to secular princes in that they may lawfully require. To whom then God said *Dii estis*: ye are gods, they are kings, princes, law-givers, and the judges of earth [ . . . ] . And again, they who are

---

[1]William Dickinson, *The King's Right*, London, 1619; sigs. B4 verso, C verso, C2, D2.

kings, and law-givers, and judges are gods, as it is in Exodus 22 [8]: Thou shalt not revile the gods, nor curse the ruler of the people. But some will say, all kings and judges do not behave themselves in their places as gods; some are usurpers, others tyrants, many are profane and wicked persons, neither fearing god, nor regarding man: But to cut these men off from their conclusion, they must understand that notwithstanding the person and power of the king, [he] is always sacred and inviolable.[2] It is not for those whom God hath appointed to obey to examine titles and pedigrees, or how kings came to their power and to be rulers over them. It sufficeth that being under we must obey, not only for fear but for conscience sake, lest through our disobedience, our conscience accuse us for resisting the ordinance of God, for the powers that be are ordained of God.[3]

[But] all men are not willing to hear of this doctrine. When passion leads the line, we may observe every particular man almost to take upon him to be a god, and the judge, and a revenger to execute wrath upon him that doth evil. Who is reviled, that back-bitheth not again? Who is threatened, that threatneth not? Who is in any sort offended and crossed, that seeketh not revenge? [ . . . ] All of us, I know not by what ill spirit set on, being desperately prone both to give and execute sentence upon our own wrongs (if happily[4] wrongs) by dint of sword and bloody death. Beloved, what high presumption is it and boldness, that for every sleight affront and idle word the king must have a subject, or two, or more ravished from him? [ . . . ] Amongst other reasons why God appointed and set up kings and princes to rule over the Sons of men, I think this was not the least, that in so quarrelling a generation, and so prone to blood and violence, every man might not be the judge and revenger of his own grief, and that wrath and passion might not take the place of law. Leave a passage for this insolence, let every man have the freedom of his own sword, suffer them to abuse their own bodies and lives unto the satisfying of the bloody purpose of their own or other mean desperate and malicious disposition, there will soon be an end of all civil society, and good order amongst the affairs of men.

---

[2]A king is beyond the power of positive law.

[3]"Let every soul be subject unto the higher powers. For there is no power but of God; the powers that be are ordained of God." Romans 13.1.

[4]Haply, by chance.

## Thomas Beard (d. 1632)

*Thomas Beard, the Puritan schoolmaster of Oliver Cromwell, is known for his treatise on the severe and immutable justice of God, superior in its providential outcomes to any that could be devised by a human judge. Beard illustrates why Christians who left vengeance to God could hope for justice in this world even under corrupt and tyrannical kings. Unlike Shakespeare's Richard III, Beard's account of Richard's reign does not mention the decisive role of Henry Richmond, afterward Henry VII, in opposing Richard's tyranny. Rather, he stresses what he regards as divinely authorized: Richard's spiritual torment when alive and the physical degradation of his body when dead.*

### from *The Theater of God's Judgments*[1]
[The fate of those who murder their rulers]

Among this rank of murderers of kings we may fitly place also Richard the third, usurper of the crown of England, and divers others which he used as instruments to bring his detestable purpose to effect: as namely, Sir James Tirrell knight, a man for nature's gifts worthy to have served a much better prince then this Richard if he had well served God, and been endued with as much truth and honesty as he had strength and wit; also Miles Forest and John Dighton, two villains fleshed in murders. But to come to the fact. It was on this sort: when Richard the usurper had enjoined Robert Brackenbury to this piece of service of murdering the young king Edward the fifth, his nephew, in the tower, with his brother the duke of York, and saw it refused by him [Brackenbury], he committed the charge of the murder to Sir James Tirrell. [He], hastening to the tower by the king's commission, received the keys into his own hands, and by the help of those two butchers, Dighton and Forest, smothered the two princes in their bed and buried them at the stair's feet; which being done, Sir James rode back to king Richard, who gave him great thanks and as some say, made him knight for his labor. All which things on every part well pondered, it appeareth that God never gave the world a notabler example, both of the inconstancy of worldly weal, and also of the wretched end which ensueth such despiteful cruelty. [F]or first to

[1]Thomas Beard, *The Theater of God's Judgments*, London, 1597; pp. 225, 229.

begin with the ministers: Miles Forest rotted away piecemeal at St Martin's; Sir James Tirrell died at the tower hill beheaded for treason; king Richard himself (as it is declared elsewhere) was slain in the field, hacked and hewed of his enemies, carried on horseback dead, his hair in despite torn and tugged like a dog. [B]esides the inward torments of his guilty conscience were more than all the rest, for it is most certainly reported that after this abominable deed done, he never had quiet in his mind. [W]hen he went abroad his eye whirled about, his body was privily fenced, his hand ever upon his dagger, his countenance and manner like one always ready to strike, his sleep short and unquiet, full of fearful dreams, insomuch that he would often suddenly start up and leap out of his bed, and run about the chamber, his restless conscience was so continually tossed and tumbled with the tedious impression of that abominable murder.

## Francis Bacon (1561–1626)

*Deeply informed by the history and philosophy of the classical past, the literary works of Francis Bacon represent the final flowering of English humanist thought. His* Essays, *written over a twenty-five-year period and published in successive editions, address topics that are central to understanding how Shakespeare's audiences responded to* Hamlet. *"Of Revenge" represents the benefits that come to an injured party who renounces revenge; it also rather daringly approves of revenge for a wrong for "which there is no law to remedy," provided that the avenger is himself free from having to give an account of his actions to the law. "Of Delays" considers the importance of fortune and its timing in a manner that recalls the decisiveness of Brutus in* Julius Caesar *("There is a tide in the affairs of men / Which taken at the flood, leads on to fortune" [4.3.218–219]) and, by contrast, Hamlet's belief that it is useless to plan ahead. What happens, Hamlet argues at the end of the play, is mandated by providence: "The readiness is all" (5.2.220). "Of Suspicion" is a virtual lesson in court politics: Bacon counsels caution and circumspection, especially when confronting "men of base natures." Consider your suspicions to be true, he warns, but act so that your suspect does not hurt you. Hamlet is tormented by suspicion, not only of his uncle but also of his mother, of Ophelia, and of the lackeys Rosencrantz and Guildenstern. He dissembles to protect himself, not always successfully.*

**from *Essays*[1]**

Of Revenge.

Revenge is a kind of wild justice; which the more man's nature runs to, the more ought law to weed it out. For as for the first wrong, it doth but offend the law; but the revenge of that wrong putteth the law out of office. Certainly, in taking revenge, a man is but even with his enemy; but in passing it over, he is superior; for it is a prince's part to pardon. And Salomon, I am sure, saith, *It is the glory of a man to pass by an offence.* That which is past is gone, and irrevocable; and wise men have enough to do with things present and to come; therefore they do but trifle with themselves, that labor in past matters. There is no man doth a wrong for the wrong's sake; but thereby to purchase himself profit, or pleasure, or honor, or the like. Therefore why should I be angry with a man for loving himself better than me? And if any man should do wrong merely out of ill-nature, why, yet it is but like the thorn or briar, which prick and scratch, because they can do no other. The most tolerable sort of revenge is for those wrongs which there is no law to remedy; but then let a man take heed the revenge be such as there is no law to punish; else a man's enemy is still beforehand, and it is two for one.[2] Some, when they take revenge, are desirous the party should know whence it cometh. This the more generous.[3] For the delight seemeth to be not so much in doing the hurt as in making the party repent. But base and crafty cowards are like the arrow that flieth in the dark. Cosmus, duke of Florence,[4] had a desperate saying against perfidious or neglecting friends, as if those wrongs were unpardonable; *You shall read* (saith he) *that we are commanded to forgive our enemies; but you never read that we are commanded to forgive our friends.* But yet the spirit of Job was in a better tune: *Shall we* (saith he) *take good at God's hands, and not be content to take evil also?* And so of friends in a proportion. This is certain, that a man that studieth revenge keeps his own wounds

---

[1]Francis Bacon, *The Works of Francis Bacon*, eds. James Spedding, Robert Leslie Ellis, and Douglas Denon Heath, 15 vols., London, 1858; vol. 6, pp. 384–385, 427–428, 454–455. (The *Essays* were first published in 1597 and thereafter, in various editions, to 1625.)

[2]A revenger puts himself in jeopardy by exposing himself to punishment.

[3]Noble.

[4]Cosimo de Medici, 1519–1574, Duke of Florence and eventually Archduke of Tuscany.

green, which otherwise would heal and do well. Public revenges are for the most part fortunate; as that for the death of Caesar; for the death of Pertinax; for the death of Henry the Third of France; and many more.[5] But in private revenges it is not so. Nay rather, vindictive persons live the life of witches, who, as they are mischievous, so end they infortunate.[6]

## Of Delays.

Fortune is like the market; where many times, if you can stay a little, the price will fall. And again, it is sometimes like Sibylla's offer[7]; which at first offereth the commodity at full, then consumeth part and part, and still holdeth up the price. For occasion (as it is in the common verse) *turneth a bald noddle, after she hath presented her locks in front, and no hold taken;* or at least turneth the handle of the bottle first to be received, and after the belly, which is hard to clasp.[8] There is surely no greater wisdom than well to time the beginnings and onsets of things. Dangers are no more light, if they once seem light; and more dangers have deceived men than forced them. Nay, it were better to meet some dangers halfway, though they come nothing near, than to keep too long a watch upon their approaches; for if a man watch too long, it is odds he will fall asleep. On the other side, to be deceived with too long shadows (as some have been when the moon was low and shone on their enemies' back), and so to shoot off before the time[9]; or to teach dangers to come on, by over early buckling[10] towards them; is another extreme. The ripeness or unripeness of the occasion (as we said) must ever be well weighed; and generally it is good to commit the beginnings of all great actions to Argus with his hundred eyes, and

---

[5] "Fortunate" because beneficial to society. Julius Caesar was assassinated in 44 BCE by Brutus and other Roman senators who worried for the safety of the republic under Caesar's ambitions. Pertinax (d. 193) was Emperor of Rome for three months, then murdered for instituting governmental reforms. Although Henri III of France (1551–1589) defended the Catholic Church, he sought to accommodate the thought and practices of the Protestant Huguenots; this provoked Jacques Clément, a Dominican monk, to murder him.

[6] Unfortunate.

[7] The Sibyls were Roman goddesses of prophecy.

[8] Opportunities prove more difficult to grasp after the first moment.

[9] To mistake the actual nearness of a danger.

[10] Movement; literally, buckling up of armor.

the ends to Briareus with his hundred hands,[11] first to watch, and then to speed. For the helmet of Pluto,[12] which maketh the politic man go invisible, is secrecy in the counsel and celerity in the execution. For when things are once come to the execution, there is no secrecy comparable to celerity; like the motion of a bullet in the air, which flieth so swift as it outruns the eye.

## Of Suspicion.

Suspicions amongst thoughts are like bats amongst birds, they ever fly by twilight. Certainly they are to be repressed, or at the least well guarded[13]: for they cloud the mind; they lose friends; and they check with business, whereby business cannot go on currently and constantly. They dispose kings to tyranny, husbands to jealousy, wise men to irresolution and melancholy. They are defects, not in the heart, but in the brain; for they take place in the stoutest natures; as in the example of Henry the Seventh of England.[14] There was not a more suspicious man, nor a more stout. And in such composition they do small hurt. For commonly they are not admitted, but with examination,[15] whether they be likely or no? But in fearful natures they gain ground too fast. There is nothing makes a man suspect much, more than to know little; and therefore men should remedy suspicion by procuring to know more, and not to keep their suspicions in smother. What would man have? Do they think those they employ and deal with are saints? Do they not think they will have their own ends, and be truer to themselves than to them? Therefore there is no better way to moderate suspicions, than to account upon such suspicions as true and yet to bridle them as false. For so far a man ought to make use of suspicions, as to provide, as if that should be true that he suspects, yet it may do him no hurt. Suspicions that the mind of itself gathers are but

---

[11]Mythical herdsman Argos had eyes all over his body (later they appeared on the tail of the peacock). Briareus was one of four giants, each of whom had a hundred hands.

[12]Roman god of the underworld.

[13]Loose.

[14]Henry VII defeated Richard III at Bosworth Field in 1485 to become king in 1486; he is reported by Edward Hall, in *The Union of the Two Noble Families of Lancastyre and Yorke* (1548), to have been suspicious of his father-in-law Lord Thomas Stanley, who might have sided with Richard III out of fear that the king would execute his son, Lord Strange.

[15]A strong man examines the basis for his doubts and so remains free of their worst effects.

buzzes; but suspicions that are artificially nourished, and put into men's heads by the tales and whisperings of others, have stings. Certainly, the best mean to clear the way in this same wood of suspicions, is frankly to communicate them with the party that he suspects; for thereby he shall be sure to know more of the truth of them than he did before; and withal shall make that party more circumspect not to give further cause of suspicion. But this would not be done to men of base natures; for they, if they find themselves once suspected, will never be true. The Italian says, *Sospetto licentia fede*[16]; as if suspicion did give a passport to faith; but it ought rather to kindle it to discharge itself.

[16] "Suspicion drives out faith."

# *Suicide*

When Hamlet considers death a "consummation devoutly to be wished" (3.1.64–65), his profound despair suggests that he may be in no condition to respect the Christian prohibition against "self-slaughter" (1.2.129–132). The fact that suicide was forbidden did not stop writers and playwrights from representing it, especially if the situations they illustrated were drawn from the literature of the classical past. In so doing, they also elucidated its causes, often with great sympathy. Both Michel de Montaigne and John Sym show a deep concern for persons so driven by fear and shame that they can see no way to escape their misery other than through a self-inflicted death.

## Michel de Montaigne (1533–1592)

*The popular* Essaies *of Michel de Montaigne, published in 1580, 1588, and 1592 in France and first translated into English by John Florio in 1603, are among the most daring expressions of sixteenth-century humanist thought. Relying on a rhetoric designed to explore rather than to define a topic, Montaigne made a practice of representing his subjects in* utremque partem, *from opposing points of view.*

*"A Custom of the Isle of Cea," while it establishes that Christian doctrine prohibits suicide, also shows why in certain circumstances it was considered a plausible course of action in the pre-Christian world. Montaigne concludes by suggesting that he, at least, might find it possible to excuse a suicide in such situations as "a grieving-smart" and fear of "a worse death." Yet these categories are so vague that they*

*could be imagined as covering many different situations. Their very
vagueness in effect leaves conclusions to the reader.*

## from "A Custom of the Isle of Cea"[1]

### [The classical view of suicide]

*Death is a remedy against all evils*: It is a most assured haven, never
to be feared and often to be sought. All comes to one period,
whether man make an end of himself, or whether he endure it;
whether he run before his day, or whether he expect it; whenceso-
ever it come, it is ever his own; wherever the thread be broken, it is
all there; it's the end of the web. The voluntariest death is the
fairest. Life dependeth on the will of others, death on ours. In nothing should we so much accommodate ourselves to our humors as in
that. Reputation doth nothing concern such an enterprise, it is folly
to have any respect unto it. To live is to serve, if the liberty to die be
wanting. The common course of curing any infirmity is ever
directed at the charge of life; we have incisions made into us, we are
cauterized, we have limbs cut and mangled, we are let blood, we are
dieted. Go we but one step further, we need no more physic, we are
perfectly whole. Why is not our jugular or throat-vein as much at
our command as the mediane?[2] To extreme sicknesses, extreme
remedies. [ . . . ]

The Stoics say, it is a convenient natural life for a wise man to
forgo life although he abound in all happiness, if he do it opportunely; and for a fool to prolong his life, albeit he be most miserable, provided he be in most part of things which they say to be
according unto nature.[3] As I offend not the laws made against
thieves, when I cut mine own purse, and carry away mine own
goods; nor of destroyers when I burn mine own wood, so am I
nothing tied unto laws made against murderers, if I deprive myself
of mine own life.

### [Another view]

But this goeth not without some contradiction. For many are of the
opinion that without the express commandment of him that hath

---

[1]Michel de Montaigne, *The Essays of Michael Lord of Montaigne*, trans. John Florio, 3 vols., London, 1910; vol. 2, pp. 27–29, 34–35, 41.

[2]One of the secondary veins of the body, i.e., the veins in the forearm.

[3]That he possess most of the things that are agreed to be essential to human nature.

placed us in this world, we may by no means forsake the garrison of it, and that it is in the hands of God only, who therein hath placed us, not for ourselves alone but for his glory and others' service, whenever it shall please him to discharge us hence and not for us to take leave; that we are not born for ourselves, but for our country. The laws for their own interest require an account at our hands for ourselves, and have a just action of murder against us; else as forsakers of our own charge, we are punished in the other world. [ . . . ] There is more constancy in using the chain that holds us, than in breaking the same; and more trial of steadfastness in Regulus than in Cato.[4]

[Extenuating circumstances, limiting cases]

Of all violences committed against conscience, the most in my opinion to be avoided is that which is offered against the chastity of women, forasmuch as there is naturally some corporal pleasure commixt[5] with it. And therefore the dissent cannot fully enough be joined thereunto: and it seemeth that force is in some sort intermixed with some will. [T]he ecclesiastical story hath in especial reverence sundry such examples of devout persons who called for death to warrant them from the outrages which some tyrants prepared against their religion and consciences. Pelagia and Sophronia [were] both canonized; the first, together with her mother and sisters, to escape the outrageous rapes of some soldiers, threw herself into a river; the other, to shun the force of Maxentius the Emperor,[6] slew herself.

[An equivocal conclusion]

Grieving-smart, and a worse death seem to me the most excusable incitations.

---

[4]As consul, Regulus led the conquest of Africa; captured by the Carthaginians, he died under torture in 249 BCE. Cato supported Pompey against Julius Caesar. At Pompey's defeat in 47 BCE, Cato went to Utica near Carthage and, believing that his own cause was hopeless, committed suicide in 46 BCE.

[5]Desire; i.e., on the part of the rape victim.

[6]St. Augustine recounts the stories of Saints Pelagia and Sophronia in *The City of God*, written sometime after 413, Book I, Chapter 26. Maxentius, Emperor of Rome from 306 to 312, was defeated by Constantine, who succeeded him.

## John Sym (1581–1631)

*John Sym, a Protestant clergyman sympathetic to Calvinism, wrote his treatise on "self-killing" in response to a growing number of reports of suicides in England during the first quarter of the seventeenth century. Although he could not excuse it on theological grounds, he described its psychological attractions: frustration or disappointment in love, hatred of a spouse, a sense of personal unworthiness, and particularly, shame at personal failure or loss of dignity. The example of the legendary Roman matron Lucretia (the heroine of Shakespeare's narrative poem "The Rape of Lucrece"), who stabbed herself after being raped, was often invoked as a limiting case. Dishonored in the terms her society professed, despairing of her reputation, traumatized by her victimization, her suicide appeared excusable. Few moralists condemned her, and some even thought that her action was highly moral.*

### from *Life's Preservative against Self-Killing*[1]
### [The causes of suicide]

[An] extreme grief of mind and trouble of conscience [and] excessive discontentment for being crossed or disappointed. [. . .] This discontentment of mind arises from two causes. First, from want of that good, true or seeming, which we desire or expect. Secondly, from suffering of that evil which we would not. [ . . . ]

First, that which ariseth from the crossing or disappointment of the will of mens' affections and lusts: as those that immoderately affect and love to have and enjoy others of the other sex and are deeply overset in carnal or conjugal love, which is an unruly passion, and being disappointed, occasions people therefore to kill themselves. A wife kills herself because her husband crosses her will; either he will not do as she would have him or he will not let her have her will to go and do as she list.[2] Or [she] is displeased with her match, which proceeds from hatred to her husband, whom she envies the enjoying of her; and so I might instance in many like particulars.[3] But it is most unreasonable that because a body cannot have their love or will that therefore such an one should revenge the same upon himself by an act of the greatest hatred and hostility in

---

[1]John Sym, *Life's Preservative against Self-Killing*, London, 1637; sigs. Gg verso–Gg3 verso.

[2]Wants; wishes.

[3]There are many instances of suicide prompted by intolerable situations.

the world; and that one should rather choose to kill himself than to live after a repulse in suit of love, or to see another brook what they impotently affected to enjoy.

The third kind of troubles of mind that sometimes occasions self-murder is shame and confusion, either for what a man hath ignominiously done or suffered or is certainly like to do or suffer, whereby he falls under contempt, scorn, and importable[4] disgrace with those whose respect he overvalues. And so, apprehending himself to be dejected and used more indignly[5] and unworthily than he thinks he hath deserved or can endure, he resolves to kill himself to free him from the same or at least from the sense of it. As did Lucretia, who, having been ravished by Tarquinius, stabbed herself to avoid the shame of it—of whom Augustine[6] says, that being sick and impatient of the villainy committed against her, she killed herself.

So intolerable a thing is shame to some, specially of the noblest natures, that they think the same worse than death, and that they had rather not to be than to live in shame; it confounds the judgment and drives [them] into desperate shifts and practices to be rid of it.

---

[4]Intolerable.

[5]Dishonorably.

[6]St. Augustine (354–430), Bishop of Hippo, gives an account of Lucretia in *The City of God*, Book I, Chapter 19.

# *Sources*

An important source for Shakespeare's *Hamlet* is the ancient story of Amleth, the heroic prince of Jutland, now modern Denmark, as told by the thirteenth-century historian Saxo Grammaticus in his *Historia Danica*. Also known as *Gesta Danorum* (that is, the deeds of the Danes), this history was first published in sixteen books in 1576 in Frankfurt. Saxo's contribution covers events through the early thirteenth century; later historians added a record of events to 1241. How this story came to Shakespeare's attention is not entirely clear: it was translated with embellishments from Saxo's Latin into Italian by Matteo Bandello (1485–1561), a writer of *novelle* or short stories, and then translated again into French with further embellishments by François de Belleforest (1530–1583), where it appears in the fifth volume of his *Histoires Tragiques* (1572). Shakespeare probably read Saxo's history as translated by Belleforest.

More recent versions of the Hamlet story existed in dramatic form and were likely to have been known to Shakespeare: one in particular, a play now lost but identified by recent critics as the Ur-Hamlet, may have been his principal source. This play is perhaps the one described by Thomas Nashe in his preface to Robert Greene's romance *Menaphon* (1589). Characterizing this play as a work by a "noverint" or public secretary, Nashe declares that it affords the audience "whole Hamlets." Nashe may be identifying a work by the playwright Thomas Kyd, whose *Spanish Tragedy* (1587) represents themes and characters somewhat similar to those in *Hamlet*, notably the character of the ghost of a murdered nobleman who converses with the figure of Revenge. The Ur-Hamlet, whether or not by Kyd, could also be implied in Thomas Lodge's reference to the character of a ghost—who cries "Hamlet, revenge"—in his *Wit's Misery and the World's Madness, Discovering the Devils Incarnate of This Age* (1596). Finally, Shakespeare may have profited from his connection with the theater. Hamlet's story is dramatized in an early version of a German play—based on the Ur-Hamlet—entitled *Der bestrafte Brudermord oder Prinz Hamlet aus Dannemark*, translated as *Fratricide Punished or Prince Hamlet in Denmark* (originally from a text dated 1710 but now lost) used by English players on tour in Europe in 1586 and afterward. In its present form, *Der bestrafte Brudermord* resembles Shakespeare's *Hamlet* in the details of its plot although not in their dramatic rendering. In the absence of any text of Ur-Hamlet, however, Saxo's account must serve as our point of comparison with Shakespeare's tragedy.

## Saxo Grammaticus (fl. 1200, d. ca. 1204)
## from *Historia Danica*[1]

*Even at its relatively far remove from* Hamlet, *Saxo's heroic tale illustrates significant elements of Shakespeare's play: fratricide, incest, a contrived or feigned madness, and a duty to avenge the murder of a father. But unlike Amleth, whose superb cunning and roguish strategies allow him to achieve his revenge in an almost comic manner, Shakespeare's Hamlet is an eminently tragic figure. Amleth never betrays self-doubt, needs no ghost to tell him that his uncle Feng murdered his father (he knows this from the moment of the murder), and does not reflect on the propriety of the revenge to which he is committed. Hamlet, by contrast, made deeply melancholic by his father's death, has to struggle with myriad doubts and anxieties after he learns that his uncle Claudius has murdered his father. The fact that he is told of this crime by his father's ghost, who then demands revenge, further troubles his situation. Ghosts were notoriously hard to identify as good rather than evil spirits, and a ghost from purgatory challenged the Protestant claim that purgatory was itself merely a clerical invention. Saxo's Amleth succeeds his father after killing his uncle Feng and lives to reign in Jutland.*

[1]Saxo Grammaticus, *Historia Danica*, trans. Oliver Elton, in *The First Nine Books of the Danish History of Saxo Grammaticus*, London, 1894; pp. 104–117.

*Shakespeare's Hamlet dies of a lethal poison administered in the course of a sword fight in which he barely manages to kill Claudius, and the succession of the crown of Denmark goes to Fortinbras of Norway.*

## [The revenge of Amleth of Jutland for the murder of his father Horwendil by his uncle Feng]

At this time Horwendil and Feng,[2] whose father Gerwendil had been governor of the Jutes, were appointed in his place by Rorik[3] to defend Jutland. But Horwendil held the monarchy for three years, and then, to win the height of glory, devoted himself to roving.[4] Then Koll,[5] King of Norway, in rivalry of his great deeds and renown, deemed it would be a handsome deed if by his greater strength in arms he could bedim the far-famed glory of the rover; and, cruising about the sea, he watched for Horwendil's fleet and came up with it. There was an island lying in the middle of the sea, which each of the rovers, bringing his ships up on either side, was holding. The captains were tempted by the pleasant look of the beach, and the comeliness of the shores led them to look through the interior of the spring-tide woods, to go through the glades, and roam over the sequestered forests. It was here that the advance of Koll and Horwendil brought them face to face without any witness. Then Horwendil endeavored to address the king first, asking him in what way it was his pleasure to fight, and declaring that one best which needed the courage of as few as possible. For, said he, the duel was the surest of all modes of combat for winning the meed[6] of bravery, because it relied only upon native courage, and excluded all help from the hand of another. Koll marvelled at so brave a judgment in a youth, and said: "Since thou hast granted me the choice of battle, I think it is best to employ that kind which needs only the endeavors of two, and is free from all the tumult. Certainly it is more venturesome, and allows of a speedier award of the victory. This thought we share, in this opinion we agree of our own accord.

---

[2]Horwendil is the basis for old king Hamlet. At this point in the "history," he appears to be merely a warrior appointed to defend Jutland (Denmark). He has actually been king of Jutland for three years, presumably in consequence of his successful defense of the kingdom. Feng is the basis for Hamlet's uncle Claudius.

[3]King of Denmark before Horwendil; he has no parallel in Shakespeare's play.

[4]Piracy.

[5]The basis for old king Fortinbras.

[6]Reward.

But since the issue remains doubtful, we must pay some regard to gentle dealing, and must not give way so far to our inclinations as to leave the last offices undone. Hatred is in our hearts; yet let piety be there also, which in its due time may take the place of rigor. For the rights of nature reconcile us,[7] though we are parted by differences of purpose; they link us together, howsoever rancor estrange our spirits. Let us, therefore, have this pious stipulation, that the conqueror shall give funeral rites to the conquered. For all allow that these are the last duties of human kind, from which no righteous man shrinks. Let each army lay aside its sternness and perform this function in harmony. Let jealousy depart at death, let the feud be buried in the tomb. Let us not show such an example of cruelty as to persecute one another's dust, though hatred has come between us in our lives. It will be a boast for the victor if he has borne his beaten foe in a lordly funeral. For the man who pays the rightful dues over his dead enemy wins the goodwill of the survivor; and whoso devotes gentle dealing to him who is no more, conquers the living by his kindness. Also there is another disaster, not less lamentable, which sometimes befalls the living—the loss of some part of their body; and I think that succor is due to this just as much as to the worst hap[8] that may befall. For often those who fight keep their lives safe, but suffer maiming; and this lot is commonly thought more dismal than any death; for death cuts off memory of all things, while the living cannot forget the devastation of his own body. Therefore this mischief also must be helped somehow; so let it be agreed, that the injury of either of us by the other shall be made good with ten talents[9] of gold. For if it be righteous to have compassion on the calamities of another, how much more is it to pity one's own? No man but obeys nature's prompting; and he who slights it is a self-murderer."

After mutually pledging their faiths to these terms, they began the battle. Nor was their strangeness in meeting one another, nor the sweetness of that spring-green spot, so heeded as to prevent them from the fray. Horwendil, in his too great ardor, became keener to attack his enemy than to defend his own body; and, heedless of his shield, had grasped his sword with both hands; and his

---

[7]Obsequies (formal ritual of prayer) owed to the dead.
[8]Event; chance occurrence. "Hap" is a medieval word for "fortune" or "chance."
[9]A talent was a unit of money.

boldness did not fail. For by his rain of blows he destroyed Koll's shield and deprived him of it, and at last hewed off his foot and drove him lifeless to the ground. Then, not to fail of his compact, he buried him royally, gave him a howe[10] of lordly make and pompous obsequies. [. . .]

He had now passed three years in valiant deeds of war; and, in order to win higher rank in Rorik's favour, he assigned to him the best trophies and the pick of the plunder. His friendship with Rorik enabled him to woo and win in marriage his daughter Gerutha,[11] who bore him a son Amleth.

Such great good fortune stung Feng with jealousy, so that he resolved treacherously to waylay his brother, thus showing that goodness is not safe even from those of a man's own house. And behold, when a chance came to murder him, his bloody hand sated the deadly passion of his soul. Then he took the wife of the brother he had butchered, capping unnatural murder[12] with incest. For whoso yields to one iniquity, speedily falls an easier victim to the next, the first being an incentive to the second. Also the man veiled the monstrosity of his deed with such hardihood of cunning, that he made up a mock pretence of goodwill to excuse his crime, and glossed over fratricide with a show of righteousness. Gerutha, said he, though so gentle that she would do no man the slightest hurt, had been visited with her husband's extremest hate; and it was all to save her that he had slain his brother; for he thought it shameful that a lady so meek and unrancorous should suffer the heavy disdain of her husband. Nor did his smooth words fail in their intent; for at courts, where fools are sometimes favored and backbiters preferred, a lie lacks not credit. Nor did Feng keep from shameful embraces the hands that had slain a brother, pursuing with equal guilt both of his wicked and impious deeds.

Amleth beheld all this,[13] but feared lest too shrewd a behavior might make his uncle suspect him. So he chose to feign dulness, and pretend an utter lack of wits. This cunning course not only concealed his intelligence but ensured his safety. Every day he remained in his mother's house utterly listless and unclean, flinging himself on

[10]Grave.

[11]The basis for Gertrude.

[12]"Unnatural murder" translates *parricidium*, the murder of the father, in Saxo's original. These are also the words of the Ghost to Hamlet, 1.5.26.

[13]Feng's crime. Amleth is not in doubt about his father's murderer.

the ground, and bespattering his person with foul and filthy dirt. His discolored face and visage smutched with slime denoted foolish and grotesque madness. All he said was of a piece with these follies; all he did savored of utter lethargy. In a word, you would not have thought him a man at all, but some absurd abortion[14] due to a mad fit of destiny. He used at times to sit over the fire, and, raking up the embers with his hands, to fashion wooden crooks, and harden them in the fire, shaping at their tips certain barbs, to make them hold more tightly to their fastenings. When asked what he was about, he said that he was preparing sharp javelins to avenge his father. This answer was not a little scoffed at, all men deriding his idle and ridiculous pursuit; but the thing helped his purpose afterwards. Now it was his craft in this matter that first awakened in the deeper observers a suspicion of his cunning. For his skill in a trifling art betokened the hidden talent of the craftsman; nor could they believe the spirit dull where the hand had acquired so cunning a workmanship. Lastly, he always watched with the most punctual care over his pile of stakes that he had pointed in the fire. Some people, therefore, declared that his mind was quick enough, and fancied that he only played the simpleton in order to hide his understanding, and veiled some deep purpose under a cunning feint. His wiliness (said these) would be most readily detected, if a fair woman were put in his way in some secluded place, who should provoke his mind to the temptations of love; all men's natural temper being too blindly amorous to be artfully dissembled, and this passion being also too impetuous to be checked by cunning. Therefore, if his lethargy were feigned, he would seize the opportunity, and yield straightway to violent delights. So men were commissioned to draw the young man in his rides into a remote part of the forest, and there assail him with a temptation of this nature. Among these chanced to be a foster-brother of Amleth, who had not ceased to have regard to their common nurture; and who esteemed his present orders less than the memory of their past fellowship. He attended Amleth among his appointed train, being anxious not to entrap, but to warn him; and was persuaded that he would suffer the worst if he showed the slightest glimpse of sound reason, and above all if he did the act of love openly. This was also plain enough to Amleth himself. For when he was bidden mount his horse, he deliberately set himself in

[14]Monster; uninduced premature births and miscarriages were commonly called "abortions."

such a fashion that he turned his back to the neck and faced about, fronting the tail; which he proceeded to encompass with the reins, just as if on that side he would check the horse in its furious pace. By this cunning thought he eluded the trick, and overcame the treachery of his uncle. The reinless steed galloping on, with the rider directing its tail, was ludicrous enough to behold.

Amleth went on, and a wolf crossed his path amid the thicket. When his companions told him that a young colt had met him, he retorted, that in Feng's stud there were too few of that kind fighting. This was a gentle but witty fashion of invoking a curse upon his uncle's riches. When they averred that he had given a cunning answer, he answered that he had spoken deliberately: for he was loth to be thought prone to lying about any mattter, and wished to be held a stranger to falsehood; and accordingly he mingled craft and candor in such wise that, though his words did lack truth, yet there was nothing to betoken the truth and betray how far his keenness went.

Again, as he passed along the beach, his companions found the rudder of a ship which had been wrecked, and said they had discovered a huge knife. "This", said he, "was the right thing to carve such a huge ham;" by which he really meant the sea, to whose infinitude, he thought, this enormous rudder matched. Also, as they passed the sandhills, and bade him look at the meal, meaning the sand, he replied that it had been ground small by the hoary tempests of the ocean. His companions praising his answer, he said that he had spoken it wittingly. Then they purposely left him, that he might pluck up more courage to practise wantonness. The woman whom his uncle had dispatched met him in a dark spot, as though she had crossed him by chance; and he took her and would have ravished[15] her, had not his foster-brother, by a secret device, given him an inkling of the trap. For this man,[16] while pondering the fittest way to play privily the prompter's part, and forestall the young man's hazardous lewdness,[17] found a straw on the ground and fastened it underneath the tail of a gadfly that was flying past; which he then drove towards the particular quarter where he knew Amleth to be: an act which served the unwary prince exceedingly well. The token was interpreted as shrewdly as it had been sent. For

[15]Raped.
[16]Hamlet's foster-brother.
[17]Dangerous sexual aggression.

Amleth saw the gadfly, espied with curiosity the straw which it wore embedded in its tail, and perceived that it was a secret warning to beware of treachery. Alarmed, scenting a trap, and fain to possess his desire in greater safety, he caught up the woman in his arms and dragged her off to a distant and impenetrable fen. Moreover, when they had lain together, he conjured her earnestly to disclose the matter to none, and the promise of silence was accorded as heartily as it was asked. For both of them had been under the same fostering in their childhood; and this early rearing in common had brought Amleth and the girl into great intimacy.

So, when he had returned home, they all jeeringly asked him whether he had given way to love, and he avowed that he had ravished the maid. When he was next asked where he did it, and what had been his pillow, he said that he had rested upon the hoof of a beast of burden, upon a cockscomb, and also upon a ceiling. For, when he was starting into temptation, he had gathered fragments of all these things, in order to avoid lying. And though his jest did not take aught of the truth out of the story, the answer was greeted with shouts of merriment from the bystanders. The maiden, too, when questioned on the matter, declared that he had done no such thing; and her denial was the more readily credited when it was found that the escort had not witnessed the deed. Then he who had marked the gadfly in order to give a hint, wishing to show Amleth that to this trick he owed his salvation, observed that latterly he had been singly devoted to Amleth. The young man's reply was apt. Not to seem forgetful of his informant's service, he said that he had seen a certain thing bearing a straw flit by suddenly, wearing a stalk of chaff fixed on its hinder parts. The cleverness of this speech, which made the rest split with laughter, rejoiced the heart of Amleth's friend.

Thus all were worsted, and none could open the secret lock of the young man's wisdom. But a friend of Feng,[18] gifted more with assurance than judgment, declared that the unfathomable cunning of such a mind could not be detected by any vulgar plot, for the man's obstinacy was so great that it ought not to be assailed with any mild measures; there were many sides to his wiliness, and it ought not to be entrapped by any one method. Accordingly, said he, his own profounder acuteness had hit on a more delicate way, which was well fitted to be put in practice, and would effectually

[18]The basis for Polonius.

discover what they desired to know. Feng was purposely to absent himself, pretending affairs of great import. Amleth should be closeted alone with his mother in her chamber; but a man should first be commissioned to place himself in a concealed part of the room and listen heedfully to what they talked about. For if the son had any wits at all he would not hesitate to speak out in the hearing of his mother, or fear to trust himself to the fidelity of her who bore him. The speaker, loth to seem readier to devise than to carry out the plot, zealously proffered himself as the agent of the eavesdropping. Feng rejoiced at the scheme, and departed on pretence of a long journey. Now he who had given this counsel repaired privily to the room where Amleth was shut up with his mother, and lay down skulking in the straw. But Amleth had his antidote for the treachery. Afraid of being overheard by some eavesdropper, he at first resorted to his usual imbecile ways, and crowed like a noisy cock, beating his arms together to mimic the flapping of wings. Then he mounted the straw and began to swing his body and jump again and again, wishing to try if aught lurked there in hiding. Feeling a lump beneath his feet, he drove his sword into the spot, and impaled him who lay hid. Then he dragged him from his concealment and slew him. Then, cutting his body into morsels, he seethed it in boiling water, and flung it through the mouth of an open sewer for the swine to eat, bestrewing the stinking mire with his hapless limbs. Having in this wise eluded the snare, he went back to the room. Then his mother set up a great wailing, and began to lament her son's folly to his face; but he said: "Most infamous of women! dost thou seek with such lying lamentations to hide thy most heavy guilt? Wantoning like a harlot, thou hast entered a wicked and abominable state of wedlock, embracing with incestuous bosom thy husband's slayer, and wheedling with filthy lures of blandishment him who had slain the father of thy son. This, forsooth, is the way that the mares couple with the vanquishers of their mates; for brute beasts are naturally incited to pair indiscriminately; and it would seem that thou, like them, hast clean forgot thy first husband. As for me, not idly do I wear the mask of folly; for I doubt not that he who destroyed his brother will riot as ruthlessly in the blood of his kindred. Therefore it is better to choose the garb of dulness than that of sense, and to borrow some protection from a show of utter frenzy. Yet the passion to avenge my father still burns in my heart; but I am watching the chances, I await the fitting hour. There is a place for all things; against so merciless and dark a spirit must be used the deeper devices of the mind.[19] And thou, who hadst been better employed in lamenting thine own disgrace, know it is superfluity to bewail my witlessness; thou shouldst weep for the blemish in thine own mind, not for that in another's. On the rest see thou keep silence." With such reproaches he rent the heart of his mother and redeemed her to walk in the ways of virtue; teaching her to set the fires of the past above the seductions of the present.

When Feng returned, nowhere could he find the man who had suggested the treacherous espial; he searched for him long and carefully, but none said they had seen him anywhere. Amleth, among others, was asked in jest if he had come on any trace of him, and replied that the man had gone to the sewer, but had fallen through its bottom and been stifled by the floods of filth, and that he had then been devoured by the swine that came up all about that place. This speech was flouted by those who heard; for it seemed senseless, though really it expressly avowed the truth.

Feng now suspected that his stepson was certainly full of guile, and desired to make away with him, but durst not do the deed for fear of the displeasure, not only of Amleth's grandsire Rorik, but also of his own wife. So he thought that the King of Britain should be employed to slay him, so that another could do the deed, and he be able to feign innocence. Thus, desirous to hide his cruelty, he chose rather to besmirch his friend than to bring disgrace on his own head. Amleth, on departing, gave secret orders to his mother to hang the hall with knotted tapestry, and to perform pretended obsequies for him a year thence; promising that he would then return. Two retainers of Feng[20] then accompanied him, bearing a letter graven on wood—a kind of writing material frequent in old times; this letter enjoined the king of the Britons to put to death the youth who was sent over to him. While they were reposing, Amleth searched their coffers, found the letter, and read the instructions therein. Whereupon he erased all the writing on the surface, substituted fresh characters, and so, changing the purport of the instructions, shifted his own doom upon his companions. Nor was he satisfied with removing from himself the sentence of death and passing the peril on to others, but added an entreaty that the King of Britain would grant his daughter in marriage to a youth of great judgment whom he was sending to him. Under this was falsely marked the signature of Feng.

---

[19]Compare Hamlet's resignation: "We defy augury" (5.2.217).

[20]The basis for Rosencrantz and Guildenstern.

Now when they had reached Britain, the envoys went to the king, and proffered him the letter which they supposed was an implement of destruction to another, but which really betokened death to themselves. The king dissembled the truth, and entreated them hospitably and kindly. Then Amleth scouted all the splendor of the royal banquet like vulgar viands, and abstaining very strangely, rejected that plenteous feast, refraining from the drink even as from the banquet. All marvelled that a youth and a foreigner should disdain the carefully-cooked dainties of the royal board and the luxurious banquet provided, as if it were some peasant's relish. So, when the revel broke up, and the king was dismissing his friends to rest, he had a man sent into the sleeping-room to listen secretly, in order that he might hear the midnight conversation of his guests. Now, when Amleth's companions asked him why he had refrained from the feast of yestereve, as if it were poison, he answered that the bread was flecked with blood and tainted; that there was a tang of iron in the liquor; while the meats of the feast reeked of the stench of a human carcass, and were infected by a kind of smack of the odor of the charnel.[21] He further said that the king had the eyes of a slave, and that the queen had in three ways shown the behavior of a bondmaid. Thus he reviled with insulting invective not so much the feast as its givers. And presently his companions, taunting him with his old defect of wits, began to flout him with many saucy jeers, because he blamed and cavilled at seemly and worthy things, and because he attacked thus ignobly an illustrious king and a lady of so refined a behavior, bespattering with the shamefullest abuse those who merited all praise.

All this the king heard from his retainer; and declared that he who could say such things had either more than mortal wisdom or more than mortal folly, in these few words fathoming the full depth of Amleth's penetration. Then he summoned his steward and asked him whence he had procured the bread. The steward declared that it had been made by the king's own baker. The king asked where the corn had grown of which it was made, and whether any sign was to be found there of human carnage? The other answered, that not far off was a field, covered with the ancient bones of slaughtered men, and still bearing plainly all the signs of ancient carnage; and that he had himself planted this field with grain in springtide, thinking it more fruitful than the rest, and hoping for plenteous abundance;

---

[21]Tomb.

and so, for aught he knew, the bread had caught some evil savor from this bloodshed. The king, on hearing this, surmised that Amleth had spoken truly, and took the pains to learn also what had been the source of the lard. The other declared that his hogs had, through negligence, strayed from keeping, and battened on the rotten carcass of a robber, and that perchance their pork had thus come to have something of a corrupt smack. The king, finding that Amleth's judgment was right in this thing also, asked of what liquor the steward had mixed the drink? Hearing that it had been brewed of water and meal, he had the spot of the spring pointed out to him, and set to digging deep down; and there he found, rusted away, several swords, the tang whereof it was thought had tainted the waters. Others relate that Amleth blamed the drink because, while quaffing it, he had detected some bees that had fed in the paunch of a dead man; and that the taint, which had formerly been imparted to the combs,[22] had reappeared in the taste. The king, seeing that Amleth had rightly given the causes of the taste he had found so faulty, and learning that the ignoble eyes wherewith Amleth had reproached him concerned some stain upon his birth, had a secret interview with his mother, and asked her who his father had really been. She said she had submitted to no man but the king. But when he threatened that he would have the truth out of her by a trial, he was told that he was the offspring of a slave. By the evidence of the avowal thus extorted he understood the whole mystery of the reproach upon his origin. Abashed as he was with shame for his low estate, he was so ravished with the young man's cleverness, that he asked him why he had aspersed the queen with the reproach that she had demeaned herself like a slave? But while resenting that the courtliness of his wife had been accused in the midnight gossip of a guest, he found that her mother had been a bondmaid. For Amleth said he had noted in her three blemishes showing the demeanor of a slave; first, she had muffled her head in her mantle as bondmaids do; next, that she had gathered up her gown for walking; and thirdly, that she had first picked out with a splinter, and then chewed up, the remnant of food that stuck in the crevices between her teeth. Further, he mentioned that the king's mother had been brought into slavery from captivity, lest she should seem servile only in her habits, yet not in her birth.

---

[22]Catacombs, a subterranean receptacle for dead bodies.

Then the king adored the wisdom of Amleth as though it were inspired, and gave him his daughter to wife; accepting his bare word as though it were a witness from the skies. Moreover, in order to fulfil the bidding of his friend, he hanged Amleth's companions on the morrow. Amleth, feigning offence, treated this piece of kindness as a grievance, and received from the king, as compensation, some gold, which he afterwards melted in the fire and secretly caused to be poured into some hollowed sticks.

When he had passed a whole year with the king he obtained leave to make a journey, and returned to his own land, carrying away of all his princely wealth and state only the sticks which held the gold. On reaching Jutland, he exchanged his present attire for his ancient demeanor, which he had adopted for righteous ends, purposely assuming an aspect of absurdity. Covered with filth, he entered the banquet-room where his own obsequies were being held, and struck all the men utterly aghast, rumor having falsely noised abroad his death. At last terror melted into mirth, and the guests jeered and taunted one another, that he whose last rites they were celebrating as though he were dead, should appear in the flesh. When he was asked concerning his comrades, he pointed to the sticks he was carrying, and said, "Here is both the one and the other." This he observed with equal truth and pleasantry; for his speech, though most thought it idle, yet departed not from the truth; for it pointed at the weregild[23] of the slain as though it were themselves. Thereon, wishing to bring the company into a gayer mood, he joined the cupbearers, and diligently did the office of plying the drink. Then, to prevent his loose dress hampering his walk, he girded his sword upon his side, and purposely drawing it several times, pricked his fingers with its point. The bystanders accordingly had both sword and scabbard riveted across with an iron nail.[24] Then, to smooth the way more safely to his plot, he went to the lords and plied them heavily with draught upon draught, and drenched them all so deep in wine, that their feet were made feeble with drunkenness, and they turned to rest within the palace, making their bed where they had revelled. Then he saw they were in a fit state for his plots, and thought that here was a chance offered to do his purpose. So he took out of his bosom the stakes he had long ago prepared, and went into the building, where the ground lay covered

[23]Compensatory payment by one responsible for a person's death to his or her family.
[24]Fearful bystanders nailed his sword in its holder.

with the bodies of the nobles wheezing off their sleep and their debauch. Then, cutting away its supports, he brought down the hanging his mother had knitted, which covered the inner as well as the outer walls of the hall. This he flung upon the snorers, and then applying the crooked stakes, he knotted and bound them up in such insoluble intricacy, that not one of the men beneath, however hard he might struggle, could contrive to rise. After this he set fire to the palace. The flames spread, scattering the conflagration far and wide. It enveloped the whole dwelling, destroyed the palace, and burnt them all while they were either buried in deep sleep or vainly striving to arise. Then he went to the chamber of Feng, who had before this been conducted by his train into his pavilion; plucked up a sword that chanced to be hanging to the bed, and planted his own in its place.[25] Then, awakening his uncle, he told him that his nobles were perishing in the flames, and that Amleth was here, armed with his old crooks to help him, and thirsting to exact the vengeance, now long overdue, for his father's murder. Feng, on hearing this, leapt from his couch, but was cut down while, deprived of his own sword, he strove in vain to draw the strange one.[26] O valiant Amleth, and worthy of immortal fame, who being shrewdly armed with a feint of folly, covered a wisdom too high for human wit under a marvellous disguise of silliness! and not only found in his subtlety means to protect his own safety, but also by its guidance found opportunity to avenge his father. By this skilful defence of himself, and strenuous revenge for his parent, he has left it doubtful whether we are to think more of his wit[27] or his bravery.

---

[25]Amleth arranges his meeting with Feng so that he fights with Feng's sword while Feng has the sword the bystanders have rendered useless. The exchange of weapons is repeated in Hamlet's sword fight with Laertes. See 5.2.305–306.

[26]Amleth's sword.

[27]Quick intelligence.

# *Performance and Interpretation*

A play is realized only in performance, animated by actors, their actions on stage, and the responses of the audience. Because a play is a living work of art, no single performance can define it. In the history of theater, there are only performances, shaped by the cultures in which they are staged. Thus past performances, even when they are described by historians of the stage, are by definition elusive. By contrast, performances created as part of a literary fiction endure even as they illustrate some of the conditions of theatricality. Henry Fielding's account of a fictional performance of *Hamlet* focuses on the playgoer, Charles Dickens' on the role of the actor. Samuel Clemens, by his satirical recreation of a ludicrous performance of Hamlet's speech "To be or not to be," tells us that, in effect, a playgoer experiences two performances: one on stage (however inept) and another in his mind, an idealized re-vision of what he is actually seeing. The critics Samuel Taylor Coleridge and William Hazlitt study the character of Hamlet to better understand the play as a whole. They see Hamlet as if he were one of them, a real man and not one playing a part on stage. A. C. Bradley follows Coleridge and Hazlitt as an analyst of character, although with an appreciation for the play as a literary work.

## Henry Fielding (1707–1754)

*In his comic novel* Tom Jones *(1749), Henry Fielding chose an inexperienced and naive spectator, the schoolmaster Partridge, to reveal the conditions in which many audiences find themselves even after years of going to plays. On the one hand, Fielding shows us that Partridge knows that* Hamlet *on stage is not continuous with daily reality; on the other hand, Fielding shows us how often Partridge cannot help but believe that* Hamlet *is, somehow, answerable to that reality. As a result, Partridge wavers between a studied detachment from and an instinctive identification with the play's characters. Not surprisingly, it is the actor who plays the King, whose performance is the most affected and therefore the least realistic, that Partridge chooses as the "best" actor—the King, at least, has not frightened him by seeming to be real.*

## from *The History of Tom Jones: A Foundling* [1]
[Partridge attends a performance of Hamlet]

As soon as the play, which was *Hamlet, Prince of Denmark*, began, Partridge was all attention, nor did he break silence till the entrance of the Ghost; upon which he asked Jones, "what man that was in the strange dress; something," said he, "like what I have seen in a picture. Sure it is not armor, it is?"

Jones answered, "That is the Ghost."

To which Partridge replied with a smile, "Persuade me to that, sir, if you can. Though I can't say I ever actually saw a ghost in my life, yet I am certain I should know one, if I saw him, better than that comes to. No, no, sir, ghosts don't appear in such dresses as that neither." In this mistake, which caused much laughter in the neighborhood of Partridge, he was suffered to continue, until the scene between the Ghost and Hamlet, when Partridge gave that credit to Mr. Garrick [2] which he had denied to Jones, and fell into so violent a trembling, that his knees knocked against each other. Jones asked him what was the matter, and whether he was afraid of the warrior upon the stage?

"Oh, la! sir," said he, "I perceive now it is what you told me. I am not afraid of anything, for I know it is but a play; and if it was really a ghost, it could do one no harm at such a distance, and in so much company: and yet if I was frightened, I am not the only person."

---

[1]Henry Fielding, *The History of Tom Jones: A Foundling*, 2 vols., London, 1882; vol. 2, pp. 125–127.

[2]David Garrick, 1717–1779, leading actor and playwright, who produced many of Shakespeare's plays at The Theater Royal, Drury Lane.

"Why, who," cries Jones, "dost thou take to be such a coward here besides thyself?"

"Nay, you may call me coward if you will: but if that little man there upon the stage is not frightened, I never saw any man frightened in my life. Ah, ah: go along with you! Lord have mercy upon such fool-hardiness! Whatever happens it is good enough for you. Follow you?—I'd follow the devil as soon. Nay, perhaps it is the devil, for they say he can put on what likeness he pleases. Oh! here he is again. No farther! No, you have gone far enough already; farther than I'd have gone for all the king's dominions." Jones offered to speak, but Partridge cried, "Hush, hush, dear sir, don't you hear him?!" And during the whole speech of the Ghost, he sat with his eyes fixed partly on the Ghost and partly on Hamlet, and with his mouth open; the same passions which succeeded each other in Hamlet succeeding likewise in him.

When the scene was over, Jones said, "Why Partridge, you exceed my expectations. You enjoy the play more than I conceived possible."

"Nay, sir," answered Partridge, "if you are not afraid of the devil, I can't help it; but to be sure it is natural to be surprised at such things, though I know there is nothing in them; not that it was the Ghost that surprised me neither, for I should have known that to have been only a man in a strange dress; but when I saw the little man so frightened himself, it was that which took hold of me."

"And dost thou imagine then, Partridge," cries Jones, "that he was really frightened?"

"Nay, sir," said Partridge, "did not you yourself observe afterwards, when he found out it was his own father's spirit, and how he was murdered in the garden, how his fear forsook him by degrees, and he was struck dumb with sorrow, as it were, just as I should have been had it been my own case. But hush! oh, la! What noise is that? There he is again. Well, to be certain though I know there is nothing at all in it, I am glad I am not down yonder where those men are." Then turning his eyes again upon Hamlet, "Ay you may draw your sword; what signifies a sword against the power of the devil?"

During the second act, Partridge made very few remarks. He greatly admired the fineness of the dresses; nor could he help observing upon the King's countenance. "Well," said he, "how people may be deceived by faces? *Nulla fides fronti*[3] is, I find, a true

---

[3]There is no proof in appearance.

saying. Who would think, by looking in the King's face, that he had ever committed a murder?" He then inquired after the Ghost; but Jones, who intended he should be surprised, gave him no other satisfaction than that he might possibly see him again soon, and in a flash of fire.

Partridge sat in fearful expectation of this; and now, when the ghost made his next appearance, Partridge cried out: "There, sir, now; what say you now? Is he frightened now or no? As much frightened as you think me; and to be sure, nobody can help some fears. I would not be in so bad a condition as what's-his-name, Squire Hamlet, is there, for all the world. Bless me! What's become of the spirit? As I am a living soul, I thought I saw him sink into the earth."

"Indeed, you saw right," answered Jones.

"Well, well," cries Partridge, "I know it is only a play; and besides, if there was anything in all this, Madame Miller[4] would not laugh so, for as to you, sir, you would not be afraid, I believe, if the devil was here in person. There, there—ay, no wonder you are in such a passion; shake the vile wicked wretch to pieces. If she was my own mother I should serve her so. To be sure, all duty to a mother is forfeited by such wicked doings. Ay, go about your business; I hate the sight of you."

Our critic was now pretty silent till the play, which Hamlet introduces before the King. This he did not at first understand, till Jones explained it to him; but he no sooner entered into the spirit of it, than he began to bless himself that he had never committed murder. Then turning to Mrs. Miller, he asked her if she did not imagine the King looked as if he was touched; "though he is," said he, "a good actor, and doth all he can to hide it. Well, I would not have so much to answer for as that wicked man there hath, to sit upon a much higher chair than he sits upon. No wonder he ran away: for your sake I'll never trust an innocent face again."

The grave digging scene next engaged the attention of Partridge, who expressed much surprise at the number of skulls thrown upon the stage. To which Jones answered, "That it was one of the most famous burial-places about town."

"No wonder then," cries Partridge, "that the place is haunted. But I never saw in my life a worse grave-digger. I had a

---

[4]Another playgoer in Tom Jones's party.

sexton, when I was clerk, that should have dug three graves while he is digging one. The fellow handles a spade as if it was the first time he had ever had one in his hand. Ay, ay, you may sing. You had rather sing than work, I believe." Upon Hamlet's taking up the skull, he cried out, "Well it is strange to see how fearless some men are: I never could bring myself to touch anything belonging to a dead man on any account. He seemed frightened enough too at the Ghost I thought. *Nemo omnibus horis sapit.*[5]"

Little more worth remembering occurred during the play; at the end of which Jones asked him, which of the players he had liked best?

To this he answered, with some appearance of indignation at the question, "The King, without doubt."

"Indeed, Mr. Partridge," says Mrs. Miller, "you are not of the same opinion with the town; for they are all agreed that Hamlet is acted by the best player who was ever on the stage."

"He the best player!" cries Partridge, with a contemptuous sneer, "why I could act as well as he myself. I am sure if I had seen a ghost, I should have looked in the very same manner, and done just as he did. And then, to be sure, in that scene, as you called it, between him and his mother, where you told me he acted so fine, why, Lord help me, any man, that is any good man, that had had such a mother, would have done exactly the same. I know you are only joking with me; but, indeed, madam, though I was never at a play in London, yet I have seen acting before in the country; and the King for my money; he speaks all his words distinctly, half as loud again as the other. Anybody may see he is an actor."

. . . . Thus ended the adventure at the playhouse; where Partridge had afforded great mirth, not only to Jones and Mrs. Miller, but to all who sat within hearing, who were more attentive to what he said than to anything that passed on the stage.

He durst not go to bed all that night for fear of the Ghost; and for many nights after, sweat two or three hours before he went to sleep, with the same apprehensions; and waked several times in great horrors, crying out, "Lord have mercy upon us! there it is."

---

[5]No one is wise all the time.

## Samuel Taylor Coleridge (1772–1834)

*A poet and critic of English Romanticism, Samuel Taylor Coleridge interpreted* Hamlet *almost as if it were a novel. In his* Notes on Some Other Plays of Shakespeare *(1806–1808) and his* Lectures on Shakespeare and Milton *(1813), he does not tell his reader how the play is to be performed or how it was performed on a particular occasion. His interest is chiefly in what makes the play's hero so disinclined to take action, to be so deeply committed to a life of contemplation. He sees in Shakespeare's hero the image of a thinker whose connection to the everyday is tenuous, who lives almost entirely in a mental world of his own construction. Coleridge sees this aspect of Hamlet's character sympathetically: To be immersed in reflection, to crave "that which is not," is, Coleridge declares, the fate of "men of genius."*

### from Notes on Some Other Plays of Shakespeare[1]
### [The character of Hamlet]

The seeming inconsistencies in the conduct and character of Hamlet have long exercised the conjectural ingenuity of critics; and, as we are always loth to suppose that the cause of defective apprehension is in ourselves, the mystery has been too commonly explained by the very easy process of setting it down as in fact inexplicable, and by resolving the phenomenon into a misgrowth or *lusus*[2] of the capricious and irregular genius of Shakespeare. The shallow and stupid arrogance of these vulgar and indolent decisions I would fain do my best to expose. I believe the character of Hamlet may be traced to Shakespeare's deep and accurate science in mental philosophy. Indeed, that this character must have some connection with the common fundamental laws of our nature may be assumed from the fact, that Hamlet has been the darling of every country in which the literature of England has been fostered. In order to understand him, it is essential that we should reflect on the constitution of our own minds. Man is distinguished from the brute animals in proportion as thought prevails over sense; but in the healthy processes of the mind, a balance is constantly maintained between the impressions from outward objects and the inward operations of the intellect; for if there be an overbal-

[1]Samuel Taylor Coleridge, *Notes on Some Other Plays of Shakespeare* and *Lectures on Shakespeare and Milton* in *Lectures and Notes on Shakespeare and Other English Poets,* London, 1885; pp. 343–345 and 473–474, respectively.
[2]Trick.

ance in the contemplative faculty, man thereby becomes the creature of mere meditation, and loses his natural power of action. Now one of Shakespeare's modes of creating characters is, to conceive any one intellectual or moral faculty in morbid excess, and then to place himself, Shakespeare, thus mutilated or diseased, under given circumstances. In Hamlet he seems to have wished to exemplify the moral necessity of a due balance between our attention to the objects of our senses, and our meditation on the workings of our minds,—an equilibrium between the real and the imaginary worlds. In Hamlet this balance is disturbed: his thoughts, and the images of his fancy are far more vivid than his actual perceptions, and his very perceptions, instantly passing through the medium of his contemplations, acquire, as they pass, a form and a color not naturally their own. Hence we see a great, an almost enormous, intellectual activity, and a proportionate aversion to real action consequent upon it, with all its symptoms and accompanying qualities. This character Shakespeare places in circumstances, under which it is obliged to act on the spur of the moment: Hamlet is brave and careless of death; but he vacillates from sensibility, and procrastinates from thought, and loses the power of action in the energy of resolve. Thus it is that this tragedy presents a direct contrast to that of *Macbeth*; the one proceeds with the utmost slowness, the other with a crowded and breathless rapidity.

The effect of this overbalance of the imaginative power is beautifully illustrated in the everlasting broodings and superfluous activities of Hamlet's mind, which, unseated from its healthy relation, is constantly occupied with the world within, and abstracted from the world without, giving substance to shadows, and throwing a mist over all common-place actualities. It is the nature of thought to be indefinite; definiteness belongs to external images alone. Hence it is that the sense of sublimity arises, not from the sight of an outward object, but from the beholder's reflection upon it; not from the sensuous impression, but from the imaginative reflex. Few have seen a celebrated waterfall without feeling something akin to disappointment: it is only subsequently that the image comes back full into the mind, and brings with it a train of grand or beautiful associations. Hamlet feels this; his senses are in a state of trance, and he looks upon external things as hieroglyphics. His soliloquy—

O! that this too too solid flesh would melt, &c.

springs from that craving after the indefinite—for that which is not—which most easily besets men of genius; and the self-delusion common to this temper of mind is finely exemplified in the character which Hamlet gives of himself:

> it cannot be
> But I am pigeon-liver'd and lack gall
> To make oppression bitter.

He mistakes the seeing his chains for the breaking of them, delays action till action is of no use, and dies the victim of mere circumstance and accident.

## from *Lectures on Shakespeare and Milton*,[3] at Bristol

The lecturer, in descending to particulars, took occasion to defend from the common charge of improbable eccentricity, the scene which follows Hamlet's interview with the Ghost. He showed that after the mind has been stretched beyond its usual pitch and tone, it must either sink into exhaustion and inanity, or seek relief by change. Persons conversant with deeds of cruelty contrive to escape from their conscience by connecting something of the ludicrous with them; and by inventing grotesque terms, and a certain technical phraseology, to disguise the horror of their practices.

The terrible, however paradoxical it may appear, will be found to touch on the verge of the ludicrous. Both arise from the perception of something out of the common nature of things, something out of place; if from this we can abstract danger, the uncommonness alone remains, and the sense of the ridiculous is excited. The close alliance of these opposites appears from the circumstance that laughter is equally the expression of extreme anguish and horror as of joy: in the same manner that there are tears of joy as well as tears of sorrow, so there is a laugh of terror as well as a laugh of merriment. These complex causes will naturally have produced in Hamlet the disposition to escape from his own feelings of the overwhelming and supernatural by a wild transition to the ludicrous, a sort of cunning bravado, bordering on the flights of delirium.

Mr. Coleridge instanced, as a proof of Shakespeare's minute knowledge of human nature, the unimportant conversation which takes place during the expectation of the Ghost's appearance; and he recalled to our notice what all must have observed in common life, that on the brink of some serious enterprise, or

---

[3]These lectures were transcribed from notes by John Payne Collier, 1789–1883, Shakespearean critic, editor, and journalist.

event of moment, men naturally elude the pressure of their own thoughts by turning aside to trivial objects and familiar circumstances. So in *Hamlet*, the dialogue on the platform begins with remarks on the coldness of the air, and inquiries, obliquely connected indeed with the expected hour of the visitation, but thrown out in a seeming vacuity of topics, as to the striking of the clock. The same desire to escape from the inward thoughts is admirably carried on in Hamlet's moralizing on the Danish custom of wassailing; and a double purpose is here answered, which demonstrates the exquisite judgment of Shakespeare. By thus entangling the attention of the audience in the nice distinctions and parenthetical sentences of Hamlet, he takes them completely by surprise on the appearance of the Ghost, which comes upon them in all the suddenness of its visionary character. No modern writer would have dared, like Shakespeare, to have preceded this last visitation by two distinct appearances, or could have contrived that the third should rise upon the two former in impressiveness and solemnity of interest.

## William Hazlitt (1778–1830)

*Like Coleridge's Hamlet, William Hazlitt's character is preeminently an intellectual. He is not a hero in the usual sense of that word; he lives unto himself and ignores "the practical consequence of things." Hazlitt reads but does not see the play; for him, it might well be a study in human psychology, one that represents the mentality of its hero, not the situations in which he finds himself. In his* Characters of Shakespeare's Plays *(1818), he observes: "We do not like to see our author's plays acted and least of all Hamlet"—a statement that reveals in a rather backhanded way how brilliantly Shakespeare dramatized the inner life of thought, conscience, and will in the most popular of his plays.*

### from *Characters of Shakespeare's Plays*[1]

This is that Hamlet the Dane whom we read of in our youth, and whom we may be said almost to remember in our after-years; he

---

[1]William Hazlitt, *Characters of Shakespeare's Plays*, London, 1901; pp. 73–81.

who made that famous soliloquy on life, who gave the advice to the players, who thought "this goodly frame, the earth," a sterile promontory, and "this brave o'er-hanging firmament, the air, this majestical roof fretted with golden fire," "a foul and pestilent congregation of vapors;" whom "man delighted not, nor woman neither"; he who talked with the grave-diggers, and moralized on Yorick's skull; the school-fellow of Rosencrantz and Guildenstern at Wittenberg; the friend of Horatio; the lover of Ophelia; he that was mad and sent to England; the slow avenger of his father's death; who lived at the court of Horwendillus[2] five hundred years before we were born, but all whose thoughts we seem to know as well as we do our own, because we have read them in Shakespeare.

Hamlet is a name; his speeches and sayings but the idle coinage of the poet's brain. What then, are they not real? They are as real as our own thoughts. Their reality is in the reader's mind. It is *we* who are Hamlet.[3] This play has a prophetic truth, which is above that of history. Whoever has become thoughtful and melancholy through his own mishaps or those of others; whoever has borne about with him the clouded brow of reflection, and thought himself "too much i' th' sun"; whoever has seen the golden lamp of day dimmed by envious mists rising in his own breast, and could find in the world before him only a dull blank with nothing left remarkable in it; whoever has known "the pangs of despised love, the insolence of office, or the spurns which patient merit of the unworthy takes"; he who has felt his mind sink within him, and sadness cling to his heart like a malady, who has had his hopes blighted and his youth staggered by the apparitions of strange things; who cannot be well at ease, while he sees evil hovering near him like a specter; whose powers of action have been eaten up by thought, he to whom the universe seems infinite, and himself nothing; whose bitterness of soul makes him careless of consequences, and who goes to a play as his best resource to shove off, to a second remove, the evils of life by a mock representation of them—this is the true Hamlet.

We have been so used to this tragedy that we hardly know how to criticize it any more than we should know how to describe our own faces. But we must make such observations as we can. It is the one of Shakespeare's plays that we think of the oftenest, because it

---

[2]Horwendil, a king of Jutland; see Saxo Grammaticus, pp. 189–201.

[3]A. C. Bradley calls this mode of engagement "sentimental" reading.

abounds most in striking reflections on human life, and because the distresses of Hamlet are transferred, by the turn of his mind, to the general account of humanity. Whatever happens to him we apply to ourselves, because he applies it so himself as a means of general reasoning. He is a great moralizer; and what makes him worth attending to is, that he moralizes on his own feelings and experience. He is not a common-place pedant. If 'Lear' is distinguished by the greatest depth of passion, 'Hamlet' is the most remarkable for the ingenuity, originality, and unstudied development of character. Shakespeare had more magnanimity than any other poet, and he has shown more of it in this play than in any other. There is no attempt to force an interest: everything is left for time and circumstances to unfold. The attention is excited without effort, the incidents succeed each other as matters of course, the characters think and speak and act just as they might do if left entirely to themselves. There is no set purpose, no straining at a point. The observations are suggested by the passing scene—the gusts of passion come and go like sounds of music borne on the wind. The whole play is an exact transcript of what might be supposed to have taken place at the court of Denmark, at the remote period of time fixed upon, before the modern refinements in morals and manners were heard of. It would have been interesting enough to have been admitted as a bystander in such a scene, at such a time, to have heard and witnessed something of what was going on. But here we are more than spectators. We have not only "the outward pageants and the signs of grief;" but "we have that within which passes show." We read the thoughts of the heart, we catch the passions living as they rise. Other dramatic writers give us very fine versions and paraphrases of nature; but Shakespeare, together with his own comments, gives us the original text, that we may judge for ourselves. This is a very great advantage.

The character of Hamlet stands quite by itself. It is not a character marked by strength of will or even of passion, but by refinement of thought and sentiment.[4] Hamlet is as little of the hero as a man can well be: but he is a young and princely novice, full of high enthusiasm and quick sensibility—the sport of circumstances, questioning with fortune and refining on his own feelings, and forced from the natural bias of his disposition by the strangeness of his situation. He seems incapable of deliberate action, and is only hurried

[4]See also Coleridge, pp. 207–210.

into extremities on the spur of the occasion, when he has no time to reflect, as in the scene where he kills Polonius, and again, where he alters the letters which Rosencrantz and Guildenstern are taking with them to England, purporting his death. At other times, when he is most bound to act, he remains puzzled, undecided, and sceptical, dallies with his purposes, till the occasion is lost, and finds out some pretence to relapse into indolence and thoughtfulness again. For this reason he refuses to kill the King when he is at his prayers, and by a refinement in malice, which is in truth only an excuse for his own want of resolution, defers his revenge to a more fatal opportunity, when he shall be engaged in some act "that has no relish of salvation in it."

He is the prince of philosophical speculators; and because he cannot have his revenge perfect, according to the most refined idea his wish can form, he declines it altogether. So he scruples to trust the suggestions of the Ghost, contrives the scene of the play to have surer proof of his uncle's guilt, and then rests satisfied with this confirmation of his suspicions, and the success of his experiment, instead of acting upon it. Yet he is sensible of his own weakness, taxes himself with it, and tries to reason himself out of it [3.8].

Still he does nothing; and this very speculation on his own infirmity only affords him another occasion for indulging it. It is not from any want of attachment to his father or of abhorrence of his murder that Hamlet is thus dilatory; but it is more to his taste to indulge his imagination in reflecting upon the enormity of the crime and refining on his schemes of vengeance, than to put them into immediate practice. His ruling passion is to think, not to act: and any vague pretext that flatters this propensity instantly diverts him from his previous purposes.

The moral perfection of this character has been called in question, we think, by those who did not understand it. It is more interesting than according to rules; amiable, though not faultless. The ethical delineations of "that noble and liberal casuist" (as Shakespeare has been well called) do not exhibit the drab-colored quakerism of morality. His plays are not copied either from the 'Whole Duty of Man,' or from 'The Academy of Compliments!'[5] We confess we are a little shocked at the want of refinement in those who are shocked at the want of refinement in Hamlet. The neglect of punctilious exactness in his behavior either partakes of the "licence

[5]Generic titles for late Renaissance tracts on conduct and manners.

of the time," or else belongs to the every excess of intellectual refinement in the character, which makes the common rules of life, as well as his own purposes, sit loose upon him. He may be said to be amenable only to the tribunal of his own thoughts, and is too much taken up with the airy world of contemplation to lay as much stress as he ought on the practical consequences of things. His habitual principles of action are unhinged and out of joint with the time. His conduct to Ophelia is quite natural in his circumstances. It is that of assumed severity only. It is the effect of disappointed hope, of bitter regrets, of affection suspended, not obliterated, by the distractions of the scene around him! Amidst the natural and preternatural horrors of his situation, he might be excused in delicacy from carrying on a regular courtship. When "his father's spirit was in arms," it was not a time for the son to make love in. He could neither marry Ophelia, nor wound her mind by explaining the cause of his alienation, which he durst hardly trust himself to think of. It would have taken him years to have come to a direct explanation on the point. In the harassed state of his mind, he could not have done much otherwise than he did. His conduct does not contradict what he says when he sees her funeral,

> "I loved Ophelia. Forty thousand brothers
> Could not with all their quantity of love
> Make up my sum."— [5.1.271–273]

Nothing can be more affecting or beautiful than the Queen's apostrophe to Ophelia on throwing the flowers into the grave.

> "Sweets to the sweet! Farewell.          [*Scattering flowers.*]
> I hoped thou shouldst have been my Hamlet's wife.
> I thought thy bride-bed to have decked, sweet maid,
> And not t' have strewed thy grave."[5.1.243–246]

Shakespeare was thoroughly a master of the mixed motives of human character, and he here shows us the Queen, who was so criminal in some respects, not without sensibility and affection in other relations of life. Ophelia is a character almost too exquisitely touching to be dwelt upon. Oh rose of May, oh flower too soon faded! Her love, her madness, her death, are described with the truest touches of tenderness and pathos. It is a character which nobody but Shakespeare could have drawn in the way that he has done, and to the conception of which there is not even the smallest approach, except in some of the old romantic ballads. Her brother,

Laertes, is a character we do not like so well: he is too hot and choleric, and somewhat rhodomontade.[6] Polonius is a perfect character in its kind; nor is there any foundation for the objections which have been made to the consistency of this part. It is said that he acts very foolishly and talks very sensibly. There is no inconsistency in that. Again, that he talks wisely at one time and foolishly at another; that his advice to Laertes is very excellent, and his advice to the King and Queen on the subject of Hamlet's madness very ridiculous. But he gives the one as a father, and is sincere in it; he gives the other as a mere courtier, a busy-body, and is accordingly officious, garrulous, and impertinent. In short, Shakespeare has been accused of inconsistency in this and other characters, only because he has kept up the distinction which there is in nature, between the understandings and the moral habits of men, between the absurdity of their ideas and the absurdity of their motives. Polonius is not a fool, but he makes himself so. His folly, whether in his actions or speeches, comes under the head of impropriety of intention.

We do not like to see our author's plays acted, and least of all, *Hamlet*. There is no play that suffers so much in being transferred to the stage. Hamlet himself seems hardly capable of being acted. Mr. Kemble[7] unavoidably fails in this character from a want of ease and variety. The character of Hamlet is made up of undulating lines; it has the yielding flexibility of "a wave o' th' sea." Mr. Kemble plays it like a man in armor, with a determined inveteracy of purpose, in one undeviating straight line, which is as remote from the natural grace and refined susceptibility of the character, as the sharp angles and abrupt starts which Mr. Kean[8] introduces into the part. Mr. Kean's Hamlet is as much too splenetic[9] and rash as Mr. Kemble's is too deliberate and formal. His manner is too strong and pointed. He throws a severity, approaching to virulence, into the common observations and answers. There is nothing of this in Hamlet. He is, as it were, wrapped up in his reflections, and only *thinks aloud*. There should therefore be no attempt to impress what

[6]Boastful.

[7]Charles Kemble, 1775–1854, a leading actor who played on the London stage for twenty years, mostly in comic roles.

[8]Edmund Kean, 1787–1833, a great charismatic tragic actor, featured in many of Shakespeare's plays.

[9]Ill-tempered, bitter.

he says upon others by a studied exaggeration of emphasis or manner; no *talking at* his hearers. There should be as much of the gentleman and scholar as possible infused into the part, and as little of the actor. A pensive air of sadness should sit reluctantly upon his brow, but no appearance of fixed and sullen gloom. He is full of weakness and melancholy, but there is no harshness in his nature. He is the most amiable of misanthropes.

## Charles Dickens (1812–1870)

*Actors, like audiences, can be inexperienced and naive. In the actor Mr. Wopsle, Charles Dickens creates the counterpart to Fielding's Mr. Partridge. Great Expectations (1860–1861) illustrates how a great play can survive inept acting. Pip and his fellow spectators can have their mocking fun of Wopsle's performance because they know well and love the play that they are not, in fact, seeing. They do not walk out of the theater, not because they are loyal to Wopsle (whom presumably many do not know), but because his touching though inadequate efforts have the power to conjure up in their minds the* Hamlet *of their dreams. Implied, perhaps, in the hopelessness of Wopsle's performance is the absolute elusiveness of the perfect performance, one that can only be imagined.*

### from *Great Expectations* [1]

[Pip goes to see his friend Mr. Wopsle act the part of Hamlet]

On our arrival in Denmark,[2] we found the king and queen of that country elevated in two arm-chairs on a kitchen-table, holding a Court. The whole of the Danish nobility were in attendance, consisting of a noble boy in the wash-leather boots of a gigantic ancestor,[3] a venerable Peer with a dirty face who seemed to have risen from the people late in life,[4] and the Danish chivalry with a comb in its hair and a pair of white silk legs, and presenting on the whole a

[1]Charles Dickens, *Great Expectations*, Boston, 1861, pp. 228–230.
[2]I.e., the theater at which *Hamlet* was to be performed.
[3]Osric.
[4]Polonius.

feminine appearance.[5] My gifted townsman stood gloomily apart, with folded arms, and I could have wished that his curls and forehead had been more probable.[6]

Several curious little circumstances transpired as the action proceeded. The late king of the country[7] not only appeared to have been troubled with a cough at the time of his decease, but to have taken it with him to the tomb, and to have brought it back. The royal phantom also carried a ghostly manuscript round its truncheon, to which it had the appearance of occasionally referring, and that too, with air of anxiety and a tendency to lose the place of reference which were suggestive of a state of mortality. It was this, I conceive, which led to the Shade's being advised by the gallery to "turn over!"—a recommendation which it took extremely ill. It was likewise to be noted of this majestic spirit that whereas it always appeared with an air of having been out a long time and walked an immense distance, it perceptibly came from a closely continuous wall. This occasioned its terrors to be received derisively. The Queen of Denmark, a very buxom lady, though no doubt historically brazen, was considered by the public to have too much brass about her; her chin being attached to her diadem by a broad band of that metal (as if she had a gorgeous toothache), her waist being encircled by another, and each of her arms by another, so that she was openly mentioned as "the kettledrum." The noble boy in the ancestral boots, was inconsistent; representing himself, as it were in one breath, as an able seaman, a strolling actor, a grave-digger, a clergyman, and a person of the utmost importance at a Court fencing-match, on the authority of whose practiced eye and nice discrimination the finest strokes were judged. This gradually led to a want of toleration for him, and even—on his being detected in holy orders, and declining to perform the funeral service—to the general indignation taking the form of nuts. Lastly, Ophelia was a prey to such slow musical madness, that when, in course of time, she had taken off her white muslin scarf, folded it up, and buried it, a sulky man who had been long cooling his impatient nose against an iron bar in the front row of the gallery, growled, "Now the baby's put to bed let's have supper!" which, to say the least of it, was out of keeping.

[5]Laertes.

[6]Hamlet, played by Mr. Wopsle.

[7]The old king Hamlet.

Upon my unfortunate townsman all these incidents accumulated with playful effect.[8] Whenever that undecided Prince had to ask a question or state a doubt, the public helped him out with it. As for example: on the question whether 'twas nobler in the mind to suffer, some roared yes, and some no, and some inclining to both opinions said "toss up for it;" and quite a Debating Society arose. When he asked what should such fellows as he do crawling between earth and heaven, he was encouraged with loud cries of "Hear, hear!" When he appeared with his stocking disordered (its disorder expressed, according to usage, by one very neat fold at the top, which I suppose to be always got up with a flat iron), a conversation took place in the gallery respecting the paleness of his leg, and whether it was occasioned by the turn the Ghost had given him. On his taking the recorders—very like a little black flute that had just been played in the orchestra and handed out at the door—he was called on unanimously for Rule Britannia. When he recommended the player not to saw the air thus, the sulky man said, "And don't you do it neither: you're a deal worse than him!" And I grieve to add that peals of laughter greeted Mr. Wopsle on every one of these occasions.

But his greatest trials were in the churchyard; which had the appearance of a primeval forest, with a kind of small ecclesiastical wash-house on one side, and a turnpike gate on the other. Mr. Wopsle in a comprehensive black cloak, being descried entering at the turnpike, the grave-digger was admonished in a friendly way, "Look out! Here's the undertaker a coming to see how you're a getting on with your work!" I believe it is well known in a constitutional country that Mr. Wopsle could not possibly have returned the skull, after moralizing over it, without dusting his fingers on a white napkin taken from his breast; but even that innocent and indispensable action did not pass without the comment "Wai-ter!" The arrival of the body for interment (in an empty black box with the lid tumbling open), was the signal for a general joy which was much enhanced by the discovery, among the bearers, of an individual obnoxious to identification. The joy attended Mr. Wopsle through his struggle with Laertes on the brink of the orchestra and the grave, and slackened no more until he had tumbled the king off the kitchen-table, and died by inches from the ankles upward.

[8] I.e., Hamlet.

We had made some pale efforts in the beginning to applaud Mr. Wopsle; but they were too hopeless to be persisted in. Therefore we had sat, feeling keenly for him, but laughing, nevertheless, from ear to ear.

## Samuel Clemens (1835–1910)

*In his* Adventures of Huckleberry Finn *(1885), Samuel Clemens, known to his readers as Mark Twain, creates a* Hamlet *designed especially for Americans. The duke's ludicrous parody of the best-known and most-quoted of* Hamlet's *lines—"To be or not to be"—paradoxically preserves this soliloquy: it expects that readers can and will recall its true form. In so doing, Clemens shows how deeply* Hamlet *has penetrated the culture of the American continent; he implies that Shakespeare's drama can and will survive its representations, however comic, even in settings quite alien to any its author could have imagined. Like Wopsle's* Hamlet, *the duke's* Hamlet *functions as a comic* aide-memoire; *it shadows the character Shakespeare actually created.*

### from *The Adventures of Huckleberry Finn* [1]

[Huck hears the king rehearse Hamlet's soliloquy[2]]

After dinner, the duke says:

"Well, Capet,[3] we'll want to make this a first-class show, you know, so I guess we'll add a little more to it. We want a little something to answer encores with, anyway."

"What's onkores, Bilgewater?[4]"

The duke told him, and then says:

---

[1]Samuel Clemens, *The Adventures of Huckleberry Finn*, New York, 1889; pp. 178–179.

[2]Huckleberry Finn, Clemens's youthful hero, is in the company of two con men, nicknamed the duke and the king. They are on their way down the Mississippi River.

[3]Probably a reference to Hugh Capet, who acceded to the French throne in 987; Capetian monarchs ruled France to 1328.

[4]Probably a reference to Francis Egerton, the last Duke of Bridgewater, 1736–1803, who built canals throughout England and was celebrated as the founder of British inland navigation.

"I'll answer by doing the Highland fling or the sailor's horn-pipe; and you—well, let me see—Oh, I've got it—you can do Hamlet's soliloquy."

"Hamlet's which?"

"Hamlet's soliloquy, you know; the most celebrated thing in Shakespeare. Ah, it's sublime, sublime! Always fetches the house. I haven't got it in the book—I've only got one volume—but I reckon I can piece it out from memory. I'll just walk up and down a minute, and see if I can call it back from recollection's vaults."

So he want to marching up and down, thinking, and frowning horrible every now and then; then he would hoist up his eyebrows; next he would squeeze his hand on his forehead and stagger back and kind of moan; next he would sigh, and next he'd let on to drop a tear. It was beautiful to see him. By-and-by he got it. He told us to give attention. Then he strikes a most noble attitude, with one leg shoved forwards, and his arms stretched away up and his head tilted back, looking up at the sky; and then he begins to rip and rave and grit his teeth; and after that, all through his speech he howled, and spread around, and swelled up his chest, and just knocked the spots out of any acting ever I see before. This is the speech—I learned it, easy enough, while he was learning it to the king:

> To be, or not to be; that is the bare bodkin
> That makes calamity of so long life;
> For who would fardels bear, till Birnam Wood do come to
>      Dunsinane,[5]
> But that the fear of something after death
> Murders the innocent sleep,
> Great nature's second course,
> And makes us rather sling the arrows of outrageous fortune
> Than fly to others that we know not of.
> There's the respect must give us pause:
> Wake Duncan with thy knocking! I would thou couldst;
> For who would bear the whips and scorns of time,
> The oppressor's wrong, the proud man's contumely,
> The law's delay, and the quietus which his pangs might take,
> In the dead waste and middle of the night, when churchyards yawn
> In customary suits of solemn black,
> But that the undiscovered country from whose bourn no traveler
>      returns,

[5]The duke interpolates phrases from *Macbeth* as well as other parts of *Hamlet* throughout this parody of Hamlet's soliloquy.

Breathes forth contagion on the world,
And thus the native hue of resolution, like the poor cat i' the adage,
Is sicklied o'er with care,
And all the clouds that lowered o'er our housetops,
With this regard their currents turn awry,
And lose the name of action.
'Tis a consummation devoutly to be wished. But soft you, the fair
    Ophelia:
Ope not thy ponderous and marble jaws,
But get thee to a nunnery—go!

Well, the old man he liked that speech, and he mighty soon got it so he could do it first rate. It seemed like he was just born for it; and when he had his hand in and was excited, it was perfectly lovely the way he would rip and tear and rair up behind when he was getting it off.

## A.C. Bradley (1851–1935)

*Shakespearean Tragedy (1905) dismisses two popular representations of Hamlet's character: the epitome of oversensitivity (as Goethe saw him) and the inward, brooding man of thought (as Coleridge read him). Rather, A. C. Bradley sees that Hamlet is beset with melancholy, a maladjustment of the psyche. Like Coleridge and Hazlitt, Bradley does not take account of Hamlet's situation, the constraints it puts on him as a prince called to avenge his father's murder. What focuses Bradley's attention is Hamlet's particular cast of mind and his unusual behavior, both symptomatic of disease.*

### from *Shakespearean Tragedy* [1]

We come next to what may be called the sentimental view of Hamlet, a view common both among his worshippers and among his defamers. Its germ may perhaps be found in an unfortunate phrase of Goethe's (who of course is not responsible for the whole view): "a lovely, pure and most moral nature, *without the strength of nerve which forms a hero,* sinks beneath a burden which it cannot

[1]A. C. Bradley, *Shakespearean Tragedy: Lectures on Hamlet, Othello, King Lear, and Macbeth*, London, 1905; pp. 101–108, 120–128.

bear and must not cast away." When this idea is isolated, developed and popularised, we get the picture of a graceful youth, sweet and sensitive, full of delicate sympathies and yearning aspirations, shrinking from the touch of everything gross and earthly; but frail and weak, a kind of Werther,[2] with a face like Shelley's[3] and a voice like Mr. Tree's.[4] And then we ask in tender pity, how could such a man perform the terrible duty laid on him?

How, indeed! And what a foolish Ghost even to suggest such a duty! But this conception, though not without its basis in certain beautiful traits of Hamlet's nature, is utterly untrue. It is too kind to Hamlet on one side, and it is quite unjust to him on another. The "conscience" theory at any rate leaves Hamlet a great nature which you can admire and even revere. But for the "sentimental" Hamlet you can feel only pity not unmingled with contempt. Whatever else he is, he is no *hero*.

But consider the text. This shrinking, flower-like youth—how could he possibly have done what we *see* Hamlet do? What likeness to him is there in the Hamlet who, summoned by the Ghost, bursts from his terrified friends with the cry:

> Unhand me, gentlemen!
> By heaven, I'll make a ghost of him that lets me;

the Hamlet who scarcely once speaks to the King without an insult, or to Polonius without a gibe; the Hamlet who storms at Ophelia and speaks daggers to his mother; the Hamlet who, hearing a cry behind the arras, whips out his sword in an instant and runs the eavesdropper through; the Hamlet who sends his 'school-fellows' to their death and never troubles his head about them more; the Hamlet who is the first man to board a pirate ship, and who fights with Laertes in the grave; the Hamlet of the catastrophe, an omnipotent fate, before whom all the court stands helpless, who, as the truth breaks upon him, rushes on the King, drives his foil right through his body, then seizes the poisoned cup and forces it violently between the wretched man's lips, and in the throes of death

---

[2]The sensitive and unfortunate artist is the hero of Goethe's novel *The Sorrows of Young Werther*, 1774.

[3]Percy Bysshe Shelley, 1792–1822, English poet of the romantic period, noted for his "feminine" beauty.

[4]Sir Herbert Beerbohm Tree, 1853–1917, actor and manager of the Haymarket Theater and later Her Majesty's Theater, produced and acted in many of Shakespeare's plays.

has force and fire enough to wrest the cup from Horatio's hand ("By heaven, I'll have it!") lest he should drink and die? This man, the Hamlet of the play, is a heroic, terrible figure. He would have been formidable to Othello or Macbeth. If the sentimental Hamlet had crossed him, he would have hurled him from his path with one sweep of his arm. This view, then, or any view that approaches it, is grossly unjust to Hamlet, and turns tragedy into mere pathos. But, on the other side, it is too kind to him. It ignores the hardness and cynicism which were indeed no part of his nature, but yet, in this crisis of his life, are indubitably present and painfully marked. His sternness, itself left out of sight by this theory, is no defect; but he is much more than stern. Polonius possibly deserved nothing better than the words addressed to his corpse:

> Thou wretched, rash, intruding fool, farewell!
> I took thee for thy better: take thy fortune:
> Thou find'st to be too busy is some danger;

yet this was Ophelia's father, and, whatever he deserved, it pains us, for Hamlet's sake, to hear the words:

> This man shall set me packing:
> I'll lug the guts into the neighbor room.

There is the same insensibility in Hamlet's language about the fate of Rosencrantz and Guildenstern; and, observe, their deaths were not in the least required by his purpose. Grant, again, that his cruelty to Ophelia was partly due to misunderstanding, partly forced on him, partly feigned; still one surely cannot altogether so account for it, and still less can one so account for the disgusting and insulting grossness of his language to her in the play-scene. I know this is said to be merely an example of the custom of Shakespeare's time. But it is not so. It is such language as you will find addressed to a woman by no other hero of Shakespeare's, not even in that dreadful scene where Othello accuses Desdemona.[5] It is a great mistake to ignore these things, or to try to soften the impression which they naturally make on one. That this embitterment, callousness, grossness, brutality, should be induced on a soul so pure and noble is profoundly tragic; and Shakespeare's business was to show this tragedy, not to paint an ideally beautiful soul unstained and undis-

[5]See *Othello* 5.2.23–109.

turbed by the evil of the world and the anguish of conscious failure. There remains, finally, that class of view which may be named after Schlegel[6] and Coleridge. According to this, *Hamlet* is the tragedy of reflection. The cause of the hero's delay is irresolution; and the cause of this irresolution is excess of the reflective or speculative habit of mind. He has a general intention to obey the ghost, but "the native hue of resolution is sicklied o'er with the pale cast of thought." He is "thought-sick." "The whole," says Schlegel, "is intended to show how a calculating consideration which aims at exhausting, so far as human foresight can, all the relations and possible consequences of a deed, cripples the power of acting. . . . Hamlet is a hypocrite towards himself; his far-fetched scruples are often mere pretexts to cover his want of determination. . . . He has no firm belief in himself or in anything else. . . . He loses himself in labyrinths of thought." So Coleridge finds in Hamlet "an almost enormous intellectual activity and a proportionate aversion to real action consequent upon it" (the aversion, that is to say, is consequent on the activity). Professor Dowden[7] objects to this view, very justly, that it neglects the emotional side of Hamlet's character, "which is quite as important as the intellectual"; but, with this supplement, he appears on the whole to adopt it. Hamlet, he says, "loses a sense of fact because with him each object and event transforms and expands itself into an idea. . . . He cannot steadily keep alive within himself a sense of the importance of any positive, limited thing,—a deed, for example." And Professor Dowden explains this condition by reference to Hamlet's life. "When the play opens he has reached the age of thirty years . . . and he has received culture of every kind except the culture of active life. During the reign of the strong-willed elder Hamlet there was no call to action for his meditative son. He has slipped on into years of full manhood still a haunter of the university, a student of philosophies, an amateur in art, a ponderer on the things of life and death, who has never formed a resolution or executed a deed."

On the whole, the Schlegel-Coleridge theory (with or without Professor Dowden's modification and amplification) is the most

---

[6]August Wilhelm von Schlegel, 1767–1845, critic and exponent of the movement of German Romanticism who wrote on theater and Shakespeare and visibly influenced Coleridge's Shakespeare criticism.

[7]Edward Dowden, 1843–1913, Professor of English at Trinity College, Dublin, a scholar who wrote on Shakespeare and the romantic poets.

widely received view of Hamlet's character. And with it we come at last into close contact with the text of the play. It not only answers, in some fundamental respects, to the general impression produced by the drama, but it can be supported by Hamlet's own words in his soliloquies—such words, for example, as those about the native hue of resolution, or those about the craven scruple of thinking too precisely on the event. It is confirmed, also, by the contrast between Hamlet on the one side and Laertes and Fortinbras on the other; and, further, by the occurrence of those words of the King to Laertes (IV. vii. 119 f.), which, if they are not in character, are all the more important as showing what was in Shakespeare's mind at the time:

> that we would do
> We should do when we would; for this "would" changes,
> And hath abatements and delays as many
> As there are tongues, are hands, are accidents;
> And then this "should" is like a spendthrift sigh
> That hurts by easing.

And, lastly, even if the view itself does not suffice, the *description* given by its adherents of Hamlet's state of mind, as we see him in the last four Acts, is, on the whole and so far as it goes, a true description. The energy of resolve is dissipated in an endless brooding on the deed required. When he acts, his action does not proceed from this deliberation and analysis, but is sudden and impulsive, evoked by an emergency in which he has no time to think. And most of the reasons he assigns for his procrastination are evidently not the true reasons, but unconscious excuses.

Nevertheless this theory fails to satisfy. And it fails not merely in this or that detail, but as a whole. We feel that its Hamlet does not fully answer to our imaginative impression. He is not nearly so inadequate to this impression as the sentimental Hamlet, but still we feel he is inferior to Shakespeare's man and does him wrong. And when we come to examine the theory we find that it is partial and leaves much unexplained. I pass that by for the present, for we shall see, I believe, that the theory is also positively misleading, and that in a most important way. And of this I proceed to speak.

Hamlet's irresolution, or his aversion to real action, is, according to the theory, the *direct* result of "an almost enormous intellectual activity" in the way of "a calculating consideration which attempts to exhaust all the relations and possible consequences of a deed." And this again proceeds from an original one-sidedness of nature, strengthened by habit, and, perhaps, by years of speculative inaction. The theory describes, therefore, a man in certain respects like Coleridge himself, on one side a man of genius, on the other side, the side of will, deplorably weak, always procrastinating and avoiding unpleasant duties, and often reproaching himself in vain; a man, observe, who at *any* time and in *any* circumstances would be unequal to the task assigned to Hamlet. And thus, I must maintain, it degrades Hamlet and travesties the play. For Hamlet, according to all the indications in the text, was not naturally or normally such a man, but rather, I venture to affirm, a man who at any *other* time and in any *other* circumstances than those presented would have been perfectly equal to his task; and it is, in fact, the very cruelty of his fate that the crisis of his life comes on him at the one moment when he cannot meet it, and when his highest gifts, instead of helping him, conspire to paralyze him. This aspect of the tragedy the theory quite misses; and it does so because it misconceives the cause of that irresolution, which, on the whole, it truly describes. For the cause was not directly or mainly an habitual excess of reflectiveness. The direct cause was a state of mind quite abnormal and induced by special circumstances,—a state of profound melancholy. Now, Hamlet's reflectiveness doubtless played a certain part in the *production* of that melancholy, and was thus one indirect contributory cause of his irresolution.[8] And, again, the melancholy, once established, displayed, as one of its *symptoms,* an excessive reflection on the required deed. But excess of reflection was not, as the theory makes it, the *direct* cause of the irresolution at all; nor was it the *only* indirect cause; and in the Hamlet of the last four Acts it is to be considered rather a symptom of his state than a cause of it. [. . .]

"Melancholy," I said, not dejection, nor yet insanity. That Hamlet was not far from insanity is very probable. His adoption of the pretence of madness may well have been due in part to fear of the reality; to an instinct of self-preservation, a fore-feeling that the pretence would enable him to give some utterance to the load that pressed on his heart and brain, and a fear that he would be unable altogether to repress such utterance. And if the pathologist calls his state melancholia, and even proceeds to determine its species, I see nothing to object to in that; I am grateful to him for emphasizing the fact that Hamlet's melancholy was no mere common depression of spirits; and I have no doubt that many readers

[8]On melancholy, see pp. 149–156.

of the play would understand it better if they read an account of melancholia in a work on mental diseases. If we like to use the word "disease" loosely, Hamlet's condition may truly be called diseased. No exertion of will could have dispelled it. Even if he had been able at once to do the bidding of the Ghost he would doubtless have still remained for some time under the cloud. It would be absurdly unjust to call *Hamlet* a study of melancholy, but it contains such a study.

But this melancholy is something very different from insanity, in anything like the usual meaning of that word. No doubt it might develop into insanity. The longing for death might become an irresistible impulse to self-destruction; the disorder of feeling and will might extend to sense and intellect; delusions might arise; and the man might become, as we say, incapable and irresponsible. But Hamlet's melancholy is some way from this condition. It is a totally different thing from the madness which he feigns; and he never, when alone or in company with Horatio alone, exhibits the signs of that madness. Nor is the dramatic use of this melancholy, again, open to the objections which would justly be made to the portrayal of an insanity which brought the hero to a tragic end. The man who suffers as Hamlet suffers—and thousands go about their business suffering thus in greater or less degree—is considered irresponsible neither by other people nor by himself: he is only too keenly conscious of his responsibility. He is therefore, so far, quite capable of being a tragic agent, which an insane person, at any rate according to Shakespeare's practice, is not. And, finally, Hamlet's state is not one which a healthy mind is unable sufficiently to imagine. It is probably not further from average experience, nor more difficult to realize, than the great tragic passions of Othello, Antony or Macbeth.

Let me try to show now, briefly, how much this melancholy accounts for.

It accounts for the main fact, Hamlet's inaction. For the *immediate* cause of that is simply that his habitual feeling is one of disgust at life and everything in it, himself included,—a disgust which varies in intensity, rising at times into a longing for death, sinking often into weary apathy, but is never dispelled for more than brief intervals. Such a state of feeling is inevitably adverse to *any* kind of decided action; the body is inert, the mind indifferent or worse; its response is, "it does not matter," "it is not worth while," "it is no good." And the action required of Hamlet is very exceptional. It is violent, dangerous, difficult to accomplish perfectly, on one side repulsive to a man of honor and sensitive feeling, on another side involved in a certain mystery (here come in thus, in their subordinate place, various causes of inaction assigned by various theories). These obstacles would not suffice to prevent Hamlet from acting, if his state were normal; and against them there operate, even in his morbid state, healthy and positive feelings, love of his father, loathing of his uncle, desire of revenge, desire to do duty. But the retarding motives acquire an unnatural strength because they have an ally in something far stronger than themselves, the melancholic disgust and apathy; while the healthy motives, emerging with difficulty from the central mass of diseased feeling, rapidly sink back into it and "lose the name of action." We *see* them doing so; and sometimes the process is quite simple, no analytical reflection on the deed intervening between the outburst of passion and the relapse into melancholy. But this melancholy is perfectly consistent also with that incessant dissection of the task assigned, of which the Schlegel-Coleridge theory makes so much. For those endless questions (as we may imagine them), "Was I deceived by the Ghost? How am I to do the deed? When? Where? What will be the consequence of attempting it—success, my death, utter misunderstanding, mere mischief to the State? Can it be right to do it, or noble to kill a defenseless man? What is the good of doing it in such a world as this?"—all this, and whatever else passed in a sickening round through Hamlet's mind, was not the healthy and right deliberation of a man with such a task, but otiose thinking hardly deserving the name of thought, an unconscious weaving of pretexts for inaction, aimless tossings on a sick bed, symptoms of melancholy which only increased it by deepening self-contempt.

Again, this state accounts for Hamlet's energy as well as for his lassitude, those quick decided actions of his being the outcome of a nature normally far from passive, now suddenly stimulated, and producing healthy impulses which work themselves out before they have time to subside. It accounts for the evidently keen satisfaction which some of these actions give to him. He arranges the play-scene with lively interest, and exults in its success, not really because it brings him nearer to his goal, but partly because it has hurt his enemy and partly because it has demonstrated his own skill (3.2.269–288). He looks forward almost with glee to countermining the King's designs in sending him away (3.4.209), and looks back with obvious satisfaction, even with pride, to the address and vigor he displayed on the voyage (5.2.1–55). These were not *the* action on which his morbid self-feeling had centered; he feels in them his old force, and escapes in them from his disgust. It accounts for the pleasure with which he meets old acquaintances, like his "school-fellows" or the actors. The former observed (and we can observe) in him a "kind of joy" at first, though it is followed by "much forcing of his disposition" as he attempts to keep this joy and his courtesy alive in spite of the misery which so soon returns upon him and the suspicion he is forced to feel. It accounts no less for the painful features of his character as seen in the play, his almost savage irritability on the one hand, and on the other his self-absorption, his callousness, his insensibility to the fates of those whom he despises, and to the feelings even of those whom he loves. These are frequent symptoms of such melancholy, and they sometimes alternate, as they do in Hamlet, with bursts of transitory, almost hysterical, and quite fruitless emotion. It is to these last (of which a part of the soliloquy, "O what a rogue," gives a good example) that Hamlet alludes when, to the Ghost, he speaks of himself as "lapsed in *passion*," and it is doubtless partly his conscious weakness in regard to them that inspires his praise of Horatio as a man who is not "passion's slave."

Finally, Hamlet's melancholy accounts for two things which seem to be explained by nothing else. The first of these is his apathy or "lethargy." We are bound to consider the evidence which the text supplies of this, though it is usual to ignore it. When Hamlet mentions, as one possible cause of his inaction, his "thinking too precisely on the event," he mentions another, "bestial oblivion"; and the thing against which he inveighs in the greater part of that soliloquy (4.4) is not the excess or the misuse of reason (which for him here and always is god-like), but this *bestial* oblivion or "*dullness*," this "letting all *sleep*," this allowing of heaven-sent reason to "fust unused":

> What is a man,
> If his chief good and market of his time
> Be but to *sleep* and feed? a *beast*, no more.

So, in the soliloquy in 2.2. he accuses himself of being "a *dull* and muddy-mettled rascal," who "peaks [mopes] like John-a-dreams, unpregnant of his cause," dully indifferent to his cause. So, when the Ghost appears to him the second time, he accuses himself of being tardy and lapsed in *time;* and the Ghost speaks of his purpose being almost *blunted*, and bids him not to *forget* (cf. "oblivion"). And so, what is emphasized in those undramatic but significant speeches of the player-king and of Claudius is the mere dying away of purpose or of love. Surely what all this points to is not a condition of excessive but useless mental activity (indeed there is, in reality, curiously little about that in the text), but rather one of dull, apathetic, brooding gloom, in which Hamlet, so far from analyzing his duty, is not thinking of it at all, but for the time literally *forgets* it. It seems to me we are driven to think of Hamlet *chiefly* thus during the long time which elapsed between the appearance of the Ghost and the events presented in the Second Act. The Ghost, in fact, had more reason than we suppose at first for leaving with Hamlet as his parting injunction the command, "Remember me," and for greeting him, on re-appearing, with the command, "Do not forget." These little things in Shakespeare are not accidents.

The second trait which is fully explained only by Hamlet's melancholy is his own inability to understand why he delays. This emerges in a marked degree when an occasion like the player's emotion or the sight of Fortinbras's army stings Hamlet into shame at his inaction. "*Why,*" he asks himself in genuine bewilderment, "do I linger? Can the cause be cowardice? Can it be sloth? Can it be thinking too precisely of the event? And does *that* again mean cowardice? What is it that makes me sit idle when I feel it is shameful to do so, and when I have *cause, and will, and strength, and means,* to act?" A man irresolute merely because he was considering a proposed action too minutely would not feel this bewilderment. A man might feel it whose conscience secretly condemned the act which his explicit consciousness approved; but we have seen that there is no sufficient evidence to justify us in conceiving Hamlet thus. These are the questions of a man stimulated for the moment to shake off the weight of his melancholy, and, because for the moment he is free from it, unable to understand the paralyzing pressure which it exerts at other times.

I have dwelt thus at length on Hamlet's melancholy because, from the psychological point of view, it is the center of the tragedy, and to omit it from consideration or to underrate its intensity is to make Shakespeare's story unintelligible. But the psychological point of view is not equivalent to the tragic; and, having once given its due weight to the fact of Hamlet's melancholy, we may freely admit, or rather may be anxious to insist, that this pathological condition would excite but little, if any, tragic interest if it were not the condition of a nature distinguished by that speculative genius on which the Schlegel-Coleridge type of theory lays stress. Such theories misinterpret the connection between that genius and Hamlet's failure, but still it is this connection which gives to his story its peculiar fascination and makes it appear (if the phrase may be allowed) as the symbol of a tragic mystery inherent in human nature. Wherever this mystery touches us, wherever we are forced to feel the wonder and awe of man's godlike "apprehension" and his "thoughts that wander through eternity," and at the same time are forced to see him powerless in his petty sphere of action, and powerless (it would appear) from the very divinity of his thought, we remember Hamlet. And this is the reason why, in the great ideal movement which began towards the close of the eighteenth century, this tragedy acquired a position unique among Shakespeare's dramas, and shared only by Goethe's *Faust*.[9] It was not that *Hamlet* is Shakespeare's greatest tragedy or most perfect work of art; it was that *Hamlet* most brings home to us at once the sense of the soul's infinity, and the sense of the doom which not only circumscribes that infinity but appears to be its offspring.

[9]*Faust*: a play by Goethe, published in two parts, 1808 and 1832. Unlike the hero of Christopher Marlowe's early 17th-century play *Dr. Faustus*, Goethe's Faust is not damned but is carried off to heaven by angels after a period of purification and service to mankind.

# Further Reading

## On Shakespeare and *Hamlet*:

Adelman, Janet. *Suffocating Mothers: Fantasies of Maternal Origin in Shakespeare's Plays, Hamlet to* The Tempest. London: Routledge, 1992.

Ayer, P. K. "Reading, Writing and *Hamlet*." *Shakespeare Quarterly* 44 (1993): 423–439.

Bate, Jonathan. *The Genius of Shakespeare*. Oxford: Oxford University Press, 1998.

Belsey, Catherine. *The Subject of Tragedy: Identity and Difference in Renaissance Drama*. London: Methuen, 1985.

Bevington, David, ed. "Hamlet." In *The Complete Works of Shakespeare*. 5th ed. New York: Longman, 2004, 1097–1149.

Booth, Stephen. "On the Value of Hamlet." In *Reinterpretations of Elizabethan Drama*. Ed. Norman Rabkin. New York: Columbia University Press, 1969, 137–176.

Bowers, Fredson Thayer. *Hamlet as Scourge and Minister*. Charlottesville: University of Virginia Press, 1989.

Cary, Louise D. "Hamlet Recycled, or the Tragical History of the Prince's Prints." *ELH* 61 (1994): 783–805.

Cohen, Walter. *The Drama of a Nation: Public Theater in Renaissance England and Spain*. Ithaca: Cornell University Press, 1985.

Colie, Rosalie. *Shakespeare's Living Art*. Princeton: Princeton University Press, 1974.

Dawson, Anthony B. "The Impasse over the Stage." *ELR* 21 (1991): 309–327.

Dollimore, Jonathan, and Alan Sinfield, eds. *Political Shakespeare: New Essays in Cultural Materialism*. Ithaca: Cornell University Press and Manchester University Press, 1985.

Eagleton, Terry. *William Shakespeare*. Oxford: Basil Blackwell, 1986.

Erickson, Peter. *Patriarchal Structures in Shakespeare's Drama*. Berkeley: University of California Press, 1985.

Foakes, R. A. Hamlet *versus* Lear: *Cultural Politics and Shakespeare's Art*. Cambridge: Cambridge University Press, 1993.

Goldman, Michael. *Shakespeare and the Energies of Drama*. Princeton: Princeton University Press, 1993, 74–93.

Grady, Hugh. *Shakespeare, Machiavelli, and Montaigne: Power and Subjectivity from* Richard II *to* Hamlet. Oxford: Oxford University Press, 2002.

Grazia, Margreta de. "*Hamlet* Before its Time." *MLQ* 62 (2001): 355–375.

Greenblatt, Stephen. *Hamlet in Purgatory*. Princeton: Princeton University Press, 2001.

———. "The Mousetrap." *Shakespeare Studies* 35 (1997): 1–32.

———. "Introduction to *Hamlet*." In *The Norton Shakespeare*. Eds. Stephen Greenblatt, Walter Cohen, Jean E. Howard, and Katharine Eisaman Maus. New York: W.W. Norton, 1997, 1659–1666.

Gross, Kenneth. "The Rumor of *Hamlet*." *Raritan* 14 (1994): 43–76.

Holland, Norman. *Psychoanalysis and Shakespeare*. New York: Octagon, 1989.

Howard, Jean, and Marion O'Connor, eds. *Shakespeare Reproduced: The Text in History and Ideology*. New York: Methuen, 1987.

Jardine, Lisa. *Still Harping on Daughters: Women and Drama in the Age of Shakespeare*. Brighton: Harvester, 1983.

Jones, Ernest. Hamlet *and* Oedipus. New York: Norton, 1976.

Kahn, Coppelia. *Man's Estate: Masculine Identity in Shakespeare*. Berkeley: University of California Press, 1981.

Kastan, David Scott. *Shakespeare and the Book*. Cambridge: Cambridge University Press, 2001.

———. "'His Semblable in His Mirror': *Hamlet* and the Imitation of Revenge." *Shakespeare Studies* 19 (1991): 111–124.

Kerrigan, William. *Hamlet's Perfection*. Baltimore: Johns Hopkins University Press, 1996.

Kliman, Bernice, ed. *Approaches to Teaching Shakespeare's* Hamlet. New York: The Modern Language Association of America, 2001.

Knight, G. Wilson. *Wheel of Fire: Interpretations of Shakespearian Tragedy*. London: Methuen, 1949.

Knights, L. C. *An Approach to* Hamlet. London: Chatto and Windus, 1960.

Kurland, Stuart. "Hamlet and the Scottish Succession?" *Studies in English Literature* 34 (1994): 279–300.

Lenz, Carolyn Ruth Swift, Gayle Greene, and Carol Thomas Neely, eds. *Woman's Part: Feminist Criticism of Shakespeare*. Urbana: University of Illinois Press, 1980.

Levao, Ronald. "King of Infinite Space: Hamlet and His Fictions." *Renaissance Minds and Their Fictions*. Berkeley: University of California Press, 1986, 334–364.

Leverenz, David. "The Woman in *Hamlet*: An Interpersonal View." *Journal of Women in Culture and Society* 4:2 (1978): 291–308.

Levin, Harry. *The Question of Hamlet*. New York: Oxford University Press, 1959.

Low, Anthony. "*Hamlet* and the Ghost of Purgatory: Intimations of Killing the Father." *ELR* 29 (1999): 443–467.

Lupton, Julia Reinhard, and Kenneth Reinhard. *After Oedipus: Shakespeare in Psychoanalysis*. Ithaca: Cornell University Press, 1993.

Mack, Maynard. "The World of *Hamlet*." *The Yale Review* 41 (1852): 502–523. Rpt. in *Twentieth-Century Interpretations of Hamlet*. Ed. David Bevington. Englewood Cliffs, New Jersey: Prentice Hall, 1968.

Mallette, Richard. "From Gyves to Graces: *Hamlet* and Free Will." *Journal of English and Germanic Philology* 93 (1994): 336–355.

Marcus, Leah. *Unediting the Renaissance: Shakespeare, Marlowe, Milton.* London: Routledge, 1996.

Neely, Carol Thomas. *Broken Nuptials in Shakespeare's Plays.* New Haven: Yale University Press, 1985.

Newman, Karen. *Fashioning Femininity and English Renaissance Drama.* Chicago: University of Chicago Press, 1991.

Novy, Marianne. *Love's Argument: Gender Relations in Shakespeare.* Chapel Hill: University of North Carolina Press, 1984.

Parker, Patricia. *Shakespeare from the Margins: Language, Culture, Context.* Chicago: Chicago University Press, 1996.

Parker, Patricia, and Geoffrey Hartman, eds. *Shakespeare and the Question of Theory.* New York: Methuen, 1985.

Paster, Gail Kern. "The Body and Its Passions." *Shakespeare Studies* 29 (2001): 44–50.

Patterson, Annabel. *Shakespeare and the Popular Voice.* Oxford: Basil Blackwell, 1989.

Rabkin, Norman. *Shakespeare and the Common Understanding.* New York: The Free Press, 1967.

Rosenberg, Marvin. *The Masks of Hamlet.* Newark: University of Delaware Press, 1992.

Sanders, Eve Rachele. *Gender and Literacy on Stage in Early Modern England.* Cambridge: Cambridge University Press, 1998.

Stoppard, Tom. *Rosencrantz and Guildenstern Are Dead.* New York: Grove Press, 1967.

Targoff, Ramie. "The Performance of Prayer: Sincerity and Theatricality in Early Modern England." *Representations* 60 (1997): 49–64.

Watson, Robert N. "Giving up the Ghost in a World of Decay: Hamlet's Revenge and Denial." *Renaissance Drama* 21 (1990): 199–223.

Wilson, J. Dover. *What Happens in* Hamlet. Cambridge: Cambridge University Press, 1951.

Wilson, Luke. *Theaters of Intention: Drama and the Law in Early Modern England.* Stanford: Stanford University Press, 2000.

Wright, George T. "Hendiadys and *Hamlet.*" *PMLA* 96 (1981): 168–193.

## On Shakespeare and the London Theater:

Agnew, Jean-Christophe. *Worlds Apart: The Market and the Theater in Anglo-American Thought, 1550–1750.* Cambridge: Cambridge University Press, 1986.

Bristol, Michael. *Big-Time Shakespeare.* London: Routledge, 1996.

Gurr, Andrew. *The Shakespearean Playing Companies.* Oxford: Oxford University Press, 1996.

———. *The Shakespearean Stage, 1574–1642.* Cambridge: Cambridge University Press, 1992.

———. *Playgoing in Shakespeare's London.* Cambridge: Cambridge University Press, 1988.

Howard, Jean E. *Shakespeare's Art of Orchestration: Stage Technique and Audience Response*. Urbana: University of Illinois Press, 1984.

Hunter, G. K. *English Drama 1586–1642: The Age of Shakespeare*. Oxford: Clarendon Press, 1997.

Kernan, Alvin. *Shakespeare, The King's Playwright, 1603–1613*. New Haven and London: Yale University Press, 1995.

Mullaney, Steven. *The Place of the Stage: License, Play and Power in Renaissance England*. Chicago: University of Chicago Press, 1988.

Thomson, Peter. *Shakespeare's Professional Career*. Cambridge: Cambridge University Press, 1994.

Wells, Stanley. *Shakespeare: A Life in Drama*. New York, London: W.W. Norton, 1995.

Yachnin, Paul Edward. *Stage-Wrights: Shakespeare, Johnson, Middleton, and the Making of Theatrical Value*. Philadelphia: University of Pennsylvania Press, 1997.

## On Shakespeare and Contemporary Culture:

Bradshaw, Graham. *Shakespeare's Scepticism*. New York: St. Martin's Press, 1987.

Berry, Ralph. *Shakespeare and Social Class*. Atlantic Highlands, NJ: Humanities Press, 1988.

Engle, Lars. *Shakespearean Pragmatism: Market of His Time*. Chicago: University of Chicago Press, 1993.

Knapp, Jeffrey. *Shakespeare's Tribe: Church, Nation, and Theater in Renaissance England*. Chicago: Chicago University Press, 2002.

Manley, Lawrence. *Literature and Culture in Early Modern London*. Cambridge: Cambridge University Press, 1995.

Marx, Steven. *Shakespeare and the Bible*. Oxford: Oxford University Press, 2000.

Orgel, Stephen. *Impersonations: The Performance of Gender in Shakespeare's England*. Cambridge: Cambridge University Press, 1996.

Shuger, Debora Kuller. *The Renaissance Bible: Scholarship, Sacrifice and Subjectivity*. Berkeley, University of California Press, 1994.

Smith, Bruce R. *Homosexual Desire in Shakespeare's England*. Chicago: University of Chicago Press, 1991.

Traub, Valerie. *Desire and Anxiety: Circulations of Sexuality in Renaissance Drama*. London: Routledge, 1992.

Woodbridge, Linda. *The Scythe of Saturn: Shakespeare and Magical Thinking*. Urbana: University of Illinois Press, 1994.

———. *Women and the English Renaissance, 1540–1620*. Urbana: University of Illinois Press, 1984.

## On the Text of *Hamlet*:

Bertram, Paul, and Bernice W. Kliman, eds. *The Three-Text* Hamlet: *Parallel Texts of the First and Second Quartos and First Folio*. New York: AMS Press, 1991.